CURRENT ECONOMIC ISSUES

15TH EDITION

READINGS IN ECONOMICS, POLITICS, AND SOCIAL POLICY FROM

EDITED BY JAMES CYPHER, SMRITI RAO, CHRIS STURR,

AND THE *DOLLARS & SENSE* COLLECTIVE

CURRENT ECONOMIC ISSUES, 15TH EDITION

Article 2.4 originally appeared in *The Nation* magazine. Used with permission.

ISBN: 978-1-878585-88-2

Published by:
Economic Affairs Bureau, Inc. d/b/a *Dollars & Sense*
29 Winter Street, Boston, MA 02108
617-447-2177; dollars@dollarsandsense.org.
For order information, contact Economic Affairs Bureau or visit: www.dollarsandsense.org.

Current Economic Issues is edited by the *Dollars & Sense* collective, which also publishes *Dollars & Sense* magazine and the classroom books *Real World Macro, Real World Micro, The Economic Crisis Reader, Real World Globalization, Real World Latin America, Real World Labor, Real World Banking and Finance, The Wealth Inequality Reader, The Environment in Crisis, Introduction to Political Economy, Unlevel Playing Fields: Understanding Wage Inequality and Discrimination, Striking a Balance: Work, Family, Life,* and *Grassroots Journalism.*

The 2011 *Dollars & Sense* Collective:
Nicole Aschoff, Arpita Banerjee, Ben Collins, Leibiana Feliz, Amy Gluckman, Ben Greenberg, Mary Jirmanus, Shirley Kressel, James McBride, John Miller, Linda Pinkow, Paul Piwko, Smriti Rao, Alejandro Reuss, Dave Ryan, Bryan Snyder, Chris Sturr, and Jeanne Winner.

Co-editors of this volume: James M. Cypher, Smriti Rao, and Chris Sturr

Cover design: Chris Sturr
Cover photo: Student protests in London, December 9, 2010. Credit: rikki, indymedia.uk. Used with permission.

Production: Chris Sturr

Printed in U.S.A.

CONTENTS

Chapter 1

THE ECONOMIC CRISIS

Article 1.1

INEQUALITY, POWER, AND IDEOLOGY

Getting It Right About the Causes of the Current Economic Crisis

BY ARTHUR MacEWAN

March/April 2009

It is hard to solve a problem without an understanding of what caused it. For example, in medicine, until we gained an understanding of the way bacteria and viruses cause various infectious diseases, it was virtually impossible to develop effective cures. Of course, dealing with many diseases is complicated by the fact that germs, genes, diet, and the environment establish a nexus of causes.

The same is true in economics. Without an understanding of the causes of the current crisis, we are unlikely to develop a solution; certainly we are not going to get a solution that has a lasting impact. And determining the causes is complicated because several intertwined factors have been involved.

The current economic crisis was brought about by a nexus of factors that involved: a growing concentration of political and social power in the hands of the wealthy; the ascendance of a perverse leave-it-to-the-market ideology which was an instrument of that power; and rising income inequality, which both resulted from and enhanced that power. These various factors formed a vicious circle, reinforcing one another and together shaping the economic conditions that led us to the present situation. Several other factors were also involved—the growing role of credit, the puffing up of the housing bubble, and the increasing deregulation of financial markets have been very important. However, these are best understood as transmitters of our economic problems, arising from the nexus that formed the vicious circle.

What does this tell us about a solution? Economic stimulus, repair of the housing market, and new regulation are all well and good, but they do not deal with the underlying causes of the crisis. Instead, progressive groups need to work to shift each of the factors I have noted—power, ideology, and income distribution—in the other direction. In doing so, we can create a *virtuous* circle, with each change reinforcing the other changes. If successful, we not only establish a more stable economy, but we lay the foundation for a more democratic, equitable, and sustainable economic order.

A crisis by its very nature creates opportunities for change. One good place to begin change and intervene in this "circle"—and transform it from vicious to virtuous—is through pushing for the expansion and reform of social programs, programs that directly serve social needs of the great majority of the population (for example: single-payer health care, education programs, and environmental protection and repair). By establishing changes in social programs, we will have impacts on income distribution and ideology, and, perhaps most important, we set in motion *a power shift* that improves our position for preserving the changes. While I emphasize social programs as a means to initiate social and economic change, there are other ways to intervene in the circle. Efforts to re-strengthen unions would be especially important; and there are other options as well.

Causes of the Crisis: A Long Time Coming

Sometime around the early 1970s, there were some dramatic changes in the U.S. economy. The twenty-five years following World War II had been an era of relatively stable economic growth; the benefits of growth had been widely shared, with wages rising along with productivity gains, and income distribution became slightly less unequal (a good deal less unequal as compared to the pre-Great Depression era). There were severe economic problems in the United States, not the least of which were the continued exclusion of African Americans, large gender inequalities, and the woeful inadequacy of social welfare programs. Nonetheless, relatively stable growth, rising wages, and then the advent of the civil rights movement and the War on Poverty gave some important, positive social and economic character to the era—especially in hindsight!

In part, this comparatively favorable experience for the United States had depended on the very dominant position that U.S. firms held in the world economy, a position in which they were relatively unchallenged by international competition. The firms and their owners were not the only beneficiaries of this situation. With less competitive pressure on them from foreign companies, many U.S. firms accepted unionization and did not find it worthwhile to focus on keeping wages down and obstructing the implementation of social supports for the low-income population. Also, having had the recent experience of the Great Depression, many wealthy people and business executives were probably not so averse to a substantial role for government in regulating the economy.

A Power Grab

By about 1970, the situation was changing. Firms in Europe and Japan had long recovered from World War II, OPEC was taking shape, and weaknesses were emerging in the U.S. economy. The weaknesses were in part a consequence of heavy spending for the Vietnam War combined with the government's reluctance to tax for the war because of its unpopularity. The pressures on U.S. firms arising from these changes had two sets of consequences: slower growth and greater instability; and concerted efforts—a power grab, if you will—by firms and the wealthy to shift the costs of economic deterioration onto U.S. workers and the low-income population.

These "concerted efforts" took many forms: greater resistance to unions and unionization, battles to reduce taxes, stronger opposition to social welfare programs, and, above all, a push to reduce or eliminate government regulation of economic activity through a powerful political campaign to gain control of the various branches and levels of government. The 1980s, with Reagan and Bush One in the White House, were the years in which all these efforts were solidified. Unions were greatly weakened, a phenomenon both demonstrated and exacerbated by Reagan's firing of the air traffic controllers in response to their strike in 1981. The tax cuts of the period were also important markers of the change. But the change had begun earlier; the 1978 passage of the tax-cutting Proposition 13 in California was perhaps the first major success of the movement. And the changes continued well after the 1980s, with welfare reform and deregulation of finance during the Clinton era, to say nothing of the tax cuts and other actions during Bush Two.

Ideology Shift

The changes that began in the 1970s, however, were not simply these sorts of concrete alterations in the structure of power affecting the economy and, especially, government's role in the economy. There was a major shift in ideology, the dominant set of ideas that organize an understanding of our social relations and both guide and rationalize policy decisions.

Alan Greenspan, Symbol of an Era

One significant symbol of the full rise of the conservative ideology that became so dominant in the latter part of the 20th century was Alan Greenspan, who served from 1974 through 1976 as chairman of the President's Council of Economic Advisers under Gerald Ford and in 1987 became chairman of the Federal Reserve Board, a position he held until 2006. While his predecessors had hardly been critics of U.S. capitalism, Greenspan was a close associate of the philosopher Ayn Rand and an adherent of her extreme ideas supporting individualism and *laissez-faire* (keep-the-government-out) capitalism.

When chairman of the Fed, Greenspan was widely credited with maintaining an era of stable economic growth. As things fell apart in 2008, however, Greenspan was seen as having a large share of responsibility for the non-regulation and excessively easy credit (see article) that led into the crisis.

Called before Congress in October of 2008, Greenspan was chastised by Rep. Henry Waxman (D-Calif.), who asked him: "Do you feel that your ideology pushed you to make decisions that you wish you had not made?" To which Greenspan replied: "Yes, I've found a flaw. I don't know how significant or permanent it is. But I've been very distressed by that fact."

And Greenspan told Congress: "Those of us who have looked to the self-interest of lending institutions to protect shareholders' equity, myself included, are in a state of shocked disbelief."

Greenspan's "shock" was reminiscent of the scene in the film *Casablanca* in which Captain Renault (played by Claude Rains) declares: "I'm shocked, shocked to find that gambling is going on in here!" At which point, a croupier hands Renault a pile of money and says, "Your winnings, sir." Renault replies, *sotto voce*, "Thank you very much."

Following the Great Depression and World War II, there was a wide acceptance of the idea that government had a major role to play in economic life. Less than in many other countries but nonetheless to a substantial degree, at all levels of society, it was generally believed that there should be a substantial government safety net and that government should both regulate the economy in various ways and, through fiscal as well as monetary policy, should maintain aggregate demand. This large economic role for government came to be called Keynesianism, after the British economist John Maynard Keynes, who had set out the arguments for an active fiscal policy in time of economic weakness. In the early 1970s, as economic troubles developed, even Richard Nixon declared: "We are all Keynesians now."

The election of Ronald Reagan, however, marked a sharp change in ideology, at least at the top. Actions of the government were blamed for all economic ills: government spending, Keynesianism, was alleged to be the cause of the inflation of the 1970s; government regulation was supposedly crippling industry; high taxes were, it was argued, undermining incentives for workers to work and for businesses to invest; social welfare spending was blamed for making people dependent on the government and was charged with fraud and corruption (the "welfare queens"); and so on and so on.

On economic matters, Reagan championed supply-side economics, the principal idea of which was that tax cuts yield an increase in government revenue because the cuts lead to more rapid economic growth through encouraging more work and more investment. Thus, so the argument went, tax cuts would reduce the government deficit. Reagan, with the cooperation of Democrats, got the tax cuts—and, as the loss of revenue combined with a large increase in military spending, the federal budget deficit grew by leaps and bounds, almost doubling as a share of GDP over the course of the 1980s. It was all summed up in the idea of keeping the government out of the economy; let the free market work its magic.

Growing Inequality

The shifts of power and ideology were very much bound up with a major redistribution upwards of income and wealth. The weakening of unions, the increasing access of firms to low-wage foreign (and immigrant) labor, the refusal of government to maintain the buying power of the minimum wage, favorable tax treatment of the wealthy and their corporations, deregulation in a wide range of industries, and lack of enforcement of existing regulation (e.g., the authorities turning a blind eye to off-shore tax shelters) all contributed to these shifts.

Many economists, however, explain the rising income inequality as a result of technological change that favored more highly skilled workers; and changing technology has probably been a factor. Yet the most dramatic aspect of the rising inequality has been the rapidly rising share of income obtained by those at the very top (see figures), who get their incomes from the ownership and control of business, not from their skilled labor. For these people the role of new technologies was most important through its impact on providing more options (e.g., international options) for the managers of firms, more thorough means to control labor, and more effective ways—in the absence of regulation—to manipulate finance. All of these gains that might be associated with new technology were

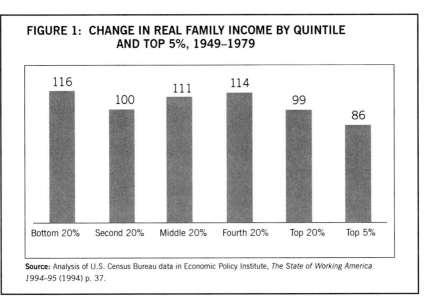

FIGURE 1: CHANGE IN REAL FAMILY INCOME BY QUINTILE AND TOP 5%, 1949–1979

Source: Analysis of U.S. Census Bureau data in Economic Policy Institute, *The State of Working America 1994–95* (1994) p. 37.

also gains brought by the way the government handled, or didn't handle (failed to regulate), economic affairs.

Several sets of data demonstrate the sharp changes in the distribution of income that have taken place in the last several decades. Most striking is the changing position of the very highest income segment of the population. In the mid-1920s, the share of all pre-tax income going to the top 1% of households peaked at 23.9%. This elite group's share of income fell dramatically during the Great Depression and World War II to about 12% at the end of the war and then slowly fell further during the next thirty years, reaching a low of 8.9% in the mid-1970s. Since then, the top 1% has regained its exalted position of the earlier era, with 21.8% of income

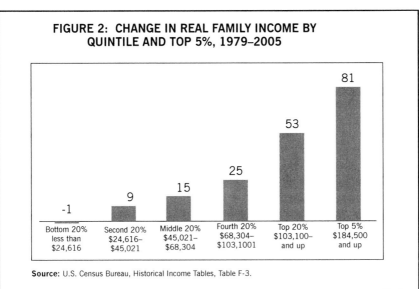

FIGURE 2: CHANGE IN REAL FAMILY INCOME BY QUINTILE AND TOP 5%, 1979–2005

Source: U.S. Census Bureau, Historical Income Tables, Table F-3.

in 2005. Since 1993, more than one-half of all income gains have accrued to this highest 1% of the population.

Figures 1 and 2 show the gains (or losses) of various groups in the 1947 to 1979 period and in the 1979 to 2005 period. The difference is dramatic. For example, in the earlier era, the bottom 20% saw its income in real (inflation-adjusted) terms rise by 116%, and real income of the top 5% grew by only 86%. But in the latter era, the bottom 20% saw a 1% decline in its income, while the top 5% obtained a 81% increase.

The Emergence of Crisis

These changes, especially the dramatic shifts in the distribution of income, set the stage for the increasingly large reliance on credit, especially consumer and mortgage credit, that played a major role in the emergence of the current economic crisis. Other factors were involved, but rising inequality was especially important in effecting the increase in both the demand and supply of credit.

Credit Expansion

On the demand side, rising inequality translated into a growing gap between the incomes of most members of society and their needs. For the 2000 to 2007 period, average weekly earnings in the private sector were 12% below their average for the 1970s (in inflation-adjusted terms). From 1980 to 2005 the share of income going to the bottom 60% of families fell from 35% to 29%. Under these circumstances, more and more people relied more and more heavily on credit to meet their needs—everything from food to fuel, from education to entertainment, and especially housing.

While the increasing reliance of consumers on credit has been going on for a long time, it has been especially marked in recent decades. Consumer debt as a share of after-tax personal income averaged 20% in the 1990s, and then jumped up to an average of 25% in the first seven years of the new millennium. But the debt expansion was most marked in housing, where mortgage debt as a percent of after-tax personal income rose from 89% to 94% over the 1990s, and then ballooned to 140% by 2006 as housing prices skyrocketed.

On the supply side, especially in the last few years, the government seems to have relied on making credit readily available as a means to bolster aggregate demand and maintain at least a modicum of economic growth. During the 1990s, the federal funds interest rate averaged 5.1%, but fell to an average of 3.4% in the 2000 to 2007 period—and averaged only 1.4% in 2002 to 2004 period. (The federal funds interest rate is the rate that banks charge one another for overnight loans and is a rate directly affected by the Federal Reserve.) Corresponding to the low interest rates, the money supply grew twice as fast in the new millennium as it had in the 1990s. (And see the box on the connection of the Fed's actions to the Iraq War.)

The increasing reliance of U.S. consumers on credit has often been presented as a moral weakness, as an infatuation with consumerism, and as a failure to look beyond the present. Whatever moral judgments one may make, however, the

Joseph Stiglitz on the War and the Economy

On October 2, 2008, on the Pacifica radio program Democracy Now!, Amy Goodman and Juan Gonzalez interviewed Joseph Stiglitz about the economic situation. Stiglitz was the 2001 winner of the Nobel Prize in Economics, former chief economist at the World Bank, and former chair of President Clinton's Council of Economic Advisers. He is a professor at Columbia University. Following is an excerpt from that interview:

AMY GOODMAN: Joseph Stiglitz, you're co-author of *The Three Trillion Dollar War: The True Cost of the Iraq Conflict.* How does the bailout [of the financial sector] connect to war?

JOSEPH STIGLITZ: Very much. Let me first explain a little bit how the current crisis connects with the war. One of the reasons that we have this crisis is that the Fed flooded the economy with liquidity and had lax regulations. Part of that was this ideology of "regulations are bad," but part of the reason was that the economy was weak. And one of the reasons the economy was weak was oil prices were soaring, and part of the reason oil prices were soaring is the Iraq war. When we went to war in 2003, before we went, prices were $23 a barrel. Futures markets thought they would remain at that level. They anticipated the increase in demand, but they thought there would be a concomitant increase in supply from the low-cost providers, mainly in the Middle East. The war changed that equation, and we know what happened to the oil prices.

Well, why is that important? Well, we were spending—Americans were spending hundreds of millions—billions of dollars to buy—more, to buy imported oil. Normally, that would have had a very negative effect on our economy; we would have had a slowdown. Some people have said, you know, it's a mystery why we aren't having that slowdown; we repealed the laws of economics. Whenever anybody says that, you ought to be suspect.

It was actually very simple. The Fed engineered a bubble, a housing bubble to replace the tech bubble that it had engineered in the '90s. The housing bubble facilitated people taking money out of their ... houses; in one year, there were more than $900 billion of mortgage equity withdrawals. And so, we had a consumption boom that was so strong that even though we were spending so much money abroad, we could keep the economy going. But it was so shortsighted. And it was so clear that we were living on borrowed money and borrowed time. And it was just a matter of time before, you know, the whole thing would start to unravel.

expansion of the credit economy has been a response to real economic forces—inequality and government policies, in particular.

The Failure to Regulate

The credit expansion by itself, however, did not precipitate the current crisis. Deregulation—or, more generally, the failure to regulate—is also an important part of the story. The government's role in regulation of financial markets has been a central feature in the development of this crisis, but the situation in financial markets has been part of a more general process—affecting airlines and trucking, telecommunications, food processing, broadcasting, and of course international trade and investment. The process has been driven by a combination of power (of large firms and wealthy individuals) and ideology (leave it to the market, get the government out).

The failure to regulate financial markets that transformed the credit expansion into a financial crisis shows up well in three examples:

The 1999 repeal of the Glass-Steagall Act. Glass-Steagall had been enacted in the midst of the Great Depression, as a response to the financial implosion following the stock market crash of 1929. Among other things, it required that different kinds of financial firms—commercial banks, investment banks, insurance companies—be separate. This separation both limited the spread of financial problems and reduced conflicts of interest that could arise were the different functions of these firms combined into a single firm. As perhaps the most important legislation regulating the financial sector, the repeal of Glass-Steagall was not only a substantive change but was an important symbol of the whole process of deregulation.

The failure to regulate mortgage lending. Existing laws and regulations require lending institutions to follow prudent practices in making loans, assuring that borrowers have the capacity to be able to pay back the loans. And of course fraud—lying about the provisions of loans—is prohibited. Yet in an atmosphere where regulation was "out," regulators were simply not doing their jobs. The consequences are illustrated in a December 28, 2008, *New York Times* story on the failed Washington Mutual Bank. The article describes a supervisor at a mortgage processing center as having been "accustomed to seeing babysitters claiming salaries worthy of college presidents, and schoolteachers with incomes rivaling stockbrokers'. He rarely questioned them. A real estate frenzy was under way and WaMu, as his bank was known, was all about saying yes."

One may wonder why banks—or other lending institutions, mortgage firms, in particular—would make loans to people who were unlikely to be able to pay them back. The reason is that the lending institutions quickly combined such loans into packages (i.e., a security made up of several borrowers' obligations to pay) and sold them to other investors in a practice called "securitization."

Credit-default swaps. Perhaps the most egregious failure to regulate in recent years has been the emergence of credit-default swaps, which are connected to securitization. Because they were made up of obligations by a diverse set of borrowers, the packages of loans were supposedly low-risk investments. Yet those who purchased them still sought insurance against default. Insurance sellers, however, are regulated—required, for example, to keep a certain amount of capital on hand to cover possible claims. So the sellers of these insurance policies on packages of loans called the policies "credit-default swaps" and thus were allowed to avoid regulation. Further, these credit-default swaps, these insurance policies, themselves were bought and sold again and again in unregulated markets in a continuing process of speculation.

The credit-default swaps are a form of derivative, a financial asset the value of which is derived from some other asset—in this case the value of packages of mortgages for which they were the insurance policies. When the housing bubble began to collapse and people started to default on their mortgages, the value of credit-default swaps plummeted and their future value was impossible to determine. No one would buy them, and several banks that had speculated in these derivatives were left holding huge amounts of these "toxic assets."

Bubble and Bust

The combination of easy credit and the failure to regulate together fueled the housing bubble. People could buy expensive houses but make relatively low monthly payments. Without effective regulation of mortgage lending, they could get the loans even when they were unlikely to be able to make payments over the long run. Moreover, as these pressures pushed up housing prices, many people bought houses simply to resell them quickly at a higher price, in a process called "flipping." And such speculation pushed the prices up further. Between 2000 and 2006, housing prices rose by 90% (as consumer prices generally rose by only 17%).

While the housing boom was in full swing, both successful housing speculators and lots of people involved in the shenanigans of credit markets made a lot of money. However, as the housing bubble burst—as all bubbles do—things fell apart. The packages of loans lost value, and the insurance policies on them, the credit-default swaps, lost value. These then became "toxic" assets for those who held them, assets not only with reduced value but with unknown value. Not only did large financial firms—for example, Lehman Brothers and AIG—have billions of dollars in losses, but no one knew the worth of their remaining assets. The assets were called "toxic" because they poisoned the operations of the financial system. Under these circumstances, financial institutions stopped lending to one another—that is, the credit markets "froze up." The financial crisis was here.

The financial crisis, not surprisingly, very quickly shifted to a general economic crisis. Firms in the "real" economy rely heavily on a well-functioning financial system to supply them with the funds they need for their regular operations—loans to car buyers, loans to finance inventory, loans for construction of new facilities, loans for new equipment, and, of course, mortgage loans. Without those loans (or with the loans much more difficult to obtain), there has been a general cut-back in economic activity, what is becoming a serious and probably prolonged recession.

What Is to Be Done?

So here we are. The shifts in power, ideology, and income distribution have placed us in a rather nasty situation. There are some steps that will be taken that have a reasonable probability of yielding short-run improvement. In particular, a large increase in government spending—deficit spending—will probably reduce the depth and shorten the length of the recession. And the actions of the Federal Reserve and Treasury to inject funds into the financial system are likely, along with the deficit spending, to "un-freeze" credit markets (the mismanagement and, it seems, outright corruption of the bailout notwithstanding). Also, there is likely to be some re-regulation of the financial industry. These steps, however, at best will restore things to where they were before the crisis. They do not treat the underlying causes of the crisis—the vicious circle of power, ideology, and inequality.

Opportunity for Change

Fortunately, the crisis itself has weakened some aspects of this circle. The cry of "leave it to the market" is still heard, but is now more a basis for derision than a guide to policy. The ideology and, to a degree, the power behind the ideology, have been severely weakened as the role of "keeping the government out" has shown to be a major cause of the financial mess and our current hardships. There is now widespread support among the general populace and some support in Washington for greater regulation of the financial industry.

Whether or not the coming period will see this support translated into effective policy is of course an open question. Also an open question is how much the turn away from "leaving it to the market" can be extended to other sectors of the economy. With regard to the environment, there is already general acceptance of the principle that the government (indeed, many governments) must take an active role in regulating economic activity. Similar principles need to be recognized with regard to health care, education, housing, child care, and other support programs for low-income families.

The discrediting of "keep the government out" ideology provides an opening to develop new programs in these areas and to expand old programs. Furthermore, as the federal government revs up its "stimulus" program in the coming months, opportunities will exist for expanding support for these sorts of programs. This support is important, first of all, because these programs serve real, pressing needs—needs that have long existed and are becoming acute and more extensive in the current crisis.

Breaking the Circle

Support for these social programs, however, may also serve to break into the vicious power-ideology-inequality circle and begin transforming it into a virtuous circle. Social programs are inherently equalizing in two ways: they provide their benefits to low-income people and they provide some options for those people in their efforts to demand better work and higher pay. Also, the further these programs develop, the more they establish the legitimacy of a larger role for public control of—government involvement in—the economy; they tend to bring about an ideological shift. By affecting a positive distributional shift and by shifting ideology, the emergence of stronger social programs can have a wider impact on power. In other words, efforts to promote social programs are one place to start, an entry point to shift the vicious circle to a virtuous circle.

There are other entry points. Perhaps the most obvious ones are actions to strengthen the role of unions. The Employee Free Choice Act may be a useful first step, and it will be helpful to establish a more union-friendly Department of Labor and National Labor Relations Board. Raising the minimum wage—ideally indexing it to inflation—would also be highly desirable. While conditions have changed since the heyday of unions in the middle of the 20th century, and we cannot expect to restore the conditions of that era, a greater role for unions would seem essential in righting the structural conditions at the foundation of the current crisis.

Shifting Class Power

None of this is assured, of course. Simply starting social programs will not necessarily mean that they have the wider impacts that I am suggesting are possible. No one should think that by setting up some new programs and strengthening some existing ones we will be on a smooth road to economic and social change. Likewise, rebuilding the strength of unions will involve extensive struggle and will not be accomplished by a few legislative or executive actions.

Also, all efforts to involve the government in economic activity—whether in finance or environmental affairs, in health care or education, in work support or job training programs—will be met with the worn-out claims that government involvement generates bureaucracy, stifles initiative, and places an excessive burden on private firms and individuals. We are already hearing warnings that in dealing with the financial crisis the government must avoid "over-regulation." Likewise, efforts to strengthen unions will suffer the traditional attacks, as unions are portrayed as corrupt and their members privileged. The unfolding situation with regard to the auto firms' troubles has demonstrated the attack, as conservatives have blamed the United Auto Workers for the industry's woes and have demanded extensive concessions by the union.

Certainly not all regulation is good regulation. Aside from excessive bureaucratic controls, there is the phenomenon by which regulating agencies are often captives of the industries that they are supposed to regulate. And there are corrupt unions. These are real issues, but they should not be allowed to derail change.

The current economic crisis emerged in large part as a shift in the balance of class power in the United States, a shift that began in the early 1970s and continued into the new millennium. Perhaps the present moment offers an opportunity to shift things back in the other direction. Recognition of the complex nexus of causes of the current economic crisis provides some guidance where people might start. Rebuilding and extending social programs, strengthening unions, and other actions that contribute to a more egalitarian power shift will not solve all the problems of U.S. capitalism. They can, however, begin to move us in the right direction. ❑

Article 1.2

BEYOND KEYNESIANISM

Irving Fisher's Depression-era debt-deflation theory, then and now.

BY JAMES M. CYPHER

January/February 2011

According to dominant economic ideas, massive government interventions beginning in 2007—by way of Keynesian fiscal stimulus programs of the Bush and Obama administrations, the TARP program (the Wall Street bailout), and unprecedented interventions by the Federal Reserve—should have reset the economy. But because these interventions have not addressed the economy's huge *structural* issues, the economy continues to stall. Structural changes have brought an end to the era when wage increases were tightly linked to productivity increases from the end of World War II through the early 1970s. Since then, in a new era of deregulation, globalization, and de-unionization, labor productivity has nearly doubled, but real hourly wages for non-supervisory workers—over 80% of the workforce—have stagnated or fallen slightly for over 30 years. This has left the working class without any viable strategy as jobs were offshored and outsourced. Instead, women flooded into the workforce, workers sought second jobs, money was pumped into 401(k)s in the hope that stock market plays could make up for declining labor opportunities, household debt reached record levels, and the dream of windfall gains from house-flipping became a major focus for millions of working-class and middle-class families. From 2007 onward, the unprecedented interventions of the Bush and Obama administrations were designed to meet the immediate needs of elite financial institutions, leaving largely unaddressed the sorry plight of the dwindling middle and working classes, now marginalized in the new era of neoliberalism.

The stimulus and rescue programs did prevent an even greater avalanche of interlocking bankruptcies from reverberating via Wall Street to Main Street and back again—as occurred for years during the Great Depression of the 1930s. Yet as of the end of 2010, the general state of the U.S. economy looks bleak. With the economy losing over 443,000 jobs from June through September and unemployment rising again in November to an official rate of 9.8%, attention shifted toward further stimulus. By September, with most of his original $787 billion stimulus plan now spent, President Obama at first urged $50 billion for new infrastructure projects. There is a bit of buzz about a "manufacturing strategy"—a belated attempt to address the long-term collapse of the manufacturing sector from nearly 30% of the economy in 1953 to only 11% in 2009. Here, Obama has offered only increased funding for the Export-Import Bank in order to meet his goal of doubling U.S. exports by 2015. And then, in December 2010 came a "second stimulus" package largely limited to extensions of existing tax breaks—nearly 25% of which will go to the richest 1% of income recipients. Additional stimulus will come only from a $110 billion one-year drop in Social Security taxes and—according to White House estimates—roughly $50 billion in new investments due a variety of tax breaks for corporations and small business. But, the same legislation eliminated the "Make

Work Pay" provision, which had been worth roughly $55 billion in tax cuts. Thus, for all the fanfare, the net new stimulus from this bill will be no more than $105 billion. In short, the administration proffers small and unimaginative policies as the economy stagnates and weakens.

Still, the interventions *have* served the purpose of putting a squishy floor underneath the collapsing edifice. All available evidence tends to support the Obama administration's claim that its fiscal interventions have saved or created some 2.7 million jobs. But these numbers constitute a counterfactual that is hard to demonstrate to the general public: the job growth owing to the stimulus has taken place in a broader context of massive job cuts—roughly 8 million jobs lost—since the downturn began. Economists Alan Blinder and Marc Zandi estimate that had it not been for a range of extremely active monetary and fiscal interventions beginning in the closing months of 2008, GDP in 2010 would have been 10.5% lower and an additional 8.5 million Americans would be out of work. Nonetheless, the public mostly rejects the assertions of Obama's economic spokespersons, either because most Americans have never learned of Keynesian economics or because they have been stampeded by a well-greased juggernaut financed by people like Pete Peterson, the Koch brothers, and the many others who would like to return the U.S. political economy to the good old days of 19th-century Social Darwinism.

Neoclassical to Neoliberal: Economic Theory in a Circular Process

The new era of neoliberalism, which has reigned since the late 1970s, has been anchored in an attempt to sweep away the New Deal policies that had guided the economy during the Keynesian interlude (1933-1978). Prior to the Great Depression economists strongly embraced the neoclassical doctrine of self-adjusting markets seamlessly functioning to bring about a full employment "equilibrium." Any time the economy tended to slow down—causing unemployment to rise as profit, production, and general business activity declined—wages would decline, raw material prices would drop, wholesale prices would plummet, etc. According to received neoclassical dogma, cheap wages, cheap raw materials, readily available credit and under-priced machinery and equipment would all constitute a seductive combination for business interests who would then jump back into the market—hiring workers, building new plants, buying up raw materials, taking on bank loans in order to enjoy an unbeatable profit-making situation. Other things remaining the same, went the argument, the deflation of the economy would create its own recovery momentum as sharp traders availed themselves of a once-in-a-lifetime opportunity.

This approach assumed the economic system functioned as if it were a mechanical apparatus that was somehow "invested with a tendency to an equilibrium." Equilibrium was noted in the fall of 1929, shortly before the great stock market crash, by the most acclaimed economist of the day, Dr. Irving Fisher. Fisher stated that stock prices had reached a "permanently high plateau," adding in September of 1929, as stocks began to crater, that there could not be "anything in the nature of a crash." In the same month President Hoover's powerful Treasury Secretary Andrew Mellon—scion of the robber baron financiers who ran the Pittsburgh-based "House of Mellon"—proclaimed that the "high tide of prosperity will continue." So ended what was, until then, the longest continuous expansion in U.S. history. Prior to the crash the era was dubbed the "New Economy," wherein recession and downturns were understood as things of the past. So, too, the information technology boom of the 1990s was dubbed a "New Economy." In the 1990s, across the United States, congenitally blind economics departments scrapped almost all of their few remaining courses on business cycles.

When the depression of 1929-1939 began, Treasury Secretary Mellon—known as a financial prodigy—ecstatically championed the neoclassical theory of downwardly flexible prices: "liquidate labor, liquidate stocks, liquidate farmers, liquidate real estate … Values will adjust … "! In other words, after a brief bought of deflation, the economy would, in machine-like fashion, quickly restore its balance; the inevitable forces of the New Economy would spring back into motion and the U.S. economic ascent would resume.

Indeed, as the real value of the GDP dropped like a stone from late 1929 through 1933, wages and prices did fall. Autoworkers' money wages fell by 64%, miners' wages plummeted by 74%, steelworkers wages dropped by 62%, and the wages of agricultural workers—one-quarter of the economy was engaged in this sector—fell by 50%. Meanwhile prices in general fell by about 25%. (However, wage and *salary* income—crucially including managerial and executive incomes—apparently fell by *less* than the price level. For a few privileged employees with outsized salaries the standard of living *rose*.)

According to neoclassical theory, the dramatic drop in real wage income—spread throughout the vast manufacturing sector—should have been an inducement for businesses to invest. Along with cheap money, cheap machinery, and cheap commodities, lower wages should have been more than sufficient inducement to restore the economy to high levels of employment at lower price levels. The New York Federal Reserve Bank—the most important in the system—dropped its interest rate from 6% in 1929 to a record low of 1.5% in May 1931. But business cut and cut its investment level: while investment accounted for only 19.3% of GDP in 1929, 56% of the total drop in GDP from 1929 through 1933 was due to *the decline* in investment! The leading sector of the New Economy of the 1920s had been the auto industry. By 1933 real auto production had fallen by 65%—hardly a situation that would encourage the expansion of plants and equipment, the low cost of labor, machinery, materials, and loans notwithstanding. Left to its own devices and the tepid interventions of the Hoover administration, the economic system became ever more dysfunctional—no mechanical apparatus was at work to bring the system back to any semblance of equilibrium.

Surprisingly, by 1933 Fisher had reflected deeply on the idea that the economy would quickly spring back to full employment. In a 180-degree turn, he now argued that the Depression had unleashed forces that were sending the economy ever downward. The U.S. economy of the 1920s had been built on mountains of business, farm, mortgage, and personal debt. Now deflation was creating its own momentum. The burden of that debt was growing greater and greater as incomes shrank under the relentless pressures of deflation. As farm and business income fell, an ever-larger portion of income was shifted to the financial sector to pay debts that had been contracted when prices were much higher. In short, the growing debt burden was driving farmers and businesses into bankruptcy, thereby leading to further layoffs and more unemployment. Those households that had accumulated mortgage debt or consumer debt were in the same boat. As wages fell, families could not possibly pay an ever-growing share of their shrinking income to make debt payments *that did not deflate with the rest of the economy*. This was Fisher's all-important debt-deflation theory; it explained how a situation of over-indebtedness would lead to declining overall demand as the economy now favored creditors over debtors.

In neoclassical theory the fact that more of the total income was now shifting to creditors should not have impeded the economy's recovery. What debtors no longer spent, went the argument, creditors would now spend. This symmetrical model, however, just did not apply in the real and non-mechanical world of economic institutions. Banks and other creditors found that their income from debt repayments gave them greater power as money *increased* in value while wages and all other components of the economy *declined* in value. But the banks did not then lend out more money because they were fearful of the endless chain of bankruptcies the Depression had unleashed. They wanted to hold lots of funds in reserve against future losses. And to the degree that the income from the creditor institutions was passed through to managers, owners, and shareholders, these well-off groups were less likely to spend the additional income than were the workers, farmers, and owners of small- and medium-sized businesses who suffered growing losses. In sum, shifting a greater share of total income into the hands of wealthy creditors served only to push the economy further downward because (1) banks hoarded funds against future losses, (2) businesses seeing low and falling sales refused to take on any more debt, and (3) the rich did not put much of their new, more powerful, dollars back into the spending stream. Deflation had a supercharger effect—downward movement in the macro-economy unleashed powerful forces that led to further, perhaps accelerating, downward movement.

Today, Fisher is far less well known than another economist who took on neoclassical economics orthodoxy in the 1930s, John Maynard Keynes. Keynes challenged the neoclassicals with his interpretation of how total final demand determined the level of production and employment. He sought to show that the macro-economy could be caught up in a "special case" wherein equilibrium was established at very high levels of unemployment. In this situation, economic forces were aligned and balanced in a way that—whatever the rate of unemployment and excess capacity—the economy could do no more than simply reproduce itself year after year. Monetary policy would not revive the economy. Keynes famously urged massive government intervention to "prime the pump," thereby inducing the economic system to return to its normal state.

Yet Fisher's model of a debt-deflation disequilibrium is much more compelling than Keynes' idea of a high-unemployment equilibrium. Inflation-adjusted GDP fell by 9.5% from 1929 to 1930, and then fell by 7%, 15%, and 2.7% in the following three years. This was a downward spiral, not an equilibrium process.

The Structural Problem

The Great Depression signaled a moment when the U.S. economic system had met with structural barriers to its own expanding reproduction. The period from the

1870s to the 1920s saw the birth and consolidation of the giant corporation and the end of competitive capitalism based on small units of production, as economist Richard DuBoff has documented. By the 1920s, competitive capitalism could be found only in the minds of economists and in the texts and lectures they fed to generations of misinformed students. Along with the consolidation of a new structure of monopoly capitalism, the dynamic engine of the system had shifted from the production of producers' goods to the production of consumer durables such as washing machines and radios. The 1920s were fueled above all by exploding consumer demand for autos and their backward linkages to the oil industry, the auto parts companies, machine-tool firms, mining corporations, and producers of other raw materials such as rubber.

But growing income inequality, of a magnitude precisely equal to that which occurred in the run-up to the financial meltdown of 2007, undermined the future growth of the U.S. auto industry. (The top 1% in the household income distribution received an incredible 24% of all income in both 1928 and 2007.) Investment in the auto industry peaked in 1926, after which stagnating demand forestalled the building of more auto plants. Weak-to-nonexistent union power was a major reason why the economy began to totter both in 1927 (and again in 2006) when the housing boom peaked—a crucial matter ignored by both Fisher and Keynes.

Deeply embedded in the popular consciousness is the idea that the stock-market crash of 1929 *caused* the depression of the 1930s. The same was true of the most severe 19th century downturn: conventional accounts of the Panic of 1873 claimed that the depression was due to the collapse of the largest financier of the time, Jay Cooke & Company, causing losses to reverberate through the financial centers, particularly New York. Similarly, many of today's commentators pin the current economic crisis on *financialization*—the growing weight of the finance, insurance and real estate sector—which, the story goes, led to Ponzi finance, excessive leverage and the collapse of Bear Stearns, Lehman Brothers, and (effectively) A.I.G.

In short, the depressions of 1873 and 1929, and the borderline depression that began in 2007, are all widely assumed to have been caused by the alchemy of financial wizards. Those who take this view generally restrict their focus to the complex world of finance, without giving due attention or weight to underlying structural changes that have resulted in unsustainable tensions among the non-financial foundational components of the economy.

In recent years, the pace of structural change has been determined by (1) the realignment of capital-labor relations resulting in the effective de-unionization of the U.S. economy; (2) the outsourcing and offshoring of millions of jobs coupled with the threat of such actions, which has caused a dramatic tilt in the distribution of national income toward capital (partly buried as the greater part of the "salary" portion of the largest national income category, "wages and salaries"); (3) the subsequent delinking of productivity increases from wages, leaving a growing mass of profits to be redirected both to conspicuous consumption on a scale never before imagined and to predatory financial gamesmanship. In brief, a profound process of capital restructuring has taken place, giving rise to a new system of globally integrated production that has left the U.S. working class puzzled, powerless, and leaderless.

A Fisher Forecast?

According to the general perspective of the economics profession, depressions are a thing of the past: clever monetary policy and/or dynamic fiscal policy can reverse any downturn. Through massive injections of cheap credit and/or some combination of tax cuts, automatic countercyclical outlays (such as unemployment benefits), and discretionary expenditures (including especially those that boost the income of military contractors), federal policymakers can induce a recovery. Since 2007 the United States has followed exactly this prescription, and federal deficits will average approximately 10% of GDP in 2009, 2010, and 2011—more than double President Roosevelt's peak New Deal deficits in 1935 and 1936.

We can credit these massive interventions with curbing the forces unleashed as a result of the overcapacity problems, but they have not addressed the Keynesians' prime focus: employment. The U-6 unemployment rate—the best measure of the health of the labor market—includes the officially registered unemployed and also those who are working part-time but are seeking full-time employment and those "discouraged" workers who are not actively seeking employment but would if they thought jobs were available. The U-6 rate started to climb in late 2007 and had already hit 10.6% in 2008. It then soared on to 16.3% in 2009 and 16.7% in the first six months of 2010. If we take these data at face value, the U.S. economy is in a borderline depression, and one that is deepening.

Of course, unemployment is not the only factor. GDP has grown at an anemic annual rate of 3.2% in the past four quarters. Recoveries entail at first merely the reestablishment of previous levels of output, yet third quarter 2010 GDP (constant dollar) was still $86 billion below the last peak, in the fourth quarter of 2007. In the most recent nine-month period (fourth quarter 2009 through second quarter 2010) much of the growth has been in inventories, not in final demand. In fact, in the second quarter of 2010 final demand grew at an annual rate of only 1.3%.

The $64 question is this: what will happen in 2011 when the Obama administration's fiscal stimulus will rapidly drop off? Even though federal fiscal stimulus in 2011 (which began October 1, 2010) will be large, it will be partially counteracted by declining spending on the part of most state and local governments. The total effect of massive cuts at the state and local level in 2011 will be to *withdraw* funds in relatively labor-intensive areas such as education and health care. An estimated 500,000 local government employees are scheduled to be terminated in 2010 and 2011. To this group should be added another 900,000 public and private sector jobs currently sustained by the 34 states that will face the need to trim their budgets to accommodate falling tax revenues in fiscal years 2011 and 2012. The roughly 1.4 million threatened state and local layoffs could eventually have a much larger impact, potentially forcing twice that number or even more into unemployment. Even with the $26 billion in emergency one-year funding that passed the Congress in 2010, sizeable state and local layoffs and wage cuts will occur in fiscal year 2011. In September local government layoffs hit their highest rate in over 30 years.

In addition, a large amount of the federal deficit in 2011 (including the net $55 billion of new stimulus due to the drop in Social Security taxes in December 2010) will, once again, bleed away as imports. That is, a significant portion of government stimulus funds received by households via unemployment insurance payments, food stamps, tax cuts, jobs saved in construction, etc., will be sent abroad to pay for imported consumer goods, oil, machinery and equipment. Further, the major share of the federal debt (54% of marketable treasury bonds in December 2009) is now owned by foreigners—so most tax payments for interest must be shipped abroad to service the debt accumulated in past years.

Major corporations have continued to avidly restructure their production processes, laying off workers right and left. For example, Ford's North American division posted a huge second-quarter 2010 profit of $1.9 billion—this after cutting its labor force by 50% and seeing its revenue drop by $20 billion since 2005. Even the touted expansion of the Louisville Ford plant in 2011 will generate only a few hundred net new hires making only $14 per hour—half of the average pay of previously hired workers. The new corporate formula is higher profits from lower sales and little investment. Real Gross Investment (new capital spending plus replacement spending for worn-out equipment, adjusted for inflation) fell by 30% from the third quarter of 2007 to the first quarter of 2009. In the second quarter of 2010 overall investment was still 17.4% below the level achieved in late 2007.

Investment, then, is weak, while profits in the third quarter of 2010 reached a 60-year record high of $1.66 *trillion*. This profit rate rose by almost 30% from its recent low in the first quarter of 2008 through the first quarter of 2010. Indeed, the profit rate is now so high—thanks to the great squeeze on workers—that it exceeds the level achieved in the third quarter of 2007 by about 13%. *If* these bloated profits were channeled back into investment, then the economy would have a tendency to recover. But they are not. Corporations are taking their profits and sitting on them—cash holdings are at their highest levels since the early 1960s.

Across the United States, wage cuts have become a front-line strategy. A 2010 survey of U.S. cities found that 51% were either cutting or freezing existing wages. At General Motors, all new hires make one-half the rate of senior production workers. Even worse, this two-tier wage system is rapidly becoming a three-tier system where jumps in demand are being met by a new cadre of "permanent" temporary workers—known as "casuals"—non-unionized workers with no benefits. In some cases casuals make up more than 25% of the peak workforce, and they are paid only 75% of the second-tier wage. As federal government spending stalls out in late 2010, as the rich pull back from their recent spending binge, as corporations pocket much of their fat profits instead of plowing them back into expanded capacity, as wages stagnate or fall, as most state and local governments retrench further, as the new Republican-dominated congress contemplates federal program cuts in 2011, and as the meager additional net stimulus from the December 2010 Social Security tax cut is considerably shrunk by household debt repayments and the purchase of imported consumer goods, it is very difficult to foresee a continuation of what is conventionally called a "recovery".

Keynesians assume that massive federal stimulus will somehow cause the forward gears of the capitalist system to mesh—but they do not explain how or why. So far, Keynesianism has gained no forward traction, although it has prevented a backward slide. This stalemate is not unprecedented. The New Deal was largely stuck in place after 1936 because of the political resistance of the captains of industry and finance to further and larger deficits. Likewise, political opposition to further huge deficits likely explains some of the current situation of stagnation and slippage. But when World War II spending ended the Depression, more was involved that just spending. The war industries created a new industrial base that generated a host of major technological changes, for example in petrochemicals, aircraft engineering, and plastics. The war broke a power logjam and financed the industrial restructuring of the U.S. economy.

Since 2008 the government has prioritized policies to push the profit rate up, thereby benefiting the top 5 million (3.7%) of all households, those with incomes above $250,000, while shrugging off the plight of the working and middle classes and the structural problems that have created the current impasse. Millions in these classes are now caught in a Fisher-style debt trap, with their incomes flat or falling and their debt-to-income ratios remaining extremely high. For most families, wealth continues to shrink: housing values lost an additional $1.7 *trillion* in 2010, with the largest proportional declines being felt in working-class neighborhoods. Aside from some largely symbolic gestures, neither the Bush nor the Obama administration's stimulus efforts have addressed the drag effect that Fisher highlighted. This has stalemated the stimulus programs and the easy-money efforts of the Fed, leaving the majority in the United States in a condition of crushing economic precariousness. ❏

Sources: Alan Blinder and Marc Zandi, "How the Great Recession was Brought to an End" (July 27, 2010); Bureau of Labor Statistics, BLS Data Series: Labor Force Statistics, Table A-15, "Alternative Measures of Labor Underutilization" ; Susan Carter et al., *Historical Statistics of the United States*, Cambridge University Press, Tables Aa9-14, Ba4218 and Ca208-212 (2006); Lester Chandler, *America's Greatest Depression*. New York: Harper & Row (1970); Richard DuBoff, *Accumulation and Power: An Economic History of the United States*, Armonk, New York: M.E. Sharpe (1989); Rendig Fels, "American Business Cycles 1865-1879,"*American Economic Review* v. 41 no. 3 (June 1951); Irving Fisher, "The Debt-Deflation Theory of Great Depression," *Econometrica* v.1, no. 4 (October 1933); John K. Galbraith, *The Great Crash*, Houghton Mifflin (1954); Steven Greenhouse, "More Workers Face Pay Cuts, not Furloughs," *New York Times* (August 8, 2010); Nicholas Johnson et al., "An Update on State Budget Cuts," Center on Budget and Policy Priorities (August 4, 2010); J. M. Keynes, Economic Consequences of the Peace, New York: Harcourt, Brace & Howe (1920); J. M. Keynes, *The General Theory of Employment, Interest and Money*, New York: Harcourt, Brace & World (1936); David Leonhardt, "Biggest Local Cuts in 30 Years," *New York Times* Economix blog (October 8, 2010); Cathrine Rampell, "Recovery Slows; Outlook on Jobs Grows Dimmer," *New York Times* (July 31, 2010); Cathrine Rampell, "Third Quarter Was Record for Profits," *New York Times* (November 24, 2010); Motoko Rich, "Wealthy Sector of Buying Public is Cutting Back," New York Times (July 17, 2010); Emanuel Saez, "Striking it Rich," (August 5, 2010); William Selway, "US Cities and Counties Poised to Cut 500,000 Jobs," (July 27, 2010); Nelson Schwartz, "Industries Find Surging Profits in Deeper Cuts," *New York Times* (July 26, 2010); Louis Uchitelle, "A White House Campaign for Factories," New York Times (September 10, 2010); Louis Uchitelle, "Unions Yield on Pay Scales to Keep Jobs" *New York Times* (November 20, 2010); Hui-yong Yu and John Gittelsohn, U.S. Home Values to Drop by $1.7 Trillion This Year, (December 9, 2010); U.S. Department of Commerce, Bureau of Economic Analysis, National Income and Product Accounts, Table 3-b (2010); U.S.

Treasury, "The Case for Temporary 100 Percent Expensing: Encouraging Business To Expand Now by Lowering the Cost of Investment" (October 29, 2010); Thorstein Veblen, "Why is Economics not an Evolutionary Science?" in *The Portable Veblen*, Max Lerner, ed., New York: Viking (1948), reprinted from the *Quarterly Journal of Economics*, (July 1898); Francis Warnock, "How Dangerous Is U.S. Government Debt?" *Capital Flows Quarterly* (Council on Foreign Relations, 2010).

Article 1.3

RANK-AND-FILE ECONOMICS
Fighting for a Jobs- and Wage-Led Recovery

BY KATHERINE SCIACCHITANO
September/October 2011

Riddle 1: When is a recovery not a recovery?
Answer: When profits are at record levels, corporations are sitting on $1.7 trillion in cash, and unemployment is still at 9.2% and rising.

Riddle 2: When is a stimulus not a stimulus?
Answer: When it's less than one-fourth the size of the hole in the economy it is intended to fill.

Riddle 3: When will it be possible to rebuild the economy?
Answer: When the U.S. labor movement joins with community and international labor allies to demand global economic development, jobs, and rising wages.

When the U.S. housing bubble burst in 2008, putting jobs first was a no-brainer. Global unions demanded immediate action. The G-20—the group of 20 nations charged with coordinating a global response to the crisis—agreed. Governments rushed to do stimulus spending. The worst was prevented.

Then in the spring of 2010 the Greek debt crisis hit. Markets plummeted. The G-20 pulled back and told countries to cut spending. Greece, Ireland, Spain, Portugal, and the U.K. have since enacted austerity packages with drastic spending and wage cuts.

The global jobs crisis is now worse than ever. Between 2007 and 2010, 30 million workers lost their jobs worldwide. In the United States, GDP is falling, jobs have declined since the recovery started, and the unemployment rate is rising again as federal stimulus funds fade and layoffs mount in the states. The Brookings Institution estimates it will take over ten years to return to normal employment levels, even at pre-crisis growth rates. Now, real wages are falling as well.

Union reps negotiating contracts with state and local governments are on the frontlines of the resulting battles. Flanked as they are by terrified members on one side, and angry tax payers and state legislatures attacking wages, benefits, and bargaining rights on the other, their problems go far beyond what can be solved at the bargaining table.

The out-of-the-box solution would be to organize for a comprehensive program of job creation. Blueprints for jobs-based recoveries do exist. But such blueprints need "rank-and-file economists" to turn them into brick and mortar. With Democrats and Republicans actively vying to impose austerity, those rank-and-file economists—community organizers as well as union reps—must tell, not ask, our elected representatives what we need. Then they have to engage in the drawn-out battle to make what we need a reality.

A major obstacle to struggle is the widespread belief—even among many union members—that there is little that government can do besides cut spending, and that only the private sector can create jobs.

Yet the fact that so many are frustrated with government over the high unemployment is evidence that on some level people do believe government action is not only possible but necessary. A rank-and-file economics needs to channel that frustration and nurture that belief. It needs to explain why the "free market" isn't going to create the jobs that are needed. It needs to educate people about the real causes of the crisis. And it needs to convince community and union members that a positive agenda for long-term growth still exists.

First, we have to arm ourselves by educating ourselves.

The Private Sector Can't Do It Alone

Here in the United States, people are surrounded by the narrative that only the private sector can create jobs. Even those who acknowledge that we need to rebuild our infrastructure and that rebuilding would create jobs are likely to say that we can't afford public investment right now. Instead, the argument goes, we should cut taxes and let corporations create the jobs and the investment we need: too much public spending got us where we are; every tax dollar spent by the government is one less dollar business could be used to create jobs.

There are three main responses to these arguments.

First, *corporations already have enough cash to invest; tax cuts for corporations and the wealthy aren't going to lead to more job creation.*

The Bush tax cuts didn't boost job creation, they didn't boost wages, and they didn't boost investment in the real economy. What they boosted was corporate profits and the deficit. Today businesses are sitting on record profits and $1.7 trillion in cash that they don't *want* to invest. What investment is being done is aimed at boosting productivity and cutting labor costs—that is, cutting jobs. The jobs problem is *not* due to businesses not having enough cash to invest. Further enriching corporations with tax cuts isn't going to fix it.

Second, *the deficit didn't cause the crisis; the crisis caused the deficit.*

Calls to cut government spending in order to spur growth ignore the fact that the economic crisis we're in has nothing to do with government spending. The deficit didn't cause the crisis. The crisis caused the deficit. The spike in the deficit is principally due to the drop in revenues as people lost jobs and businesses lost sales. What additional spending we have done in the past three years—for the stimulus program and for TARP—was temporary. And as economist Dean Baker from the Center for Economic and Policy Research (CEPR) has calculated, in the long run the U.S. budget deficit would virtually disappear if it brought its health-care spending in line with other industrialized countries, all of which have universal health coverage.

Third, *there are times when government spending is essential to help the economy over a crisis and when failure to spend will make the deficit worse.*

In the short term, the best way to reduce the deficit without increasing unemployment is to recover from the crisis, not cut spending and create more joblessness while the economy is still weak. This is a lesson we should have learned from the last great global economic collapse, the Depression of the 1930s.

Before the 1930s, most economists believed that economies recovered naturally from recessions: in a downturn, either prices would fall and stimulate spending, or wages would fall and stimulate hiring, or both. But when consumers and businesses stopped spending during the Depression, falling wages and prices made the economy worse. It took the New Deal to get the economy growing. From 1933 through the end of the Depression, GDP rose and fell with government spending. By 1936 unemployment had fallen from 23% to 9%. But in 1937 unemployment rose again after Roosevelt cut the budget to reduce the deficit. After that it took massive spending for World War II to return the economy to full employment.

Stimulus Isn't Enough Either

Given the lessons from the Depression of the 1930s, why didn't the Obama stimulus plan work better than it did?

One reason is that the housing bubble drained nearly $1.4 trillion in annual spending, yet the Obama administration proposed a stimulus that was only $825 billion spread over several years. Congressional Republicans then reduced that number to $727 billion. They also cut proposed spending for infrastructure, green energy, and aid to states so they could increase tax cuts, even though tax cuts are known to create fewer jobs.

But the deeper reason the Obama stimulus failed is that the administration misunderstood the nature of the crisis. The country needs more than stimulus spending for recovery. It needs a sustained program for rebuilding the real economy and raising wages. The problem isn't just that cutbacks over the past decades have left us with a shortage of over two trillion dollars in infrastructure spending. It's that growing inequality has created too big a hole in demand.

During the boom following World War II, the United States regularly used government spending to ease recessions. The idea was that instead of waiting for unemployment to push down wages in the hopes that low wages would boost hiring, the government should boost job creation, and hence wages, by plugging holes in private consumption with public expenditures.

This worked because during the post-war boom, wages as a matter of policy rose with productivity. Recessions were due to short-term policy missteps or the "business cycle"—production temporarily getting ahead of demand. When that happened, businesses made fewer profits and investment would fall. Government spending would boost demand. And demand would spur investment.

In the current economy, stimulus spending can't accomplish what it did in the post-war economy. Not only have we just had a massive financial crisis rather than a dip in the business cycle, but the crisis happened after decades of stagnating wages. Since the 1980s, demand has been based not on rising wages, as it was in the post-war era, but on household debt backed by the rising prices of assets such as stocks and real estate.

With the bursting of the housing bubble, 28% of homeowners are now under water. Under these circumstances, households that get a temporary bump in disposable income from a stimulus package are as likely to pay down debt as they are to increase spending. Even households that aren't in debt may save instead of spending because of fear of unemployment. The economy may get a small boost. But businesses correctly see that demand isn't there and hold back from investing. The economy remains in a hole unless the government embarks on a sustained program of rebuilding wages, jobs, and the real economy.

How We Unlearned Equality

To understand what it will take to rebuild the economy, we have to understand the strength of the post-war economy and how it was reversed.

The great economic lesson of the post-war era was the importance of equality for economic growth and stability. The period before the Great Depression had been marked by steep inequality, debt, and bubbles. Following World War II, the governments of the United States and most of Western Europe made commitments to full employment and rising wages in order to avoid another similar collapse. Global growth reached record rates. Inequality declined. And there were no serious global financial crises.

In the United States, real hourly wages roughly doubled during this period. The policies that made this wage growth and stability possible included corporate acceptance of collective bargaining; a strong social safety net; high quality public services; regulation of business; progressive tax systems—where corporations and the wealthy are taxed at higher rates—to help pay for public services and the cost of regulation; deficit spending to stimulate the economy during economic downturns, thereby preventing wages from falling; and a willingness to lower interest rates when unemployment rose.

Corporate tolerance for these pro-labor policies was transitory and grudging: it lasted as long as the extraordinary post-war levels of profit lasted. Once global profit rates slowed, corporations fought to reverse wage growth and restore profit rates under the guise of the policy mix that came to be known as neoliberalism. They attacked labor rights, the minimum wage, and unemployment insurance. They pushed to reduce taxes on corporations and the wealthy, shifting the tax burden to working people instead. They lobbied to privatize public services and deregulate industries—opening opportunities for profits, denigrating the role of government, and increasing the likelihood of financial crises. The rhetoric of balanced budgets and self-reliance replaced support for a strong safety net and stimulus spending to stabilize wages during recessions. And interest rate hikes were used to minimize inflation—now touted as a primary threat to living standards—by *raising* unemployment and keeping wages low.

There were changes in international policy as well. After World War II, U.S. trade policy had focused on opening up markets for U.S. exports, which meant not only higher profits but higher domestic employment. Under neoliberalism, boosting profits meant moving production to lower cost areas overseas and exporting back to the United States. It meant cutting jobs at home as well as and pushing down wages abroad.

In short, while the post-war strategy supported rising incomes in the United States and much of the rest of the world, the strategy from the 1980s onward was built on stagnating or falling wages for workers generally. The result was that the global rate of profit rose while hourly wages stagnated or fell, with few exceptions, throughout the globe—not just in the United States and developing countries, but in Europe as well.

Going Global: Coordination, not Competition

Jobs debates tend to focus on national needs. We're told repeatedly that competition is the key to a country's economic success: increase productivity, decrease labor costs, hone our technology, and we'll beat out the other guy to get the jobs. But the kind of development the world needs for recovery isn't a zero-sum game. U.S. labor needs healthy manufacturing and wage growth in other countries every bit as much as we need a revival of manufacturing and wages in the United States.

Achieving the objectives proposed in this article—rising wages, demand-led growth, and global development—will require both struggle and international coordination. Labor is familiar with many of the economic tools that will be needed to achieve these core objectives, but it is used to applying them in a national context only, not advocating for their use as part of a global development agenda. Here are a few of the most familiar tools that will be needed and what labor can add by pressing for international coordination:

Fiscal and monetary policy to support employment growth. Governments need to return to wider use of fiscal and monetary policy to stimulate demand and put a floor on unemployment. But in a global economy, stimulus spending can end up "leaking" out of a country when consumers buy imports. Stimulus is most effective when countries act together so one country can't "steal" demand from another by keeping its wages and demand low while another country raises wages and expands demand.

Labor rights and employment regulation to raise wages. Using fiscal and monetary policy to put a floor on unemployment can help keep wages from falling. But wage growth needs a vigorous commitment to collective bargaining, social benefits such as health care and pensions, minimum and living wage laws, and a strong safety net for unemployed and underemployed workers. These policies are most effective when widely adopted, both because widespread adoption raises global demand and also because it discourages low-wage competition.

Tax reform to provide adequate revenues. Tax reform is needed to ensure that the wealthy and corporations pay their share of the costs for the economic crisis, and to provide revenue for rebuilding and development. Corporate tax reform in particular needs to be coordinated to prevent corporations from gaming differences in countries' tax rates by relocation or transfer pricing. Since the crisis began, a vigorous global movement has sprung up for a financial transaction tax, which could raise hundreds of billions globally from the finance industry.

Industrial policy to nurture high-wage manufacturing sectors. Ultimately, strong job growth is needed to support strong wage growth. Countries that have developed successfully—including the United States and Britain in their early years, Europe and Japan after World War II, the Asian Tigers in the 1980s, and now China—have done so by using industrial policies to nurture infant industries and growth. These policies have included such measures as regulation of the movement of capital in and out of the country; government investment in infrastructure, education, research and development; requirements that corporations purchase inputs locally and train local workforces; and facilitating the availability of credit for key industries and sectors. Since the eighties and nineties, neoliberal policies and trade agreements have sought to ban many of these policies and make countries dependent on transnational corporations instead. International labor campaigns to eliminate these bans will be critical for reversing this dependence and the advantage it gives corporations over labor. Freeing countries to use industrial policy will in turn be critical for the growth of green manufacturing and energy production as the world grapples with climate change.

Sources: Damian Paletta and David Enrich, "Banks Gain in Rules Debate," Wall Street Journal, July 15, 2010; Damian Paletta and David Enrich, "Risks Rulebooks Is Nearly Done—Key Aspects of Banks' New Restraints Are Agreed Upon," Wall Street Journal, July 27, 2010; Damien Paletta, "Banks Get New Restraints," Wall Street Journal, September 13, 2010.

To compensate for stagnating purchasing power, U.S. consumers borrowed, and the finance industry made credit more available: between 1981 and 2007, the last year of the housing bubble, household debt doubled as a percentage of GDP. The U.S. consumer became the consumer of last resort for the world. And the global economy balanced precariously on U.S. consumer debt and the dollar.

By the early 2000s, balancing on U.S. consumer debt meant balancing on the housing bubble: dollars exited the country to pay for imports and were recycled back, not as demand for U.S. exports, but as demand for investment in U.S. mortgage securities and other financial assets. The world found out how painful a balancing act this was when the U.S. housing bubble burst, homeowners defaulted on mortgages, and the banking system nearly collapsed, cutting off the supply of easy credit. Global demand plummeted. It hasn't recovered since.

Tackling Inequality Head-on

In its own terms, neoliberalism worked: it increased profits, suppressed wages, and shifted tax burdens from the wealthy to lower income workers. Proponents have seized on the deficits created by the crisis to slash social spending, helping insure against future tax increases for those at the top.

The contradictions *should* be obvious to all: suppressing wages suppresses demand, and balancing consumer spending on debt rather than wages destabilizes the U.S. economy *and* the global economy. Cutting government spending before we rebuild private demand will throw the country and the world back into recession. It will keep U.S. unemployment at Depression-era levels. And it will result in larger, not smaller, deficits.

Yet the contradictions don't register because people have a deep-seated belief that the very inequality that is crashing the system is essential to growth and jobs— that by limiting inequality we are limiting our ability to generate wealth.

To build momentum for a jobs- and wage-based recovery, the labor movement has to tackle the belief in inequality head on. It needs to show that the jobs crisis can only be addressed by rebuilding and rebalancing the national and global economies with higher wages and greater equality.

Rebuild and Rebalance

A broad consensus is developing within the global labor movement on how this rebuilding and rebalancing needs to take place. There are three main goals:

Raise wages, raise demand. The most pressing economic problem today isn't government debt or deficits. It's the hole in demand left by 30 years of wage suppression, and the danger of another period of bubble-fueled growth. To be sustainable, demand has to be based on wages, not on household debt. Inequality isn't just painful for workers. It's destabilizing for the global economy. Correcting inequality isn't a matter of charity. It's a matter of economic survival.

First and foremost, rebalancing the global economy means correcting the global wage imbalance by creating jobs and raising wages. This imbalance isn't primarily about high- versus low-income countries. It's about the share of national incomes going to workers wages and the share going to profit. Since 1980, the share of income going to labor has fallen steadily in all regions of the world, with the possible exceptions of East and Central Asia. The decline hasn't been due to shifts to low-wage occupations. It hasn't been limited to low-wage countries. And it has occurred at all income levels. It's also getting worse. In the current recovery, U.S. corporations captured a whopping 88% of the growth in national income through the beginning of 2010, while only 1% went to labor. Compare that to the recovery after the 1991 recession, when 50% of the growth in national income went to labor.

Replace growth based on low-wage exports with wage- and demand-led growth around the world. As U.S. corporations moved overseas in the eighties and nineties, the U.S. government used the carrot and the stick—as well as its powers over the IMF and the World Bank—to persuade destination countries to cut government spending, let wages fall, remove regulations on movement of foreign capital known as "capital controls," and "devalue" currencies to artificially force down the price of exports. The result was intensified global competition and the emergence of an "export-led" model of growth: economies grew not because rising wages grow domestic demand, but because suppressed wage growth (or falling wages) pushed down the price of exports. Regardless of their income level, countries that adopt the export-led model suppress both wage growth and demand for imports. They export more than they import. And they run permanent trade surpluses while their trading partners lose jobs and run deficits.

European countries that are sharply reducing deficits to deal with the current crisis and letting wages stagnate or fall are turning to the export-led growth model in hopes of becoming "more competitive." This kind of "competitiveness" as a primary strategy for global growth isn't the solution for lagging incomes. It's a recipe for an intensified race to the bottom and permanently depressed wages. It's also impossible for a majority of the world to "export" its way out of the crisis and back to growth; for every country that exports, another must be able to import. The solution, whether in Europe or the developing world, is to trade in the model of export-led growth for one based on rising wages and domestic demand.

Create a global model for economic development and decent work. The idea of stimulus spending is that it "jumpstarts" a cycle of demand, investment, and job creation when a basically healthy economy stalls. Today, living on the "other side" of the export-led model the United States helped create, U.S. consumers are too mired in debt, corporations too addicted to outsourcing and cutting jobs and wages, and the country too far behind in infrastructure spending for this kind of stimulus to be effective. We need to rebuild, not "jumpstart," the U.S. economy. The same is true overseas. Developing countries mired in the export-led model also suffer from a long-term lack of public investment and infrastructure.

To replace the export-led growth model unions need to demand a global agenda for decent work. This in turn requires a program for sustainable development that includes support for public services such as education and health care, funds for infrastructure, and support for sustainable manufacturing and green energy in both advanced and developing countries. The jobs and wages created by this investment will in turn build the base of demand needed for sustained demand-led growth.

Closer Than We Think

There are ways out of the current jobs crisis. Budget-cutting, austerity, and intensified wage competition aren't among them. Unionists need to keep their eyes on the ball: The chief barrier to recovery is the lack of global demand. A main cause of the current crisis is a multi-decade, multi-pronged strategy of wage suppression across the world. And the response must include global coordination for economic development—a global New Deal.

Governments committed to neoliberal policies won't be the prime movers behind a global New Deal. That's labor's job. So is forging the ties with other labor movements that will be needed to carry on the struggle both nationally and internationally. (See sidebar, pp. 16-17.)

This struggle must take place country by country. Over the past decade U.S. unionists have fought successful battles for living wage ordinances. They have won community benefits agreements from corporations receiving public funds, locking in pledges to create jobs and respect labor rights. They've renewed the battle for single-payer health care and made common cause with immigrant workers working at the margins of the U.S. economy. There is crucial organizing for a national infrastructure bank, withdrawal from Iraq and Afghanistan, putting a floor on foreclosures, and taxing the wealthy. Learning new strategies is not going to be the hard part of U.S. labor. Nor will forging international linkages with unions in other countries—a process which will deepen understanding of common problems and exponentially increase the energy and clarity of struggle.

The hard part will be unlearning the indoctrination we've received about the crisis, the role of government in the economy, and the free market. Once we do that, we can build successful movements at home and abroad. We're closer than we think to the army of rank-and-file economists that we need. ❑

Sources: Gerald Friedman, "Bernanke's Bad Teachers," *Dollars & Sense*, July/August 2009 (stimulus spending during the Depression); Michael Greenstone and Adam Looney, "The Great Recession's Toll on Long-Term Unemployment," Brookings Institution UP Front Blog, November 5, 2010; Dean Baker, "The Economic Illiterates Step Up Attacks on Social Security and Medicare," August 2, 2011, cepr.net (inadequate size of the Obama stimulus); Dean Baker, "Barack Obama's Big Stimulus," *The Guardian*, Jan 19th, 2009 (original composition of the Obama stimulus); Katherine Sciacchitano, "W(h)ither the Dollar?," *Dollars & Sense*, May/June 2010; Resolution on a Sustainable and Just Development Model for the 21st Century, International Trade Union Confederation, 2nd World Congress, Vancouver, 21-25 June 2010 (2CO/E/6.4 final); Francisco Rodriguez and Arjun Jayadev, "The Declining Share of Labor Income," UNDP Human Development Research Paper 2010/36; Steven Greenhouse, "The Wageless, Profitable Recovery," *New York Times*, June 30th, 2011; Andrew Sum, Ishwar Khatiwada, Joseph McLaughlin and Sheila Palma, "The 'Jobless and Wageless' Recovery from the Great Recession of 2007- 2009: The Magnitude and Sources of Economic Growth Through 2011 I and Their Impacts on Workers, Profits, and Stock Values," Center for Labor Market Studies Northeastern University Boston, Massachusetts, May 2011; National Infrastructure Development Bank press release, May 20, 2009; Ha Joon Chang, Bad Samaritans: The Myth of Free Trade and the Secret History of Capitalism (Bloomsbury Press, 2008); Thomas I. Palley, "The Rise and Fall of Export-led Growth," Levy Economics Institute of Bard College, Working Paper No. 675, July 2011.

Article 1.4

UNEMPLOYMENT: A JOBS DEFICIT OR A SKILLS DEFICIT?

BY JOHN MILLER AND JEANNETTE WICKS-LIM

January/February 2011

Millions of Americans remain unemployed nearly a year and a half after the official end-date of the Great Recession, and the nation's official unemployment rate continues at nearly 10%.

Why? We are being told that it is because—wait for it—workers are not qualified for the jobs that employers are offering.

Yes, it's true. In the aftermath of the deepest downturn since the Great Depression, some pundits and policymakers—and economists—have begun to pin persistently high unemployment on workers' inadequate skills.

The problem, in this view, is a mismatch between job openings and the skills of those looking for work. In economics jargon, this is termed a problem of "structural unemployment," in contrast to the "cyclical unemployment" caused by a downturn in the business cycle.

The skills-gap message is coming from many quarters. Policymaker-in-chief Obama told Congress in February 2009: "Right now, three-quarters of the fastest-growing occupations require more than a high school diploma. And yet, just over half of our citizens have that level of education." His message: workers need to go back to school if they want a place in tomorrow's job market.

The last Democrat in the White House has caught the bug too. Bill Clinton explained in a September 2010 interview, "The last unemployment report said that for the first time in my lifetime, and I'm not young … we are coming out of a recession but job openings are going up twice as fast as new hires. And yet we can all cite cases that we know about where somebody opened a job and 400 people showed up. How could this be? Because people don't have the job skills for the jobs that are open."

Economists and other "experts" are most likely the source of the skills-gap story. Last August, for instance, Narayana Kocherlakota, president of the Federal Reserve Bank of Minneapolis, wrote in a Fed newsletter: "How much of the current unemployment rate is really due to mismatch, as opposed to conditions that the Fed can readily ameliorate? The answer seems to be a lot." Kocherlakota's point was that the Fed's monetary policy tools may be able to spur economic growth, but that won't help if workers have few or the wrong skills. "The Fed does not have a means to transform construction workers into manufacturing workers," he explained.

The skills-mismatch explanation has a lot to recommend it if you're a federal or Fed policymaker: it puts the blame for the economic suffering experienced by the 17% of the U.S. workforce that is unemployed or underemployed on the workers themselves. Even if the Fed or the government did its darndest to boost overall spending, unemployment would be unlikely to subside unless workers upgraded their own skills.

The only problem is that this explanation is basically wrong. The weight of the evidence shows that it is not a mismatch of skills but a lack of demand that lies at the heart of today's severe unemployment problem.

High-Skill Jobs?

President Obama's claim that new jobs are requiring higher and higher skill levels would tend to support the skills-gap thesis. His interpretation of job-market trends, however, misses the mark. The figure that Obama cited comes from the U.S. Department of Labor's employment projections for 2006 to 2016. Specifically, the DOL reports that among the 30 fastest growing occupations, 22 of them (75%) will typically require more than a high school degree. These occupations include network systems and data communications analysts, computer software engineers, and financial advisors. What he fails to say, however, is that these 22 occupations are projected to represent less than 3% of all U.S. jobs.

What would seem more relevant to the 27 million unemployed and underemployed workers are the occupations with the *largest* growth. These are the occupations that will offer workers the greatest number of new job opportunities. Among the 30 occupations with the largest growth, 70%—21 out of 30—typically do not require more than a high school degree. To become fully qualified for these jobs, workers will only need on-the-job training. The DOL projects that one-quarter of all jobs in 2016 will be in these 21 occupations, which include retail salespeople, food-preparation and food-service workers, and personal and home care aides.

In fact, the DOL employment projections estimate that more than two-thirds (68%) of the jobs in 2016 will be accessible to workers with a high school degree or less. Couple this with the fact that today, nearly two-thirds (62%) of the adult labor force has at least some college experience, and an alleged skills gap fails to be convincing as a driving force behind persistent high unemployment.

LABOR MARKET MUSICAL CHAIRS

To understand the data discussed here, try picturing the U.S. labor market as a game of musical chairs, with a few twists. At any time, chairs (job openings) can be added to the circle and players can sit down (get hired). When the music stops at the end of the month, not all the chairs are filled. Still, many people—far more people than the number of empty chairs—are left standing.

Each month, the Bureau of Labor Statistics reports on what happened in that month's game of labor market musical chairs in its various measures of unemployment and in the Job Openings and Labor Turnover Survey (JOLTS). Here's how the BLS scorecard for labor market musical chairs works.

- **Job openings** is a snapshot of the number of jobs available on the last day of the month—the number of empty chairs when the music stops.

- **Hires** are all the new additions to payroll during the month—the number of people who found a chair to sit in while the music was playing. Because many chairs are added to the circle and filled within the same month, the number of hires over a month is typically greater than the number of openings available on the last day of that month.

- **Unemployed persons** are those who looked for a job that month but couldn't find one—the number of people who played the game but were left standing when the music stopped at the end of the month.

Low-Skill Workers?

If employers were having a hard time finding qualified workers to fill job openings, you'd think that any workers who are qualified would be snapped right up. But what the unemployment data show is that there remains a substantial backlog of experienced workers looking for jobs or for more hours in their existing part-time jobs in those major industries that have begun hiring—including education, healthcare, durable goods manufacturing, and mining.

Most telling are the *underemployed*—those with part-time jobs who want to work full-time. Today there are more underemployed workers in each of the major industries of the private economy than during the period from 2000 to 2007, as Arjun Jayadev and Mike Konczal document in a recent paper published by the Roosevelt Institute. Even in the major industries with the highest number of job openings— education and health services, professional and business services, transportation and utilities, leisure and hospitality, and manufacturing—underemployment in 2010 remains at levels twice as high or nearly twice as high as during the earlier period (measured as a percentage of employed workers).

Purveyors of the mismatch theory would have a hard time explaining how it is that underemployed workers who want full-time work do not possess the skills to do the jobs full time that they are already doing, say, 20 hours a week.

More broadly, workers with a diverse set of skills—not just construction workers—lost jobs during the Great Recession. Workers in manufacturing, professional and business services, leisure and hospitality, transportation and utilities, and a host of other industries were turned out of their jobs. And many of these experienced workers are still looking for work. In each of the 16 major industries of the economy unemployment rates in September 2010 were still far higher than they had been at the onset of the Great Recession in December 2007. In the industries with a large number of (cumulative) job openings during the recovery—education and health services, professional and business services, and manufacturing—experienced workers face unemployment rates twice what they were back in December 2007.

There are plenty of experienced workers still looking for work in the industries with job openings. To be faithful to the data, Kocherlakota and the other mismatch proponents would need to show that experienced workers no longer possess the skills to work in their industry, even though that industry employed them no more than three years ago. That seems implausible.

Statistical Errors

Still, the statistical oddity that Bill Clinton and many economists have pointed to does seem to complicate the picture. If the number of job openings is rising at a good clip yet the number of new hires is growing more slowly and the unemployment rate is stagnant, then maybe employers *are* having trouble finding qualified folks to hire.

Once you take a closer looks at the numbers, though, there is less here than meets the eye.

First, the *rate* at which job openings and new hires numbers change over time is not the right place to look. What we really need to know is how the number of unfilled job posts compares to the number of qualified workers employers hire over the same month. If employers in today's recovery are having a hard time finding workers, then the job openings left unfilled at the end of the month should be relatively high compared to the number of newly hired workers that month. In other words, if the number of positions left unfilled at the end of the month relative to the number of new hires rises *above* what we've seen during past recoveries, this would mean that employers are finding it harder to fill their positions with the right workers this time around.

But it turns out that the ratio of unfilled job openings to new hires is approximately the same during this recovery as in the recovery from the 2001 recession. In September 2010, fifteen months into the current economic recovery, the ratio of job posts left unoccupied at the end of the month to the number of monthly new hires stood at 69%—very close to its 67% level in February 2003, fifteen months into the last recovery. In other words, today's employers are filling their job openings with the same rate of success as yesterday's employers.

Comparisons that focus on the unemployment rate rather than on the number of new hires are even less meaningful. As hiring picks up at the beginning of an economic recovery, workers who had given up the job search start looking again. This brings them back into the official count of the unemployed, keeping the unemployment rate from dropping even as both job openings and new hires rise.

WHERE MISMATCHES MAY MATTER

The skills-mismatch theory does not go very far toward explaining stubbornly high U.S. unemployment. Still, there are unquestionably some unemployed and underemployed workers whose job prospects are limited by "structural" factors.

One kind of structural unemployment that does seem to fit the contours of the Great Recession to at least some degree is that caused by a mismatch of geography: the workers are in one part of the country while the jobs they could get are in another. The housing crisis surely has compromised the ability of unemployed workers to unload their single largest asset, a house, and move to another part of the country. Plus, job losses have been particularly heavy in regions where the housing crisis hit hardest.

But at the same time, lost jobs have been widespread across industries and there is little real evidence of geographic mismatch between job openings and unemployed workers. As labor economist Michael Reich reports, "economic decline and the growth of unemployment have been more widespread than ever before, making it unclear where the unemployed should migrate for greater job opportunities."

Even where there is a skills mismatch, that doesn't mean the government shouldn't get involved. On the contrary, government policies to boost economic demand can help significantly. When demand is high, labor markets become very tight and there are few available workers to hire. Workers previously viewed as "unemployable" get hired, get experience and on-the-job training, and see their overall career prospects brighten.

And, of course, government can fund expanded job-training programs. If the economy continues to slog along with low growth rates and persistent unemployment, the ranks of the long-term unemployed will rise. As they go longer and longer without work, their skills will atrophy or become obsolete and they will face a genuine skills-mismatch problem that will make job-training programs more and more necessary.

Not Enough Jobs

The reality of the situation—the widespread job losses and the long, fruitless job searches of experienced workers—make it clear that today's employment problem is a jobs deficit across the economy, not a skills deficit among those looking for work.

While it's true that any given month ends with some number of unfilled job openings, the total number of jobs added to the economy during this recovery has simply been inadequate to put the unemployed back to work. In fact, if every job that stood open at the end of September 2010 had been filled, 11.7 million officially unemployed workers would still have been jobless.

This recovery has seen far fewer job openings than even the so-called "jobless" recovery following the 2001 recession. Economists Lawrence Mishel, Heidi Shierholz, and Kathryn Edwards of the Economic Policy Institute report that cumulative job openings during the first year of this recovery were roughly 25% lower than during the first year of the recovery following the 2001 recession—that's 10 million fewer jobs. Even in the industries generating the most job openings in the current recovery—education and health services, professional and business services, leisure and hospitality, and manufacturing—the cumulative number of job openings has lagged well behind the figure for those industries during the first year of the recovery from the 2001 recession. (Only the mining and logging category, which accounted for just 0.5% of employment in 2007, has had more job openings during the first year of this recovery than during the first year of the 2001 recovery.)

Why has the pick-up in jobs following the Great Recession been worse than usual? The simple answer is that the recession was worse than usual. The sharp and extreme decline of output and employment in the Great Recession has severely dampened demand—that is, people have not had money to buy things. With the resulting lack of sales, businesses were not willing to either invest or hire; and this in turn has meant a continuing lack of demand.

If businesses have barely resumed hiring, it has not been for lack of profits. By the middle of 2010, corporate profits (adjusted for inflation) were about 60% above their low point at the end of 2008, well on their way back to the peak level of mid-2006. Also, in early 2010 non-financial firms were sitting on almost $2 trillion in cash. There was no lack of ability to invest and hire, but there was a lack of incentive to invest and hire, that is, a lack of an expectation that demand (sales) would rise. As is well known, small businesses have generally accounted for a disproportionately large share of job growth. Yet, since the onset of the Great Recession, small business owners have consistently identified poor sales as their single most important problem—and thus, presumably, what has prevented them from expanding employment.

The Role of Demand

Regardless of the lack of evidence to support it, the skills-mismatch story has seeped into media coverage of the economy. Take, for example, National Public Radio's recent Morning Edition series titled "Skills gap: holding back the labor market." In one segment, reporter Wendy Kaufman presents anecdotes about employers turning down record numbers of applicants and leaving job openings unfilled. Economist Peter Capelli then comes on and remarks, "You know, a generation ago you'd never expect that somebody could come into a reasonably skilled, sophisticated position in your organization and immediately make a contribution. That's a brand new demand." Now, that comment does not point to today's workers possessing fewer skills or qualifications. Rather, it suggests that employers have raised the bar: they are pickier than in the past.

That makes sense. We've seen that employers are successfully filling positions at about the same rate as in the recent past. What's different this time around is that employers have had up to six unemployed workers competing for every job opening left vacant at the close of the month. This is by far the highest ratio on record with data back to 2000. During the 2001 recession, that ratio rose to just over two unemployed workers for each opening. (In the first years of the "jobless recovery" following the 2001 recession, the ratio continued to rise, but it remained below three to one.) Clearly, these numbers favor the alternative explanation. Unfortunately, Kaufman doesn't even consider it.

That's too bad. Recognizing that a lack of demand for goods and services is to blame for the severe crisis of unemployment puts the focus squarely back on the federal government and on the Fed, which could help to remedy the problem —*if* they had the political will to do so. Millions of unemployed workers, organized and armed with an accurate diagnosis of the problem, could create that political will— unless they are distracted by a wrong-headed diagnosis that tries to blame them for the problem. ❑

Sources: Bureau of Labor Statistics Table A-14, Unemployed persons by industry and class of workers, not seasonally adjusted, historical data (bls.gov); Lawrence Mishel, Heidi Shierholz, and Kathryn Anne Edwards, "Reasons for Skepticism About Structural Unemployment," Economic Policy Institute, Briefing Paper #279, September 22, 2010 (epi.org); Arjun Jayadev and Mike Konczal, "The Stagnating Labor Market," The Roosevelt Institute, September 19, 2010 (rooseveltinstitute. org); Bureau of Labor Statistics, Job Openings and Labor Turnover (JOLTS) Highlights, September 2010 (bls.gov); Michael Reich, "High Unemployment after the Great Recession: Why? What Can We Do?," Policy Brief from the Center on Wage and Employment Dynamics, Institute for Research on Labor and Employment, University of California, Berkeley, June 2010 (irle.berkeley.edu/cwed); Narayana Kocherlakota, President Federal Reserve Bank of Minneapolis, "Inside the FOMC," Marquette, Michigan, August 17, 2010 (minneapolisfed.org); Lawrence Mishel and Katherine Anne Edwards, "Bill Clinton Gets It Wrong," Economic Policy Institute, Economic Snapshot, September 27, 2010 (epi.org); "Remarks of President Barack Obama—Address to Joint Session of Congress," February 24, 2009 (whitehouse.gov); "The Skills Gap: Holding Back the Labor Market," Morning Edition, National Public Radio, November 15, 2010 (npr.org).

Article 1.5

HOW BLACKS MIGHT FARE IN THE JOBLESS RECOVERY

BY SYLVIA ALLEGRETTO AND STEVEN PITTS
October 2010

There have been seemingly contradictory announcements recently concerning the economy. In September another 95,000 jobs were shed as the official unemployment rate remained at 9.6%. Unemployment has been at 9.5% or higher for well over a year now. About the same time this bad news about employment came out, it was announced that the recession, which began in December 2007, had actually ended in June of 2009—thus we are several months into the second year of recovery.

How could the recession be over, even amidst continued job losses and stubbornly high unemployment? And how might black workers, whose levels of unemployment have (as usual) been much higher than white workers' in this recession, fare in a "jobless recovery"?

The Dating of the Business Cycle

The task of officially declaring the start and end dates of recessions is performed by the Business Cycle Dating Committee of the National Bureau of Economic Research. The Committee is currently comprised of seven economists (an eighth is on leave) from prominent universities. The Committee examines the data trends of several economic indicators, including measures of:

- Overall output
- Overall national income
- Total employment
- Aggregate hours worked

The Committee did not say that the economy had returned to its pre-recession level of activity or that the economy was strong; it just stated that the decline in several economic measures that began in December 2007 had ended and any new decline in economic activity would represent a new recession. That the economy is not officially in recession does not mean that it doesn't feel as if it is for many workers and their families. There is often not a palpable difference between a recessionary economy and a weak recovery—this is especially true with what are called "jobless recoveries."

What Is Meant by a "Jobless Recovery"?

An economy officially in recovery that continues to shed jobs as if in recession, or experiences prolonged tepid job growth, is deemed a "jobless recovery." In a jobless recovery it takes an inordinate amount of time to recoup the jobs lost during the downturn. While the recession officially ended in June 2009, the employment picture remains quite dismal. At the lowest point for jobs, in December 2009, 8.4 million jobs were lost, which represented 6.1% of all jobs. To date job losses are still at 7.7 million, which represents 5.6% of all jobs. Since the onset of recovery, the monthly employment reports have been mixed, but the net employment level has fallen by an additional 439,000.

Figure 1 depicts the dynamics of recessionary job losses and jobless recoveries. Each line represents the trajectory of job growth from the onset of recession until jobs were finally recouped (when the line crosses the horizontal axis—which represents months since the onset of recession). The solid black line represents average job losses for recessions prior to 1990. (On average the pre-1990 recessions were about eleven months long and it took about 21 months to recoup pre-recessionary job level.)

Job losses due to the 1990 recession (the solid gray line) were just about 1.5%—quite shallow comparatively and the recession was officially just eight months long. But employment lingered at the trough for a long time and it took about 31 months to recoup those lost jobs. The downturn in 2001 (dotted black line) was also eight months long and about 2% of jobs were lost—again relatively mild—but it took 46 months to recoup those lost jobs.

It is clear from the figure that the recession that started in December 2007 (dotted gray line) led to a reduction in employment that far exceeded that of the previous recessions. This recession was 18 months long and ended in June 2009. Job losses were catastrophic. At its worst point jobs were down 8.4 million. Job growth turned positive in the spring of 2010—mostly due to the temporary hiring of Census workers. But shortly after Census workers were hired they were let go, and job growth once again turned negative. At this point it is clear that the labor market is in the realm of a jobless recovery—a prolonged period of negative or weak job growth. It will be a very long time before this economy recoups the enormous amount of jobs lost over this recession.

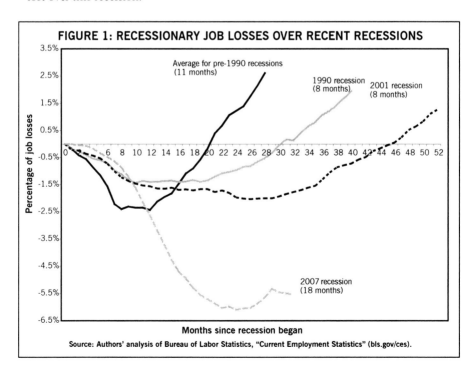

FIGURE 1: RECESSIONARY JOB LOSSES OVER RECENT RECESSIONS

Percentage of job losses

Average for pre-1990 recessions (11 months)

1990 recession (8 months)

2001 recession (8 months)

2007 recession (18 months)

Months since recession began

Source: Authors' analysis of Bureau of Labor Statistics, "Current Employment Statistics" (bls.gov/ces).

How Might Blacks Fare?

While it is difficult to predict exactly what might happen to black workers during this jobless recovery, it is instructive to examine what happened to black unemployment during the last jobless recovery, which followed the 2001 recession. Chart 2 provides key information.

The gray bars in the chart mark key dates of the last two recessions and recoveries. In examining the trend in black unemployment since the 2001 recession, there are six key dates:

- The beginning of the recession (March 2001)
- The official end of the recession (November 2001)
- When job creation turned positive (September 2003)
- When the employment levels returned to pre-recession level (January 2005)
- The beginning of recession (December 2007)
- The official end of the recession (June 2009)

As Figure 2 indicates, unemployment rates continued to rise after the official end of the recession in November 2001. Over the jobless recovery—from November 2001 to September 2003—unemployment increased from 9.8% to 11% for blacks and 4.9% to 5.4% for whites. Black unemployment rates did not begin to steadily fall until the total number of jobs had reached the pre-recession level (January 2005). The unemployment rates for whites started to fall just prior to September 2003—near the end of the jobless recovery.

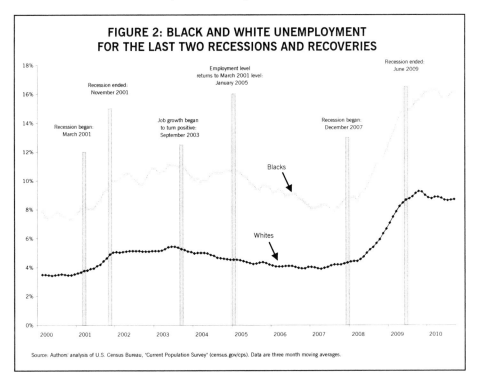

FIGURE 2: BLACK AND WHITE UNEMPLOYMENT FOR THE LAST TWO RECESSIONS AND RECOVERIES

Source: Authors' analysis of U.S. Census Bureau, "Current Population Survey" (census.gov/cps). Data are three month moving averages.

Starting with the onset of the 2007 recession, again the black unemployment rate increased at a faster rate than did that of whites. Since the onset of recovery—in June 2009—the unemployment rate of blacks has increased by 1.4 percentage points, from 14.8% to 16.2%. The rate for whites at the start of recovery was 8.7%, and after an initial increase it is back to that same rate today.

If the 2001 pattern holds, it may well be that the current black unemployment rates will not begin to significantly abate until the employment level returns to its pre-recessionary level of December 2007. This will almost certainly take several years as the shortfall in jobs is currently at 7.7 million. In order to return the national unemployment rate to its December 2007 rate, the economy would need to create 290,000 jobs per month for five years; so far this year job creation has averaged 68,000 per month, even as the last four months have averaged -98,000.

In other words, for many black workers and their families, the recovery will continue to feel like a deep recession for many years to come. ❑

Resources: Bureau of Labor Statistics, "Current Employment Statistics" (bls.gov/ces); National Bureau of Economic Research, "The NBER's Business Cycle Dating Committee" (nber.org/cycles/recessions.html and nber.org/cycles/sept2010.html).

Article 1.6

STILL BANKING ON FRAUD
Reforms fail to address the "control fraud" that caused the financial crisis.

BY WILLIAM K. BLACK
Janurary/February 2011

A truly amazing thing has happened in banking. After the worst finan-cial crisis in 75 years sparked the "Great Recession," we have

- Failed to identify the real causes of the crisis
- Failed to fix the defects that caused the crisis
- Failed to hold the CEOs, professionals, and anti-regulators who caused the cri-sis accountable—even when they committed fraud
- Bailed out the largest and worst financial firms with massive public funds
- Covered up banking losses and failures—impairing any economic recovery
- Degraded our integrity and made the banking system even more encouraging of fraud
- Refused to follow policies that have proved extremely successful in past crises
- Made the systemically dangerous megabanks even more dangerous
- Made our financial system even more parasitic, harming the real economy

And pronounced this travesty a brilliant success.

The Bush and Obama administrations have made an already critically flawed financial system even worse. The result is that the banking industry's future is bad for banking, terrible for the real economy, horrific for the public—and wonderful for the top executives at the largest banks. This is significantly insane, especially given that over the past 30 years, the savings-and-loan fiasco and other crises pro-vided ample opportunity to learn about those flaws. It appears that we will need to suffer another depression before we are willing to put aside the crippling dogmas that have so degraded the financial system, the real economy, democracy, and the ethical standards of private and public elites.

The Economics Blindfold

Why did most of the experts neither foresee nor understand the forces in the U.S. banking industry that caused this meltdown? The short answer is: their dogmatic belief in neoclassical economic theory that is impervious to the facts, or what I like to call "theoclassical" economics.

Theoclassical economics is premised on the asserted effectiveness of private mar-ket discipline. This (oxymoronic) discipline is the basis for the "efficient markets" and "efficient contracts" hypotheses that are the pillars of faith supporting mod-ern finance theory and much of neoclassical microeconomics. Collectively, these hypotheses lead to absolute faith that markets exclude fraud. "A rule against fraud is not an essential or even necessarily an important ingredient of securities markets," wrote eminent corporate law scholars Frank Easterbrook and Daniel Fischel in their 1991 *The Economic Structure of Corporate Law*, in a typical statement of that faith.

How are markets supposed to exclude fraud? Easterbrook and Fischel offer two reasons. The first, a circular argument, lies in theoclassical economists' core belief that markets are by nature efficient. Markets that allow frauds cannot be efficient. Therefore, markets must exclude fraud.

The other argument rests on "signaling" theory. The logical premise is that honest firms have a financial incentive to signal to investors and creditors that they are honest. The false premise is that honest firms have the *unique* ability to signal that they are honest. Easterbrook and Fischel claim that there are three signals of honesty that only honest firms can transmit: hiring a top-tier audit firm, having the CEO own substantial stock in the firm, and operating with extreme leverage, i.e., a high ratio of debt to capital.

The reality, which Fischel knew before he co-authored the treatise, was that firms engaging in so-called control fraud can mimic each of these signals. Control fraud occurs when the executives at a seemingly legitimate firm use their control to loot the firm and its shareholders and creditors. In banking, accounting is the weapon of choice for looting. Accounting control frauds have shown the consistent ability to get "clean" accounting opinions from top tier audit firms; their CEOs use their stock ownership to loot the firm; and they love to borrow extensively, as that allows them to loot the firm's creditors.

In fact, the claim that markets inherently exclude fraud runs contrary to all of our experience with securities markets. The role of epidemics of accounting control frauds in driving recent financial crises is well documented. The national commission that investigated the causes of the savings-and-loan debacle found that at the "typical large failure," "fraud was invariably present." Similarly, the Enron and WorldCom scandals were shown to be accounting control frauds.

Theoclassical economists, however, refused to acknowledge these frauds because recognizing the existence of control fraud would challenge the assumptions underlying their faith-based economic theories. This economic dogma was so dominant that it drove regulatory policy in the United States, Europe, and Japan during the last three decades. Regulations ignored control fraud and assumed that paper profits produced by fraud were real. The result, from the mid-1990s on, was regulatory complacency endorsed by economists who actually praised the worst of the emerging control frauds because of their high reported profits.

So it is no surprise that the recent U.S. banking crisis was driven by an epidemic of lending fraud, primarily mortgage lenders making millions of "liar's loans" annually. According to Credit Suisse, for instance, 49% of all mortgage originations in 2006 were stated-income loans, meaning loans based on applicants' self-reported incomes with no verification. MARI, the Mortgage Bankers Association experts on fraud, warned in 2006 that these loans caused endemic fraud:

Stated income and reduced documentation loans ... are open invitations to fraudsters. It appears that many members of the industry have little historical appreciation for the havoc created by low-doc/no-doc products that were the rage in the early 1990s. Those loans produced hundreds of millions of dollars in losses for their users.

One of MARI's customers recently reviewed a sample of 100 stated income loans upon which they had IRS Forms 4506. When the stated incomes were compared to the IRS figures, the resulting differences were dramatic. Ninety percent of the stated incomes were exaggerated by 5% or more. More disturbingly, almost 60% of the stated amounts were exaggerated by more than 50%. These results suggest that the stated income loan deserves the nickname used by many in the industry, the "liar's loan."

Why would scores of lenders specialize in making liar's loans after being warned by their own experts and even by the FBI that such loans led to endemic fraud? (Not that they needed any warnings. Bankers have known for centuries that underwriting is essential to survival in mortgage lending. Even the label "liar's loan," widely used in the industry, shows that bankers knew such loans were commonly fraudulent.) How could these fraudulent loans be sold to purportedly the most sophisticated underwriters in the history of the world at grossly inflated values blessed by the world's top audit firms? How could hundreds of thousands of fraudulent loans be pooled into securities, the now-infamous collateralized debt obligations (CDOs), and receive "AAA" ratings from the top rating agencies? How could markets that are supposed to exclude all fraud instead accommodate millions of fraudulent loans that hyper-inflated the largest financial bubble in history and triggered the Great Recession?

The answer is the financial system is riddled with incentives so perverse that it is criminogenic—it creates fraud epidemics instead of preventing fraud. When compensation levels for banking executives and professionals are very large and based substantially on reported short-term income, financial firms become superb vehicles for control fraud. Add in deregulation and desupervision, and the result is an environment ripe for a fraud epidemic.

Accounting is the weapon of choice for financial sector control frauds. The recipe for a lender to maximize (fictional) reported accounting income has four ingredients:

- Extremely rapid growth
- Lending regardless of borrower creditworthiness, at premium yields
- Extreme leverage
- Minimal loss reserves

The first two ingredients are related. A U.S. housing lender operates in a mature, reasonably competitive industry. A mortgage lender cannot grow extremely rapidly by making high-quality mortgages. If it tried to do so, it would have to cut its yield substantially in order to gain market share. Its competitors would respond by cutting their yields and the result would be modest growth and a serious loss of yield, reducing reported profits. Any lender, however, can guarantee extremely rapid growth and charge borrowers a premium yield simply by making loans to borrowers who most likely cannot repay them. Worse, hundreds of lenders can follow this same recipe because there are tens of millions of potential homebuyers in the United States who would not be able to repay their loans. Indeed, when hundreds of firms follow the same recipe, they hyper-inflate the resultant financial bubble, which in turn allows borrowers to refinance their loans and thereby delay their defaults for years.

Economists George Akerlof and Paul Romer explained in 1993 that accounting fraud is a "sure thing" and explained why it caused bubbles to hyper-inflate, then burst. Note that the same recipe that produces record *fictional* income in the short-term eventually produces catastrophic *real* losses. The lender will fail (unless it is bailed out or able to sell to the "greater fool"), but with their compensation largely based on reported income, the senior officers can walk away wealthy. This paradox—the CEO prospers by causing the firm's collapse—explains Akerlof and Romer's title, *Looting: The Economic Underworld of Bankruptcy for Profit.*

Senior executives can also use their ability to hire, promote, compensate, and fire to suborn employees, officers, and outside professionals. As Franklin Raines, chairman and CEO of Fannie Mae, explained to *BusinessWeek* in 2003:

Investment banking is a business that's so denominated in dollars that the temptations are great, so you have to have very strong rules. My experience is where there is a one-to-one relation between if I do X, money will hit my pocket, you tend to see people doing X a lot. You've got to be very careful about that. Don't just say: "If you hit this revenue number, your bonus is going to be this." It sets up an incentive that's overwhelming. You wave enough money in front of people, and good people will do bad things.

Raines knew what he was talking about: he installed a compensation system at Fannie Mae that produced precisely these perverse incentives among his staff and made him wealthy by taking actions that harmed Fannie Mae.

In an earlier work, Akerlof had explained how firms that gained a competitive advantage through fraud could cause a "Gresham's" dynamic in which bad ethics drove good ethics from the marketplace. The national commission that investigated the savings and loan debacle documented this criminogenic dynamic: "[A]busive operators of S&L[s] sought out compliant and cooperative accountants. The result was a sort of "Gresham's Law" in which the bad professionals forced out the good." The same dynamic was documented by N.Y. Attorney General Andrew Cuomo's 2007 investigation of appraisal fraud, which found that Washington Mutual blacklisted appraisers who refused to inflate appraisals. An honest secured lender would never inflate, or permit the inflation of, appraisals.

Failure to Respond

The U.S. government's response to the meltdown has been not merely inadequate, but actually perverse. The Bush and Obama administrations' banking regulators have left frauds in charge of failed banks and covered up the banks' losses, allowed the behemoths of the industry to become even larger and more dangerous, and passed a "reform" law that fails to mandate the most critical reforms.

In March 2009, Congress, with the explicit encouragement of Federal Reserve Board Chairman Bernanke and the implicit acceptance of the Obama administration, successfully extorted the Financial Accounting Standards Board on behalf of the banking industry to force it to change the banking rules so that banks did not have to recognize losses on their bad assets until they sold them. Normal accounting rules sensibly require banks to recognize losses on bad loans when the problems with the loans are not "temporary." The losses at issue in the recent crisis were caused by system-wide fraud and the collapse of the largest financial bubble in world history. They were not temporary—moreover, they were (and are) massive. If banks had recognized these losses as they were required to do under pre-existing accounting rules, many of them would have had to report that they were unprofitable, badly undercapitalized, or even insolvent.

Gimmicking the accounting rules so bankers could lie about their asset values has caused the usual severe problems. First, it allows CEOs to pretend that unprofitable banks are profitable and so continue to pay themselves massive bonuses. This is not only unfair; it contributes to a broadly criminogenic environment. Second, it leads banks to hold onto bad home loans and other assets at grossly inflated prices, preventing markets from clearing and prolonging the recession. This is the Japanese scenario that led to the country's "lost decade" (now extended). Third, it makes it harder for regulators to supervise vigorously, should they try to do so, because many regulatory powers are triggered only when losses occur with the resulting failure to meet capital requirements. Indeed, the assault on honest accounting was launched with the express purpose of evading the Prompt Corrective Action law, passed in 1991 on the basis of bitter experience: when savings-and-loan CEOs who had looted "their" institutions were allowed to remain in control of them by using fraudulent accounting, the losses and the fallout of the S&L crisis kept growing. Fourth, it embraces dishonesty as an official policy. Indeed, it implies that the solution to the accounting fraud that massively inflated asset valuations is to change the accounting rules to encourage the massive inflation of those same asset values. Effective regulation is impossible without regulatory integrity; lying about asset values destroys integrity.

Even in the case of the roughly 20 massive U.S. financial institutions considered "too big to fail," the public policy response has been perverse. The terminology itself demonstrates how economists err in their analysis—and how much they identify with the CEOs who helped cause the Great Recession. They refer to the largest banks as "systemically important institutions," as if these banks deserved gold stars. By the prevailing logic, however, the massive banks are the opposite: ticking time bombs that can take down the global financial system if they fail. So "systemically dangerous institutions," or SDIs, would be more apt.

It should be a top public policy priority to end the ability of any single bank to pose a global systemic risk. That means that the SDIs should be forbidden to grow, required to shrink over a five-year period to a size at which they no longer pose a systemic risk, and intensively supervised until they shrink to that size. These reforms are vital for all banks but particularly urgent for the SDIs, with their potential to cause massive damage.

Instead, the opposite has been done. Both administrations have responded to the financial crisis by allowing (indeed, encouraging) SDIs, even insolvent ones, to acquire other failed financial firms and become even larger and more systemically dangerous to the global economy. The SDIs' already perverse incentives were made worse by giving them a bailout plus the accounting cover-up of their losses on terms that made the U.S. Treasury and the Federal Reserve the "fools" in the market.

With small- and medium-size banks likely to continue to fail in high numbers due to residential and commercial real estate losses, the financial crisis has increased the long-term trend toward extreme concentration in the financial industry. The SDIs will pursue diverse business strategies. Some will continue their current strategy of borrowing short-term at extremely low interest rates and reinvesting the proceeds primarily in government bonds. They will earn material, not exceptional, profits but will do little to help the real economy recover. Others will invest in whatever asset category offers the best (often fictional) accounting income. They will drive the next U.S.-based crisis.

What about the long-awaited bank reform law, which Congress finally delivered in July 2010 in the form of the Dodd-Frank Act? The law does not address the fundamental factors that have caused recurrent, intensifying financial crises: fraud, accounting, executive and professional compensation, and regulatory failure. The law does create a regulatory council that is supposed to identify systemic risks. The council, however, will be dominated by economists of the same theoclassical stripe who not only failed to identify the systemic risks that produced the recent financial crises, but actually praised the criminogenic incentives that caused those crises.

The chief international reform, the Basel III accord, shares the fundamental deficiency of the Dodd-Frank Act. Dominated as they were by theoclassical economists, the Basel negotiations not surprisingly produced an agreement that ignores the underlying causes of the crisis. Instead, it focuses on one symptom of the crisis—extreme leverage, the third ingredient of the recipe for optimizing accounting control fraud. The remedy was to restore capital requirements to roughly the levels required under Basel I (Basel II eviscerated European banks' capital requirements). Fortunately, the United States did not fully implement the Basel II capital reserve reductions, which means that the leverage of non-fraudulent U.S. banks has been significantly lower than their European counterparts. However, capital requirements only have meaning under honest accounting. Once one takes into account the fictional "capital" produced by fraudulent lending—along with the revised accounting rules that are helping banks hide their losses—the irrelevance of the proposed Basel III capital requirements becomes clear. (For more on the Dodd-Frank Act as well as Basel III, see "Underwater" in this volume.)

If the Dodd-Frank Act of 2010 and the Basel III proposals are the limits of our response to the crisis, then the most probable outcome in the near- and medium-term is the Japanese scenario—a weak, delayed, and transitory recovery followed by periodic recessions. Banks will remain weak and a poor provider of capital for economic expansion.

With private market "discipline" having become criminogenic, the only hope for preventing the current crisis was vigorous regulation and supervision. Effective supervision *is* possible. For instance, in 1990-91, savings-and-loan regulators used their hard-won understanding of accounting control fraud to stop a developing pattern of fraud in California involving S&Ls making stated-income loans. Unfor-tunately, at the federal level the dogmatic belief that markets automatically prevent fraud led to complacency and the appointment of anti-regulators chosen for their willingness to praise and serve their banking "customers."

(The "reinventing government" initiative championed by former Vice President Al Gore and by George W. Bush when he was Texas' governor indeed instructed banking regulators to refer to bankers as their "customers.") President Obama has generally left in office, reappointed, or promoted the heads (or their "acting" successors) of the Office of the Comptroller of the Currency, the Office of Thrift Supervision, the Federal Reserve, the Federal Reserve Bank of New York, and the Federal Housing Finance Agency. Several of these leaders did not simply fail as federal regulators; they actually made things worse by aggressively preempting state regulatory efforts against fraudulent and predatory mortgage lenders.

None of the reforms to date addresses the fundamental criminogenic incentive structures that have produced recurrent, intensifying financial crises. True, liar's loans have been largely eliminated, and in 2008 the Federal Reserve finally used its regulatory authority under the Home Ownership and Equity Protection Act of 1994 to regulate mortgage bankers (after most of the worst ones had failed), but none of this came soon enough to contain the current crisis and none of it will prevent the next one. The accounting control frauds merely need to switch to a different asset category for a time. ❏

Sources: George A. Akerlof, 1970, "The Market for 'Lemons': Quality Uncertainty and the Market Mechanism," *Quarterly Journal of Economics* 84(3):488–500; George A. Akerlof and Paul G. Romer, 1993, "Looting: The Economic Underworld of Bankruptcy for Profit," in W. Brainard and G. Perry, eds., *Brookings Papers on Economic Activity* 2:1-73; William K. Black, 2003, "Reexamining the Law-and-Economics Theory of Corporate Governance," *Challenge* 46(2):22-40; William K. Black, 2005, *The Best Way to Rob a Bank Is to Own One: How Corporate Executives and Politicians Looted the S&L Industry*, Austin: University of Texas Press; Frank Easterbrook and Daniel Fischel, 1991, *The Economic Structure of Corporate Law,* Cambridge, Mass.: Harvard University Press; National Commission on Financial Institution Reform, Recovery and Enforcement (NCFIRRE), 1993, *Origins and Causes of the S&L Debacle: A Blueprint for Reform.* Washington, D.C.: Government Printing Office.

Chapter 2

PUBLIC-SECTOR WORKERS

Article 2.1

AMERICA'S PUBLIC-SECTOR WORKERS UNDER ATTACK
It's not about their pay and benefits—it's about what they do.

BY GERALD FRIEDMAN
November/December 2011

From California to Massachusetts, from Texas to Wisconsin, whether by fiat or through bargaining, state governments would balance their budgets by taking a meat ax to public employee wages, benefits, and jobs. Behind the headlines, the relative strength of public-sector unions has long made them a target for economists and conservatives hostile to all forms of working-class collective action and any regulation of the capitalist marketplace. Labor economist Leo Troy set the tone for many when he warned in 1994 of "A New Society" that was emerging, dominated by unions of public employees and a redistributive state. While market competition had beaten back the threat of private-sector unionism, public employee unions, in his view, had renewed the socialist challenge to free enterprise.

Ideologues like Troy inspired an ongoing attack on public-sector unions to defend America from socialism. When he accepted the Republican presidential nomination in 1996, for example, Bob Dole singled out the teachers' unions for attack. While this was a great applause line, Dole lost the election. This has been the outcome of most of the right's attack on public-sector workers and unions: applause from the far right and some of the media but little resonance among a public that generally supports public services and those who provide them.

It may be that those who would attack public employees and their unions as sponsors of incipient socialism have learned to conceal their real motives. Instead of attacking public services, they present themselves as advocates for private-sector workers and insist that they only seek to eliminate inequities between private- and public-sector workers. New Jersey Gov. Chris Christie denounces public-sector unions as creating "two classes of citizens: one that receives rich health and pension benefits, and all the rest who are left to pay for them."

It is odd to find such touching concern for equity among those who have campaigned relentlessly to widen disparities between rich and poor and between managers and workers. In any case, such equity concerns should be relieved by the growing body of empirical studies showing that public-sector workers are *not* overpaid compared with private-sector workers. Nor is there evidence that public-sector unions have been diverting national income towards their exorbitant salaries and staffing. State and local taxes took 9% of income in 1990 and 9% in 2007. As a share of national income, state and local employee compensation has fallen since the 1990s despite rising demands on the public sector—to improve education, repair infrastructure, clean up the environment, and provide health care to growing numbers left out of our private health care system.

When neither evidence nor popular opinion can deflect political attacks on public-sector workers, then we should look for some deeper ideological hostility rather than rational explanation. Public-sector workers and their unions are not under attack because their salaries have grown, because of a groundswell of popular hostility, nor because their pay and employment benefits are swamping the capacity of the public. They are under attack because their very existence and the commitment of public-sector workers to provide services without regard to ability to pay or the market distribution of income challenges the legitimacy of markets. Public schools, public health services, public roads and parks, even public police and fire protection offend those who would restrict such services to those who can pay for them, denying them to the poor, the young, and the disabled. Their view may be shaped by racial and gender animosity: not only are a disproportionate share of public employees women and people of color, but so are their young and low-income clientele.

If the reactionaries are now winning where Dole had earlier failed, it may be because they have new allies, enablers who have turned against public employees in a misguided attempt to protect public services and liberal values. Republicans have been the face of the attack on public employees but Democrats, even liberals, have been right there with them. New York's Governor Andrew Cuomo, Massachusetts's Deval Patrick and California's Jerry Brown have all found political advantage in attacking public employee unions. Indeed, in his 2011 state of the state address, Christie found support for his anti-worker stance in the words of Cuomo and Brown, whose calls for austerity and wage cuts, Christie declared, were inspired by New Jersey's example. By lending credibility to reactionaries like Christie, liberals like Brown and Cuomo provide political cover for attacks on public-sector workers.

But there is more here than simple political opportunism. The anti-public employee rhetoric from Cuomo, Patrick, and other liberals reflects the frustration of pro-government liberals five years into the worst economic recession since the 1930s. Years of falling revenues and rising state and local deficits have forced liberal politicians to make agonizing choices among competing needs. After cutting schools to save road repair and cutting Medicaid to save drug rehabilitation programs, liberal politicians have come to look covetously at public employee salaries and benefits. In the labor-intensive work of education and providing social services, everything liberals want to do comes up against the cost of paying workers; and a chance to reduce those costs means a chance to save services in times of austerity. As Assemblyman Angel Fuentes, a Camden Democrat who represents one of the neediest cities in the United States, said in endorsing Governor Christie's program, "These reforms are unquestionably bitter pills for us to swallow, but they are reasonable and they are necessary" because "towns across this state" are laying off workers to pay for health benefits for their employees.

One can understand how these liberal enablers would try to protect spending even by cutting public employee pay. The problem is that they have accepted a false choice that pits public services against each other rather than against other uses of the public's money, including private consumption. There is no economic logic in taking the pool of government revenue as fixed rather than considering whether public services should be preserved by reducing *private* expenditure by raising taxes. But if we are to argue that liberals are wrong to accept the need to cut government spending, then we need to develop alternatives to austerity. We need to articulate not only a defense of the work of the public sector, but also a coherent way to fund it.

Here's how:

- "Flip" the state and federal tax systems. A recent report by United for a Fair Economy demonstrates how shifting the tax burden so that the wealthiest would pay the rates currently borne by the poorest would eliminate state budget deficits; under such a plan, for example, New Jersey would raise some $12 billion in additional revenue, more than enough to restore all of Governor Christie's spending cuts while dramatically increasing state support for communities like Camden. Since 1979, federal tax cuts have saved households in the top 0.1% nearly $90 billion a year. Reversing those cuts would supply enough revenue to balance state budget deficits for the current fiscal year.

- Federal revenue sharing. This program was established during the Nixon administration, repealed under Reagan and brought back briefly and under a different name under Obama. It could eliminate the need for state and local spending cuts by sharing with these governments the abundant revenues of the national government and its capacity to borrow.

- Upgrade Social Security and establish universal, single-payer health coverage. By dramatically reducing their labor costs, improved national pensions and health insurance would immediately solve the fiscal problems of states and localities. Even enacted on a state level, universal pensions and single-payer health systems would realize huge savings. For example, a single-payer health insurance program on the state level, such as Vermont is currently establishing, could save between 15% and 30% of the current cost of health care, savings of between 3% and 6% of state income. In addition to being a boon for business and consumers, this would produce huge savings throughout state and local governments. In Massachusetts, for example, cities and towns could save over $320 million on their current health care spending and the state government would save over $2 billion, more than this year's budget deficit.

It is time to stop playing defense against the often absurd and always misguided attacks on public employees. There are alternatives to austerity. All that we need is the political will to demand them. ❑

Sources: Michael Cooper and Megan Thee-Brenan, "Majority in Poll Back Employees in Public Sector Unions," *New York Times*, February 28, 2011; David M. Halbfinger, "Gov. Chris Christie of New Jersey Lays Out Tight Budget," *New York Times*, February 22, 2011; Jeffrey Keefe, "Debunking the Myth of the Overcompensated Public Employee: The Evidence," Economic Policy Institute, September 15, 2010; Karen Kraut, Shannon Moriarty, and Dave Shreve, *Flip it to Fix it: An Immediate, Fair Solution to State Budget Shortfalls,* United for a Fair Economy, May 25, 2011; Elizabeth McNichol, Phil Oliff, and Nicholas Johnson, "States Continue to Feel Recession's Impact," Center on Budget and Policy Priorities, June 17, 2011; Richard Pérez-Peña, "N.J. Legislature Moves to Cut Benefits for Public Workers," *New York Times*, June 23, 2011; Jeffrey Thompson and John Schmitt, "The Wage Penalty for State and Local Government Employees in New England," Political Economy Research Institute and CEPR, September 2010; Leo Troy, *The New Unionism in the New Society: Public Sector Unions in the Redistributive State*, Fairfax, Va.: George Mason University Press, 1994.

Article 2.2

WHAT WISCONSIN MEANS

BY ROGER BYBEE
May/June 2011

When Wisconsin Gov. Scott Walker addressed the Milwaukee Press Club on Friday Feb. 11 about public-sector union rights, he sounded less like a rookie governor floating a legislative proposal than a uniformed *generalissimo* issuing a demand for total capitulation.

Citing a $137 million state budget "crisis," Walker called for the legislature to act immediately on a bill that would effectively gut the union rights of state and local public employees (except for police and firefighters) by, among other things, prohibiting collective bargaining over any issue besides wages, limiting contracts to one year, eliminating dues check-off, and forcing unions to win annual re-certification votes. His address was followed by a carefully timed barrage of radio and TV ads funded by the right-wing lobby group Club for Growth. Highlighting recent concessions made by workers at several private-sector companies in the state, the ads called for sacrifices from supposedly overpaid public workers in the name of "fairness."

Then, as everyone knows, all hell broke loose.

The dramatic events of the month that followed—from the massive daily demonstrations, to the self-imposed exile of Democratic state senators to an Illinois hotel, to Gov. Walker's revealing 20-minute phone conversation with an activist impersonating one of his wealthiest patrons—inspired labor activists across the nation and captured international headlines. The state capital was under a non-violent siege for some six weeks. Outdoor rallies drew as many as 100,000 people despite frigid weather, while inside, the ornate Capitol was occupied by protesters who held sleep-ins and organized clean-up patrols to keep the halls neat. The protests drew a mixture of public employees (including firefighters, police, and state troopers whose unions were exempt from Walker's proposal), private-sector union members, high school students who had walked out of their classes, university students, and a 50-strong "tractor-cade" of farmers. Smaller but equally diverse groups of protesters staged rallies in cities and towns across Wisconsin.

In a narrow sense the protests failed: the new law passed in the early morning hours of March 9 following questionable procedural maneuvers that will likely keep it tied up in the courts for months. Now, some of the progressive energy evident in February and March has been channeled into recall campaigns against several Republican legislators. In a closely watched election, a pro-labor challenger unexpectedly took on an incumbent conservative for a seat on the state supreme court. How the state's unions of teachers and other public-sector workers will carry on if the new law is upheld is an open question.

In the meantime, Walker's eroding popularity testifies to at least some weakness in a corporate-Right coalition effort to target hapless public employees as a means of crippling labor, weakening the Democrats' electoral chances, and preventing public resentment over widespread economic insecurity from turning upward.

The Right Pushes Its Luck

The massive outburst of labor-based protest exploded in Wisconsin just three months after this Democratic-leaning state (e.g., Wisconsin has voted for every Democratic presidential candidate since 1988, giving Barack Obama a 14-point edge) went through the nation's sharpest turn to the right in the mid-term elections last November. The Democrats lost a U.S. Senate seat, two U.S. House seats, and the governor's chair, and both houses of the state legislature flipped to big Republican majorities.

Nonetheless, Walker was taking a big chance when he pushed not only to force significant wage and benefit cuts on the state's public employees but also to go after their rights to collective bargaining. But the stakes were high, and Walker was not

Making Union Representation Futile

In 1959, Wisconsin, under Democratic Gov. Gaylord Nelson, was the first state to legalize collective bargaining by local public employees. In 1967, Republican Gov. Warren Knowles expanded these rights to state employees. Today, the state's new law on public-employee unions would make it nearly impossible for them to function. Among its provisions:

- Public-employee unions would be restricted to bargaining only over wages.

- Public-employee contracts would be restricted to a length of one year.

- Unions would be required to hold an annual re-certification election.

- Unions would no longer be allowed to collect dues via dues checkoff, nor could they assess non-members "agency fees" for the costs of representing them.

- Wage increases above the inflation rate could be granted only with the passage of a local referendum.

- State and local public employees would pay 12.6% of their health costs, a doubling of their present share. Pension payments for public employees would rise to 5.6%. This would amount to a pay cut of approximately 8%.

- Limited-term employees would lose all health-care benefits.

- University of Wisconsin faculty, granted collective-bargaining rights for the first time in 2009, would again be deprived of any union rights.

- Graduate teaching and research students would be required to pay about 20% of their income to cover health-care benefits.

acting alone. His election last November and his policy agenda as governor owe much to networks of right-wing and pro-corporate lobbies, think tanks, and individuals, from the billionaire Koch brothers to organizations like the Club for Growth, Americans for Prosperity, FreedomWorks, and the American Legislative Exchange Council. In Wisconsin and around the country, the offensive against public-sector unions has the potential to accomplish many of the aims of these networks.

Billionaire David Koch, with his brother Charles, gave $43,000 in direct contributions to Walker's campaign and another $1 million to the Republican Governors Association, which spent $3.4 million on negative ads targeting Walker's Democratic opponent last fall. The Koch brothers have been major funders of a national crusade to essentially extinguish unionism as a force on the U.S. landscape, as Judith Davidoff described in a Feb. 23 *Capital Times* article. Koch Industries, the largest privately held corporation in the United States, has 3,000 employees in Wisconsin at facilities including a Georgia-Pacific toilet-paper plant, several power plants, and numerous pipelines. (Interestingly, Walker's budget-repair bill would give the governor the power to sell state-owned power plants under no-bid procedures.)

In this vein, Walker's effort would have provided a model, showing other Republican governors how to crush what is now the last bastion of union strength in the United States. In the private sector, union density nationally has fallen to 6.9%, compared to 36.2% in the public sector. In some states, public employees make up more than half of all union members.

Walker did not openly characterize his bill as aimed at sacking unions. Instead he focused his public statements on the need for severe spending cuts to balance the state's budget.

On one level this strategy backfired when the major public unions, the 23,000-member Wisconsin State Employees Union and the Wisconsin Education Association Council, representing 98,000 teachers and other school employees, agreed to the economic concessions but declared that their union rights were sacrosanct. Walker was left sputtering, "There is no room to compromise. We are broke." By refusing to take "Yes" for an answer, Walker's aim of destroying public-sector unions was unmasked.

In the long run, strong public-employee unions do raise their members' pay and benefits, with consequences for state and municipal budgets, as Jane Slaughter of *Labor Notes* has pointed out. But those effects do not constitute a crisis; for Walker, the real crisis was not a budget problem to be solved, rather an opportunity to be seized. Besides inspiring his fellow Republican governors, a quick "shock therapy" success against public unions would have set the stage for further shifting Wisconsin from its generally progressive traditions toward a low-wage, de-unionized, Southern-style model where the undisputed first priority of state government is to subsidize large corporations.

Weakening public-employee unions would confer political benefits as well, depriving the Democrats of a key on-the-ground organizational asset and a major source of funds. The *Capital Times*'s Davidoff summarized labor's vital electoral role: "As the 2010 elections showed, public sector unions were the only groups with enough cash and people power to counter the corporate money that flowed to

Republicans once spending restrictions were lifted by the U.S. Supreme Court ruling in the Citizens United case."

State Senate Majority Leader Scott Fitzgerald offered a blunt admission of the GOP's political motives on Fox-TV: "If we win this battle, and the money is not there under the auspices of the unions, certainly what you're going to find is President Obama is going to have a much difficult, much more difficult time getting [re-]elected and winning the state of Wisconsin."

Labor Pushes Back

Walker and his advisers no doubt miscalculated. They evidently believed that a recent round of painful concessions endured by private-sector union workers—for instance, at Mercury Marine, Harley-Davidson, and Kohler, where profitable firms had extorted massive wage cuts via two-tier wage structures, using the threat of relocating the jobs—would serve to justify an all-out attack on public-sector workers in the name of "fairness" and "shared sacrifice."

During the campaign, Walker depicted public-sector workers as a pampered, privileged class shielded from the free-market solution to excessive wage costs. "We can no longer live in a society where the public employees are the haves and taxpayers who foot the bills are the have-nots," he declared.

In reality, public employees are implausible villains: studies show they earn less than their peers in the private sector for comparable work. (See "State Workers Face a Compensation Penalty," *D&S,* March/April 2011.) An Economic Policy Institute study of Wisconsin wages found a private-sector pay and benefit advantage of 4.2% to 8.4% when educational differences are taken into account. And the allegedly high-end pension benefits public employees receive actually average just $19,000 nationally.

This time, divide-and-conquer did not work so well. Instead of blaming their own and the state's fiscal troubles on teachers and highway workers, a broad swath

MORE DRACONIAN THAN TAFT-HARTLEY

Wisconsin's new law on public-employee unions "goes further than anything since the Taft-Hartley Act of 1947," according to labor historian Stephen Meyer of UW-Milwaukee. Taft-Hartley was the law that brought the New Deal-era expansion of collective-bargaining rights to a sudden halt. Among other provisions, it allowed states to adopt "right-to-work" laws which ban union shops yet mandate unions to undertake the cost and responsibility of representing members and non-members alike.

"In fact," says Meyer, "Walker's plan is worse than the 'right-to-work' laws because it requires that unions get certified by their members yearly, at the same time that the unions are prevented from accomplishing anything for their members."

"Right-to-work" laws alone make it hard for unions to first get established and then to survive over the long haul. The shift of much U.S. industry to the South, where right-to-work laws are ubiquitous, has helped to drive private-sector unionization in the entire nation to 6.9%, down from about 35% in the mid-1950s.

of Wisconsinites seemed to recognize Walker's action as a concerted effort to drive down wages for working people generally, and his manufactured budget crisis as a ploy to compensate for the non-payment of taxes by Wisconsin corporations. Somehow, perhaps because of their over-the-top arrogance, the new governor's tactics quickly re-ignited Wisconsin's still-smoldering pro-labor tradition. As observed by political scientist and sociologist Frances Fox Piven, author of numerous works on social movements like *Poor People's Movements* and *Challenging Authority*, "The Wisconsin uprising was largely unpredictable. It's always hard to assess when people are going to be able to see beyond the clichés and fabrications of politically powerful."

"In Wisconsin, maybe this maneuver was just too obvious, maybe the elites have tried it too many times," Piven reflected. "When it becomes this transparent, when we are told that we must have cuts in rights and earnings for public sector workers, food and health while taxes are being cut for corporations, it becomes clear that it is a manufactured crisis."

The Wisconsin protests are crucial to build upon, says Piven, because they have reflected a profound rejection of the elite notion that state and federal deficits necessitate more sacrifices for working people but continued incentives and tax cuts for corporations and the wealthy.

Other observers agree that the Wisconsin uprising revealed a major progressive opening in the state. The level of support for labor and against corporate domination of state government was evident not just in major rallies in Madison and Milwaukee, but also in unprecedented crowds of 2,000 showing up in tiny hamlets like Burnett. On a single day, pro-labor rallies were held in 19 different cities, showing a much greater reach than past protest movements.

The strength of the pro-labor, anti-Walker movement reflects a growing awareness that middle-class jobs are under systematic attack. As Mike Imbrogno, a cook at UW-Madison who makes $28,000 a year, put it: "[Walker's] basically trying to smash the last remaining organized upward pressure on wages and benefits in Wisconsin." This message clearly resonated with thousands of non-union members around the state.

The issue of tax fairness is also emerging with a new force, as evidenced by the proliferation of protest signs denouncing corporate tax loopholes. "I'm pleased with recent polls saying that nearly 70% of Wisconsinites support higher taxes as part of a balanced solution to the budget challenges. People are always much more favorable toward taxes when they know the money will go to something important that matters to them, such as public education, services for the frail elderly or severely disabled, or garbage collection," says Jack Norman, research director of the Institute for Wisconsin's Future.

Labor attorney and former gubernatorial candidate Ed Garvey sees the recent uprising as a turning point for labor and progressives after years of defeats. "Labor had lacked the confidence that it could win the middle class to its side until the Wisconsin eruption. But the now the movement really has the confidence that it will win in the recall elections and frustrate Walker's efforts to obliterate unions."

Labor's rebellion in Wisconsin has created a large group of new leaders with the potential for building a very broad movement to challenge corporate power, in the view of Michael Rosen, president of American Federation of Teachers

Local 212. "Right now, there's enormous potential for a genuine workers movement that is broader than just labor, incorporating low-wage immigrant workers, environmentalists, church and neighborhood groups," says Rosen. "Labor brings organizational strength and resources while the new movements bring energy, passion, courage, and numbers."

While Walker's anti-union moves are on hold in the courts, labor and progressives have a chance to do something even more important than recalling Republican state legislators: to build a durable coalition that will support union rights and oppose draconian budget cuts. ❑

Sources: Judith Davidoff, "Walker's Plan to End Bargaining Has Deep Roots in GOP," *The Capital Times*, February 23, 2011; Ethan Pollack, "State Workers Face a Compensation Penalty," *Dollars & Sense*, March/April 2011; William P. Jones, "Public employees: Low-wage workers would be the hardest hit," *Milwaukee Journal Sentinel*, February 14, 2011; Roger Bybee, "Class War Heats Up in Wisconsin," *Z Magazine*, April 2011; Les Leopold, *The Looting of America*, Chelsea Green Publishing, 2009; David Kocieniewski, "G.E.'s Strategies Let It Avoid Taxes Altogether," *The New York Times*, March 24, 2011, Jane Slaughter, "Collective Bargaining Rights: A Money Issue," *Labor Notes*, March 19, 2011.

Article 2.3

STATE WORKERS FACE A COMPENSATION PENALTY

BY ETHAN POLLACK
March/April 2011

The campaign against state and local workers is often justified with claims that they are privileged relative to their private-sector peers or have somehow been cushioned from the effects of the recent recession and slow recovery. Data from Wisconsin as well as Indiana, New Jersey, and Ohio prove that these claims are clearly false.

In Wisconsin, which has become a focal point in this debate, public servants already take a pretty hefty pay cut just for the opportunity to serve their communities, according to findings by Rutgers economist Jeffrey Keefe. The figure below shows that when comparing the total compensation (which includes non-wage benefits such as health care and pensions) of workers with similar education, public-sector workers consistently make less than their private-sector peers. Workers with a bachelor's degree or more—who make up nearly 60% of the state and local workforce in Wisconsin—are compensated between $20,000 a year less (if they just have a bachelor's degree) to over $82,000 less (if they have a professional degree).

True apples-to-apples comparisons require controlling for worker characteristics such as education in order to best measure a worker's potential earnings in a different sector or industry. Controlling for a larger range of earnings predictors—including not just education but also age, experience, gender, race, etc., Wisconsin public-sector workers face an annual compensation penalty of 11%. Adjusting for the slightly fewer hours worked per week on average, these workers still face a compensation penalty of 5% for choosing to work in the public sector.

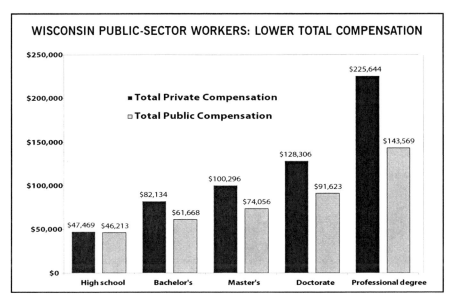

WISCONSIN PUBLIC-SECTOR WORKERS: LOWER TOTAL COMPENSATION

PUBLIC- AND PRIVATE-SECTOR WORKERS COMPARED					
		Job experience		% w/ 4-yr degree	
	Public-sector Penalty	Public	Private	Public	Private
Indiana	7.5%	24.1 years	21.6	49%	24%
New Jersey	4.1%	24	22	57%	40%
Ohio	6%	23.2	21.7	49%	26%
Wisconsin	11%	22.5	21.3	59%	30%

The story is similar in Indiana, New Jersey, and Ohio. Public-sector workers in all of these states also face an annual compensation penalty—of 7.5%, 4.1%, and 6%, respectively. As in Wisconsin, a higher percentage of public-sector workers than private-sector workers in these states have a four-year college degree, as well as more job experience on average (see table).

The deficit that these states face is caused by the economic downturn and, in Wisconsin, a recent tax-cut package. It has nothing to do with the compensation of the people that educate our children, keep the streets safe and clean, keep dangerous chemicals out of our water, and keep insurance companies from taking advantage of us. These public servants are already paid less than those in the private sector, and nationally, this gap has actually been increasing over the past few decades, according to a report by University of Wisconsin-Milwaukee economists Keith Bender and John Heywood.

Instead of opportunistically using these hard times to target workers who—because of their public service—already take a substantial pay cut, state politicians should focus on creating jobs and boosting the incomes of all workers. ❑

A version of this article originally appeared as a "Snapshot" at the Economic Policy Institute website (epi.org).

Sources: Keith Bender and John Heywood, "Out of Balance: Comparing Public and Private Sector Compensation over 20 Years," National Institute on Retirement Security, Washington, D.C., April 2010, (sige.org); Jeffrey H. Keefe, "Are Wisconsin Public Employees Overcompensated?," Economic Policy Institute, Washington, D.C., February 10, 2011 (epi.org); Economic Policy Institute, Reports on public-sector worker undercompensation in Ohio, Indiana, and New Jersey, Washington, D.C., February 18, 2011 (epi.org).

Article 2.4

THE BETRAYAL OF PUBLIC WORKERS

*It's not only bad politics for states to use their budget crises to bust unions—
it's bad economics.*

BY ROBERT POLLIN AND JEFFREY THOMPSON

March 2011; The Nation

The Great Recession and its aftermath are entering a new phase in the United States, which could bring even more severe assaults on the living standards and basic rights of ordinary people than we have experienced thus far. This is because a wide swath of the country's policy- and opinion-making elite have singled out public sector workers—including schoolteachers, healthcare workers, police officers and firefighters—as well as their unions and even their pensions as deadweight burdens sapping the economy's vitality.

The Great Recession did blow a massive hole in state and municipal government finances, with tax receipts—including income, sales and property taxes—dropping sharply along with household incomes, spending and real estate values. Meanwhile, demand for public services, such as Medicaid and heating oil assistance, has risen as people's circumstances have worsened. But let's remember that the recession was caused by Wall Street hyper-speculation, not the pay scales of elementary school teachers or public hospital nurses.

Nonetheless, a rising chorus of commentators charge that public sector workers are overpaid relative to employees in comparable positions in the private sector. The fact that this claim is demonstrably false appears not to matter. Instead, the attacks are escalating. The most recent proposal gaining traction is to write new laws that would allow states to declare bankruptcy. This would let them rip up contracts with current public sector employees and walk away from their pension fund obligations. Only by declaring bankruptcy, Republican luminaries Jeb Bush and Newt Gingrich argued in the *Los Angeles Times*, will states be able to "reform their bloated, broken and underfunded pension systems for current and future workers."

But this charge is emanating not only from the Republican right; in a front-page story on January 20, the *New York Times* reported on a more general trend spreading across the country in which "policymakers are working behind the scenes to come up with a way to let states declare bankruptcy and get out from under crushing debts, including the pensions they have promised to retired public workers."

Considered together, state and local governments are the single largest employer in the US economy. They are also the country's most important providers of education, healthcare, public safety and other vital forms of social support. Meanwhile, the official unemployment rate is stuck at 9%—a more accurate figure is 16.1%—a full eighteen months after the recession was declared over. How have we reached the point where the dominant mantra is to dismantle rather than shore up state and local governments in their moment of crisis?

Why States Need Support During Recessions

The Wall Street–induced recession clobbered state and local government budgets. By 2009, state tax revenues had fallen by fully 13% relative to where they were in 2007, and they remained at that low level through most of last year. By comparison, revenues never fell by more than 6% in the 2001 recession. Even during the 1981–82 recession, the last time unemployment reached 9%, the decline in state tax revenues never exceeded 2%. These revenue losses, starting in 2008, when taken together with the increased demand for state services, produced an average annual budget gap in 2009–11 of $140 billion, or 21% of all state spending commitments.

Unlike the federal government, almost all state and local governments are legally prohibited from borrowing money to finance shortfalls in their day-to-day operating budgets. The state and local governments do borrow to finance their long-term investments in school buildings, roads, bridges, sewers, mass transit and other infrastructure projects. They have established a long record of reliability in repaying these debt obligations, even during the recession. Nevertheless, these governments invariably experience a squeeze in their operating budgets during recessions, no matter how well they have managed their finances during more favorable economic times.

If, in a recession, states and municipalities are forced to reduce their spending in line with their loss in tax revenues, this produces layoffs for government employees and loss of sales for government vendors. These cutbacks, in turn, will worsen conditions in the private market, discouraging private businesses from making new investments and hiring new employees. The net impact is to create a vicious cycle that deepens the recession.

As such, strictly as a means of countering the recession—on behalf of business interests as well as everyone else in the community—the logic of having the federal government providing stimulus funds to support state and local government spending levels is impeccable. The February 2009 Obama stimulus—the American Recovery and Reinvestment Act (ARRA)—along with supplemental funds for Medicaid, has provided significant support, covering about one-third of the total budget gap generated by the recession. But that leaves two-thirds to be filled by other means. ARRA funds have now run out, and the Republican-controlled House of Representatives will almost certainly block further funding.

In 2010 roughly another 15% of the budget gap was covered by twenty-nine states that raised taxes and fees-for-services. In general, raising taxes during a recession is not good policy. But if it must be done to help fill deepening budgetary holes, the sensible way to proceed is to focus these increases on wealthier households. Their ability to absorb such increases is obviously strongest, which means that, unlike other households, they are not likely to cut back on spending in response to the tax hikes. In fact, ten states—New York, Illinois, Connecticut, North Carolina, Wisconsin, Oregon, Hawaii, Vermont, Rhode Island and Delaware—have raised taxes progressively in some fashion.

Of course, the wealthy do not want to pay higher taxes. But during the economic expansion and Wall Street bubble years of 2002–07, the average incomes of the richest 1% of households rose by about 10% per year, more than three times that for all households. The richest 1% received fully 65% of all household income growth between 2002–07.

One charge against raising state taxes in a progressive way is that it will encourage the wealthy to pick up and leave the state. But research on this question shows that this has not happened. We can see why by considering, as a hypothetical example, the consequences of a 2% income tax increase on the wealthiest 5% of households in Massachusetts. This would mean that these households would now have $359,000 at their disposal after taxes rather than $370,000—hardly enough to affect spending patterns significantly for these households, much less induce them to relocate out of the state. At the same time, a tax increase such as this by itself will generate about $1.6 billion for the state to spend on education, healthcare and public safety.

But even with the ARRA stimulus funds and tax increases, states and municipalities have had to make sharp cuts in spending. More severe cuts will be coming this year, with the ARRA funds now gone. These include cuts that will reduce low-income children's or families' eligibility for health insurance; further cuts in medical, homecare and other services for low-income households, as well as in K–12 education and higher education; and layoffs and furloughs for employees. The proposed 2012 budgets include still deeper cuts in core areas of healthcare and education. In Arizona, the governor's budget would cut healthcare for 280,000 poor people and reduce state support for public universities by nearly 20%. In California, Governor Brown is proposing to bring spending on the University of California down to 1999 levels, when the system had 31% fewer students than it does today.

State and Local Government Workers Are Not Overpaid

Even if state and local government employees are not responsible for the budgetary problems that emerged out of the recession, are they nevertheless receiving bloated wage and benefits packages that are holding back the recovery? Since the recession began, there has been a steady stream of media stories making such claims. One widely cited 2009 Forbes cover article reported, "State and local government workers get paid an average of $25.30 an hour, which is 33% higher than the private sector's $19.... Throw in pensions and other benefits and the gap widens to 42%."

What figures such as these fail to reflect is that state and local government workers are older and substantially better educated than private-sector workers. Forbes is therefore comparing apples and oranges. As John Schmitt of the Center for Economic Policy Research recently showed, when state and local government employees are matched against private sector workers of the same age and educational levels, the public workers earn, on average, about 4% less than their private counterparts. Moreover, the results of Schmitt's apples-to-apples comparison are fully consistent with numerous studies examining this same question over the past twenty years. One has to suspect that the pundits who have overlooked these basic findings have chosen not to look.

State Pension Funds Are Not Collapsing

Not surprisingly, state and local government pension funds absorbed heavy losses in the 2008–09 Wall Street crisis, because roughly 60% of these pension fund assets were invested in corporate stocks. Between mid-2007 and mid-2009, the total value of these pension funds fell by nearly $900 billion.

This collapse in the pension funds' asset values has increased their unfunded liabilities—that is, the total amount of benefit payments owed over the next thirty years relative to the ability of the pension funds' portfolio to cover them. By how much? In reality, estimating the total level of unfunded liabilities entails considerable guesswork. One simply cannot know with certainty how many people will be receiving benefits over the next thirty years, nor—more to the point—how much money the pension funds' investments will be earning over this long time span. The severe instability of financial markets in the recent past further clouds the picture.

Thus, these estimates vary by huge amounts, depending on the presumed rate of return for the funds. The irony is that right-wing doomsayers in this debate, such as Grover Norquist, operate with an assumption that the fund managers will be able to earn returns only equal to the interest rates on riskless US Treasury securities. Under this assumption, the level of unfunded liabilities balloons to the widely reported figure of $3 trillion. To reach this conclusion, the doomsayers are effectively arguing that the collective performance of all the Wall Street fund managers—those paragons of free-market wizardry—will be so anemic over the next thirty years that the pension funds may as well just fire them and permanently park all their money in risk-free government bonds. It follows that the profits of private corporations over the next thirty years will also be either anemic or extremely unstable.

But it isn't necessary to delve seriously into this debate in order to assess the long-term viability of the public pension funds. A more basic consideration is that before the recession, states and municipalities consistently maintained outstanding records of managing their funds. In the 1990s the funds steadily accumulated reserves, such that by 2000, on average, they were carrying no unfunded liabilities at all. Even after the losses to the funds following the previous Wall Street crash of 2001, the unfunded share of total pension obligations was no more than around 10%. By comparison, the Government Accountability Office holds that to be fiscally sound, the unfunded share can be as high as 20% of the pension funds' total long-term obligations.

A few states are facing more serious problems, including New Jersey, Illinois and California. New Jersey is in the worst shape. But this is not because the state has been handing out profligate pensions to its retired employees. The average state pension in New Jersey pays out $39,500 per year. The problem is that over the past decade, the state has regularly paid into the system less than the amount agreed upon by the legislature and governor and stipulated in the annual budgets. For 2010 the state skipped its scheduled $3.1 billion payment altogether. However, even taking New Jersey's worst-case scenario, the state could still eliminate its unfunded pension fund liabilities—that is, begin running a 100% fully funded pension fund—if it increased the current allocation by about 4% of the total budget, leaving 96% of the state budget allocation unchanged.

In dollar terms, this worst-case scenario for New Jersey would require the state to come up with roughly $4 billion per year to cover its pension commitments in an overall budget in the range of $92 billion. Extracting this amount of money from other programs in the budget would certainly cause pain, especially when New

Jersey, like all other states, faces tight finances. But compare this worst-case scenario with the bankruptcy agenda being discussed throughout the country.

To begin with, seriously discussing a bankruptcy agenda will undermine the confidence of private investors in all state and municipal bonds—confidence that has been earned by state and municipal governments. When the markets begin to fear that states and municipalities are contemplating bankruptcy, this will drive up the interest rates that governments will have to pay to finance school buildings, infrastructure improvements and investments in the green economy.

Then, of course, there is the impact on the pensioners and their families. For the states and municipalities to walk away from their pension fund commitments would leave millions of public sector retirees facing major cuts in their living standards and their sense of security. Something few Americans understand is that roughly one-third of the 19 million state and local employees—i.e., those in fifteen states, including California, Texas and Massachusetts—are not eligible for Social Security and will depend exclusively on their pensions and personal savings in retirement. In addition, public sector pensions are not safeguarded by the federal Pension Benefit Guaranty Corporation. Unlike Wall Street banks, state pensioners will receive no bailout checks if the states choose to abrogate their pension fund agreements.

Getting Serious About Reforming State Finances

Of course, there are significant ways the public pension systems, as well as state and local finances more generally, can be improved. The simplest solution, frequently cited, involves "pension spiking"—that is, practices such as allowing workers to add hundreds of hours of overtime at the end of their careers to balloon their final year's pay and their pensions. This has produced serious additional costs to pension obligations in some states and municipalities, but it is still by no means a major factor in explaining states' current fiscal problems.

But states and municipalities also have to follow through on the steps they have taken to raise taxes on the wealthy households that are most able to pay. They should also broaden their sources of tax revenue by taxing services such as payments to lawyers, as well as by taxing items purchased over the Internet. And they have to stop giving out large tax breaks to corporations as inducements to locate in their state or municipality instead of neighboring locations. This kind of race to the bottom generates no net benefit to states and municipalities.

Finally, state and local governments are in the same boat as the federal government and private businesses in facing persistently rising healthcare costs. As was frequently noted during the healthcare debates over the past two years, the United States spends about twice as much per person on healthcare as other highly developed countries do, even though these other countries have universal coverage, longer life expectancies and generally healthier populations. These costs weigh heavily on the budgets of state and local governments, which finance a large share of Medicaid and health benefits for state employees. The problem is that we spend far more than other countries on medications, expensive procedures and especially insurance and administration. We also devote less attention to prevention. It remains to be seen how much the Obama healthcare reform law—the 2010 Patient Protection and Affordable Care Act—will remedy this situation. It is certainly the case that more must be done, especially in establishing effective controls on the drug and insurance industries.

These are some of the long-run measures that must be taken to bolster the financing of education, healthcare, public safety and other vital social services, as well as to support investments in infrastructure and the green economy. If states declare bankruptcy they will break their obligations to employees, vendors, pensioners and even bondholders, which will undermine the basic foundations of our economy. As we emerge, if only tentatively, from the wreckage of the Great Recession, this is precisely the moment we need to strengthen, not weaken, the standards of fairness governing our society. ❑

Article 2.5

TEACHERS, SECRETARIES, AND SOCIAL WORKERS: THE NEW WELFARE MOMS?

BY RANDY ALBELDA
May/June 2011

Conservatives have had their sights on public-sector workers for a while and for good reason. Public-sector workers represent two favorite targets: organized labor and government. I am a public-sector employee and union member, so I can't help but take these attacks and struggles personally. I am also a veteran of the welfare "reform" battles of the 1990s, and the debates over public-sector workers are strikingly similar.

Like welfare moms, public-sector workers have been painted as greedy [fill-in-the-blank barnyard animals], feeding from the public trough and targeted as the primary source of what's wrong with government today.

Like 1990s welfare-reform debates, this one is dominated by more fiction than fact. For example, previous and recent research consistently shows public-sector workers actually earn less than private-sector workers with comparable skills and experience. While many, but not all, public-sector workers who work long enough for the public sector have a defined-benefit pension, the unfunded portions of those pensions are often due to bad state policy, not union negotiations.

In some states, like my own, Massachusetts, current workers are paying most of their pension costs through their own contributions into interest-bearing pension funds. Because state and local governments with defined pensions do not contribute to social security, there are currently cost savings. The upshot is that the cost of pensions may not be as high as some are arguing.

It is true that health-insurance costs for current retirees are expensive and worrisome. But this is because of the rising costs in private health insurance. Making workers pay more for their health-care benefits will erode the compensation base of public-sector workers, but it won't get at the real problem of escalating health-care costs.

During the welfare debates, one of the arguments used to justify punitive legislative changes was spun around the fact that welfare moms who did get low-wage employment could also get child-care assistance—while other moms could not. Sound familiar? Public-sector workers do have employer-sponsored benefits many private-sector workers no longer get. But benefits haven't improved in the public sector over the last 20 years; indeed most public-sector workers are paying more for the same benefits.

Over the same period, many private-sector workers have been stripped of their employer-provided benefits even as profits have soared. Instead of asking why corporate America is stripping middle-class workers of decent health-care coverage and retirement plans, the demand is to strip public-sector workers of theirs.

The new Cadillac-driving welfare queens are the handful of errant politicians who game the pension system and a few highly paid administrators getting handsome pensions. Sure they exist, but are hardly representative. The typical public-sector worker is a woman, most often working as a teacher, secretary or social worker. Women comprise 60% of all state and local workers (compared to their 47% representation in the private work force). And those three occupations make up 40% of the state and local work force.

Shaking down public-sector unions may make some feel better about solving government fiscal problems, but the end result will be more lousy jobs for educated and skilled workers. It will also not stem the red ink that is causing states to disinvest in much-needed human and physical infrastructure with budget cuts. But eroding wages and benefits combined with public-sector bashing will send a very loud market signal to the best and brightest currently thinking about becoming teachers, librarians, or social workers to do something else.

Wisconsin Governor Scott Walter is leading the attack on public-sector workers today. In the 1990s it was another Wisconsin governor, Tommy Thompson, who was a leader in demanding and implementing punitive changes to his state's welfare system. His plan became a model for the rest of the states and federal welfare legislation in 1996. Then there were horror stories and welfare bashing, but not much in the way of discussing the real issue of decent paying jobs that poor and low-income mothers on and off welfare needed to support their families. The main result of welfare reform was the growth in working-poor moms.

There is one important difference. Public-sector workers, unlike welfare moms, have unions and a cadre of supporters behind them. ❏

Chapter 3

UNIONS AND WORKING CONDITIONS

Article 3.1

WRONG ABOUT RIGHT-TO-WORK

Laffer throws another curve-ball.

BY JOHN MILLER
July/August 2011

BOEING AND THE UNION BERLIN WALL

Two policies have consistently stood out as the most important in predicting where jobs will be created and incomes will rise. First, states with no income tax generally outperform high income tax states. Second, states that have right-to-work laws grow faster than states with forced unionism.

As of today there are 22 right-to-work states and 28 union-shop states. Over the past decade (2000-09) the right-to-work states grew faster in nearly every respect than their union-shop counterparts: 54.6% versus 41.1% in gross state product, 53.3% versus 40.6% in personal income, 11.9% versus 6.1% in population, and 4.1% versus -0.6% in payrolls.

The Boeing incident makes it clear that right-to-work states have a competitive advantage over forced-union states. So the question arises: Why doesn't every state adopt right-to-work laws?

—Arthur B. Laffer and Stephen Moore, *Wall Street Journal* op-ed, May 13, 2011

What do you get when you mix a *Wall Street Journal* editorial writer with a supply-side economist?

That's right: more of the same.

This time, however, it's right-to-work laws, not taxes, that come in for the full Laffer treatment (although without the illustration on the back of a cocktail napkin).

In May of this year, the National Labor Relations Board (NLRB) issued an injunction to stop defense giant Boeing from moving a jet production line from its unionized factories in Washington state to right-to-work South Carolina. The

International Association of Machinists & Aerospace Workers union had filed a complaint that the planned move was in retaliation against strikes the union conducted over the last decade, and thus illegal.

The NLRB decision amounts to "a regulatory wall with one express purpose: to prevent the direct competition of right-to-work states with union-shop states," insist Arthur Laffer, the supply-side economist, and Stephen Moore, former head of the far-right economics think tank Club for Growth and now on the *Wall Street Journal*'s editorial board. Right-to-work laws enforced in 22 states, mostly in the southern and western United States, prohibit businesses and unions from agreeing to contracts that stipulate that an employer will hire only workers who join the union or pay union dues. In right-to-work states, unions confront a free-rider problem: they have to organize workers who can benefit from collective bargaining without joining (or staying in) the union or paying dues.

The disadvantages that right-to-work states impose on unions give those states a competitive advantage that will enrich them, according to Laffer and Moore. And their report, "Rich States, Poor States," has the numbers to prove it, or so they claim. Right-to-work states grow faster, add more income, create more jobs, and attract more people than states hamstrung by pro-union labor laws.

But it turns out that the claim that right-to-work laws lead states to prosper is no more credible than Laffer's earlier claim that cutting income taxes would spur such an explosion of economic growth that government revenues would actually rise despite the lower tax rates. Much like what Laffer had to say about tax cuts and economic growth, Laffer and Moore make the case for right-to-work laws as the key to economic prosperity through sleight of hand and half-truths.

Let's take a look at exactly where their story goes wrong.

Something Up Their Sleeve

To begin with, Laffer's and Moore's report needs to be read carefully. Their claim is that the economies of states with right-to-work laws grow faster, not that their citizens are better off.

And they are not. For instance, while it is true that both output and income have grown faster in right-to-work states than in other states over the last decade, the growth is from a much lower starting point. In fact, output and income in those states still lag well behind the levels in non-right-to-work states. Personal income per capita averaged $37,134 (in 2010) and real GDP per capita averaged $39,365 (in 2009) in right-to-work states, but $41,312 and $42,513 respectively in the other 28 states.

The positive job creation numbers that Laffer and Moore report for right-to-work states over the last decade haven't resulted in superior job prospects for those out of work. With their faster growing populations, right-to-work states had unemployment rates averaging 8.0% in April of this year, just below the 8.2% average in non-right-to-work states.

And in practice, right-to-work laws are very much "right-to-work-for-less" laws, as union critics call them. In a recent Economic Policy Institute briefing paper, economists Elise Gould and Heidi Shierholz looked closely at the differences in compensation between right-to-work and non-right-to-work states. Controlling for the demographic and job characteristics of workers as well as state-level economic conditions and cost-of-living differences across states, they found that in 2009:

- Wages were 3.2% lower in right-to-work states vs. non-right-to-work states–about $1,500 less annually for a full-time, year-round worker.

- The rate of employer-sponsored health insurance was 2.6 percentage points lower in right-to-work states compared with non-right-to-work states.

- The rate of employer-sponsored pensions was 4.8 percentage points lower in right-to-work states. On top of that, in 2008 the rate of workplace deaths was 57% higher in right-to-work states than non-right-to-work states, while the 2009,poverty rate in right-to-work states averaged 15.0%, considerably above the 12.8% average for non-right-to-work states.

But here is the real kicker: once their effect is isolated from the effects of other factors, right-to-work laws seem to have little or no impact even on economic growth itself. For instance, a 2009 study conducted by economist Lonnie Stevans concludes that:

While ... right-to-work states are likely to have more self-employment and less bankruptcies on average relative to non-right-to-work states, there is certainly no more business capital. ... Moreover, from a state's economic standpoint, being right-to-work yields little or no gain in employment and real economic growth. Wages and personal income are both lower in right-to-work states, yet proprietors' income is higher.

Those lower wages and lower personal incomes are especially detrimental in today's fragile economic recovery, still plagued by a lack of consumer spending.

A Bad Move

The evidence above militates against the notion that right-to-work laws are the key to economic prosperity for state economies, and in favor of the notion that anti-union laws, much like deregulation and tax cuts targeted at the rich, are another mechanism for securing more and more for the well-to-do at the expense of most everyone else.

That is especially clear when it comes to Boeing's planned move from Washington state to South Carolina. Ironically, union-heavy Washington tops right-to-work South Carolina in Laffer's and Moore's Economic Outlook Rankings for 2010 and in their Economic Performance Rankings for 1998- 2008. Personal income, output, and employment all grew considerably faster in Washington state than in South Carolina from 1998 to 2008. And personal income per capita and GDP per capita in Washington state ($43,564 and $45,881 respectively) far exceed their levels in South Carolina ($33,163 and $30,845).

Beyond that, unemployment and poverty rates in Washington state are both well below those in South Carolina. By all those measures, Washington's economy is far and away the more vibrant of the two.

Working conditions are a lot better in Washington state too, something not lost on Boeing. Wage workers in Washington state on average make $11,020 a year more than their counterparts in South Carolina. Production workers in Washington state earn $5,560 a year more. South Carolina workers are 69% more likely to die on the job than workers in Washington. And not surprisingly, just 6.2% of wage and salary workers in right-to-work South Carolina were union members in 2010, versus more than 20% in Washington.

So then why does Boeing want to leave the Evergreen State for the Palmetto State? To benefit from a more vibrant economy? Or to take advantage of workers whose ability to organize is hindered by right-to-work laws, whose bargaining power has been eroded by high unemployment and poverty, who have few alternatives than to endure working in far more dangerous conditions while getting paid less than workers in Washington? The numbers speak for themselves.

No wonder the NLRB filed an injunction against Boeing's planned move. Labor board members saw it for what it is: not a mere relocation, but an exercise of raw power intended to bust a union.

Sources: Arthur B. Laffer and Stephen Moore, "Rich States, Poor States: ALEC-Laffer State Economic Competitiveness Index, 3rd edition," Wall Street Journal, April 7, 2010; Lonnie K. Stevans, "The Effect of Endogenous Right-to-Work Laws on Business and Economic Conditions in the United States: A Multivariate Approach," Review of Law & Economics, Vol. 5, Issue 1, 2009; Elise Gould and Heidi Shierholz, "The Compensation Penalty of 'Right-to-Work' Laws," Economic Policy Institute Briefing Paper #299, February 17, 2011 (epi.org); Gordon Lafar, "'Right-to-Work': Wrong in New Hampshire," Economic Policy Briefing Paper #302, April 5, 2011 (epi.org); Carl Horowitz, "NLRB Sues Boeing; Seeks End to Commercial Jet Production in South Carolina," National Legal and Policy Center, May 4, 2011 (nlpc.org).

Article 3.2

CONFLICTING DREAMS
The Strikes That Made Boeing a Flashpoint

BY JOSH EIDELSON
September/October 2011

Boeing makes the future. That's the recurring message of Boeing's "Future of Flight" tour, which brings visitors from around the world through its Everett factory in Washington State. The tour begins with a sign announcing that Boeing will "shape the future," and then carries you through employee elevators encouraging riders to "embrace the future."

Now Boeing is in a high-profile legal battle with national implications. It's the latest round in a decades-long labor struggle. At stake: Do workers at Boeing get to shape their own future, and Boeing's? Or do they just have to embrace—or rather, submit to—the corporation's plan?

The National Labor Relations Board case against Boeing drew national head-lines this summer, and it will again as the case winds through the board's process and Republicans seize more opportunities to bash President Obama for appointing board members who may actually enforce labor law against employers. Though several media outlets have run with Republican claims that the case is an effort to punish South Carolinians for their state's right-to-work law, it's actually about Boeing's alleged effort to punish its Puget Sound workers for striking by moving work to South Carolina. The NLRB's General Counsel issued the complaint (roughly comparable to an indictment) after Boeing executives publicly and repeatedly declared that they would be producing a new line of Dreamliner aircraft in South Carolina because Puget Sound workers kept going on strike—four times since 1989. The National Labor Relations Act protects the right of workers to strike without actual or threatened retaliation.

Last month I went to Puget Sound to hear directly from workers there why they've chosen time and again to strike.

The International Association of Machinists represents 29,000 workers at Boeing's Puget Sound plants in Renton, Seattle, and Everett. A dozen of them told me how strikes have allowed them to achieve and sustain their standard of living.

Safety and Sane Scheduling

Workers went on strike in 1989 to win protections for safety and restrictions on overtime. John Jorgenson, who just retired from Boeing after 45 years, is one of six employees in his building who were diagnosed with kidney cancer, which he blames in part on the chemicals they worked with before the 1989 strike. The strike won new protective gear and the elimination of dozens of chemicals judged unsafe.

Jorgenson says excessive overtime is one reason that so many Boeing workers from the pre-1989 period are now divorced, himself included. He remembers working eleven hours a day without a day off for 16 weeks. He would worry about falling asleep at work or while driving home. Brian Pelland, who started work at Boeing in 1988, says he hardly saw his kids in his first year on the job. "You're always looking at the future," Pelland says, "and you think you're always going to have time." But eventually the mandatory overtime left him feeling "deadbeat" and "numb." Since the 1989 strike he's been able to make enough money at Boeing to support his kids, while spending enough time outside of work to be in their lives. Without the strike, he says, "I wouldn't know them. They wouldn't know me."

When I asked Jorgenson what his life would be like without that strike, he said "I'd probably still have to work," despite the back injuries that put him out on medical leave for the final six months prior to his retirement at age 65. Before he could describe what that would be like, his wife cut him off. "I don't think so, John. I think with all those chemicals and the stuff you were exposed to … you wouldn't be here."

Defending Their Dream

Though workers have won additional improvements over the past two decades, the dozen employees I spoke to all described the strikes since 1989 primarily as defensive actions aimed at simply maintaining what had been won before. That includes robust pensions and an affordable family health-care plan for workers and retirees.

(Reached by phone, Boeing labor relations spokesperson Tim Healy said that both sides share responsibility for the frequency of strikes.)

The Boeing medical coverage pays for prescription medicine for 15-year employee Jason Redrup's stepson, who's had a liver transplant. Without Boeing benefits, Redrup said, "It would bankrupt me." Then he paused, contemplating what would happen next. "He'd be dead."

Bob Merritt, a 32-year employee, described rushing his daughter to the emergency room after she collapsed on the volleyball court. As he drove, he watched her fingers ball up as she lay in a fetal position in the back seat. "Talk about scared," he says. "We got her in [the ER] and I flashed my health card—damn right I got that insurance." He questioned whether his daughter, who fully recovered, would have gotten adequate treatment if she hadn't had adequate insurance. "There goes your whole life."

The strikes have also given workers confidence that their contract can be enforced. Pelland believes that without the credibility the union has established through striking, Boeing would have found an excuse to fire him. Twenty years ago, working under pressure on a wing line, Pelland slipped on leaking oil and badly sprained his thumb. His doctor sent him back to work with instructions not to grasp with his right hand for two weeks. With a mix of anger and embarrassment, he described his manager announcing at a morning crew meeting, "Oh Brian, he's got some pussy restriction—he can't do his job." "That changed me for life," said Pelland. Without strikes, he said, "they'd throw me away," and the union would lack the clout to stop them.

Dave Swann, who was hired in 1989, says the contract language and clout won through the strikes created opportunities for him to advance at Boeing despite management racism. Growing up, Swann was one of three or four African-American students bussed into a majority white school district in West Seattle. For years before the recent strikes won a new promotions system, managers looked at him "like I was a ghost."

A Changed Membership

The strikes were transformative experiences. For Jorgenson, the scariest was in 1977, when he was recently married to his first wife and making house payments. He says he went into the strike unsure "whether I'm going to have a job or not." He remembers managers swerving their cars towards picketing strikers on their way into work, and then taking photos of picketers from inside the plant.

Jorgenson joined a group calling itself the "Everett Raiders" that worked to discourage replacement workers and keep the spirits of the other strikers up. He compared going through a strike together to going through a war. "You're not really going to desert each other, and you're a lot more willing to endure the pain of going through all of it. And it is painful." The percentage of the workforce on strike went up during the course of the strike rather than down. By the end, he felt "pretty powerful," and when he went back to work, co-workers told him he had helped give them the strength to stay out on strike.

Wilson "Fergie" Ferguson, a military veteran who plays Santa at union Christmas parties, says going on strike for the first time in 1977 "scared the shit out of me." But "anger trumps fear every time. I'm scared until you piss me off."

Pelland says if he had crossed the picket line, "a part of me would have died, and I wouldn't be who I am." Having been guided through the 1989 strike by the veterans, by the time of the 2008 strike Pelland was seeking out newer employees on the picket line. "Can I talk to you about how the company bluffs?" he would ask them. "We hold a straight flush and the company's always bluffing."

Several workers mentioned they were struck by the degree of support from the community. Twenty-five-year employee Diana Loggins was moved in 1989 when her mailman, seeing the strike stickers on her car, would say, "Hang in there, you're on strike for us." Jorgenson says Boeing provides most of the middle-class jobs in Puget Sound. Boeing workers make significant contributions to the local tax base and the demand for local businesses. The other major private employer in the area is Microsoft, whose educational requirements leave its jobs out of reach for many.

A History of Retaliation

None of the dozen workers I met with doubted that Boeing was retaliating for Puget Sound strikes by locating production of its new Dreamliner line in South Carolina. For these workers, threats to shift production are more of the same. What's new is that this time, Boeing is actually making good on its threat to build commercial airplanes outside of Puget Sound.

Several workers said they've heard managers threaten to shut down or transfer production during past contract fights. Pelland says prior to "every strike" he's heard managers threaten to move lines of airplanes out of state. He says friends of his in management told him they were specifically instructed to warn workers that "they could take their business somewhere else." Merritt says co-workers informed him that managers told them, "We're pretty sick of this—you keep striking, we'll move your jobs."

During the 2002 contract fight, Jorgenson was pulled into a meeting where managers tried to convince him and other shop stewards to support the company's offer. Jorgenson says a manager told them that if the workers voted to strike, a Sonic Cruiser line planned for Everett would be built somewhere else instead. Jorgenson and other stewards did their best anyway to round up the two-thirds support the union requires to authorize a strike. But with the airline industry still recovering from 9/11, they fell just short. That meant management's final offer was accepted, including weakened subcontracting protections and language that prevented the union from filing charges over past threats. Fifteen-year employee Paul Veltkamp thinks that after managers "managed to scare just enough people" to vote against striking in 2002, they convinced themselves they were "vote-counting wizards" who could get workers to agree to more concessions in subsequent contracts. But after Boeing lost the 2005 and 2008 strikes, says Veltkamp, now the company is "trying something else, a different kind of threat."

Some workers said their co-workers have been intimidated by managers telling reporters that Boeing denied Puget Sound the second line of airliners because of strikes. Veltkamp, a shop steward, says he was approached by employees holding up newspapers and telling him that in the 2012 contract negotiations "we're just going to have to give them what they want." However, he says, "We don't stay scared for long."

Boeing spokesperson Healy said the lesson Puget Sound employees should take from the choice of South Carolina is that "we need to be competitive," and added that Boeing would "talk to our unionized employees here" about paying a greater share of health care costs in their next contract.

Different Dreams

Machinists Union members at Boeing are defending a dream too few American workers have in place or see in reach: Work hard, and don't live paycheck to paycheck. Get sick, and don't worry whether you can afford a doctor's visit. Put in enough decades, and expect a comfortable retirement. They didn't just win that dream through the beneficence of their bosses or the worthiness of their work (though the particulars of the industry make strikers less vulnerable to permanent replacement). It was birthed and maintained through strikes. Four times over the past 22 years, they held together and outlasted the company.

Dave Swann proudly relates that his great-grandfather was a porter, "one of the highest-paid jobs an African-American could have back in those days … Everybody came to their house to eat, because he was in the union and they made good money." His grandfather was a longshoreman and his father, like him, was a Machinists member at Boeing. "I feel threatened," he says, because if his sons can't land their dream jobs of moviemaker and sportscaster, he wants union jobs at Boeing to be there for their whole lives. "It's a hurting feeling, because you want to see your kids do better than you."

Boeing has its own dreams. Take its tour and you'll hear about a future of faster, smoother production. When all the pieces are in place, my tour guide said, parts will arrive from several sources and become a Dreamliner in three days. "Most of the people who will ride on this plane," a pre-tour video brags, "haven't been born yet."

Bob Merritt describes the attitude he gets now from the company: "We want our airplanes to be plug and play, we want our workers to be plug and play." Pelland says Boeing is trying to become "a Lego building company" more focused on assembling parts than creating them. "They're sending a message to their customers and their shareholders that they're done with us," said Redrup. He says Boeing is trying "to break our stranglehold on their production system" just as General Motors did to the UAW half a century ago. "They've got to deal with the workers, and they don't like that. If they can't housebreak us, they gotta find a way to get away from us."

Now Boeing is at the center of a national controversy over how robust the right to strike should be. The workers I spoke to were divided over whether the company had arrogantly stumbled into legal danger or intentionally set out to see what they could get away with. It's good to see that, under the Obama-era labor board, publicly declaring you are denying production of a line of airplanes to a group of workers because they keep going on strike at least earns you a labor board complaint (Obama has been at pains to keep his distance from the case).

Reached by phone, Boeing government operations spokesperson Tim Neale maintained that management has "been honest about the fact that strikes have harmed the company and that we as a company very much are looking for production stability," but insisted Boeing hasn't broken the law. Its Republican defenders claim that the complaint signifies a shift toward Soviet-style central planning or Chicago-style machinations. But it's the prospect of an acquittal—or a management-friendly settlement—that would signal a further departure from the stated purpose and promise of the National Labor Relations Act, which set forth as its intent the promotion of collective bargaining and enshrined a right to collective action without threat of retaliation.

And if Boeing does pay a heavy price for telling its employees that their collective action cost them an expansion of their plant, it won't take a high-priced anti-union consultant to interpret the lesson for other companies: Don't be so obvious. All too often, employers get away with anti-union retaliation when they don't go bragging about it in the newspaper.

So whatever the result, the Boeing case is less a story about the potency of current labor law than about the power of the strike on the one hand and the threat of retaliation on the other. It's the story of workers who have refused to believe that they should cede a hard-won package of middle-class wages and workplace protections in the face of a major company's multi-year effort to persuade or intimidate them into backing down. Now, after decades during which Puget Sound has been the only place Boeing assembles commercial aircraft, workers are right to recognize that the power to move work elsewhere has become a powerful weapon in management's arsenal.

Boeing workers expect to have to strike every few years until they retire. One can imagine new attacks from Boeing spurring them to leverage their solidarity in other ways as well, be it international coordination, secondary picketing, or directing their political mobilization (which has successfully helped the company win tax breaks) towards demanding that the U.S. government, a major Boeing customer, insist on better behavior. As Boeing and the Machinists both look to the future, their struggle across decades shows both the enduring power of collective action and the still-unmet challenge that capital mobility poses for the labor movement.

Successive generations of Boeing workers have figured out that it's better to shape the future than to passively accept it. Meanwhile, Boeing and its peers are working to foist their own dreams on the rest of us—sometimes loudly, often not. My "Future of Flight" tour guide boasted about the ways the Dreamliner represents a new achievement in illusion. Scientific innovations in materials and lighting mean that passengers won't feel the altitude, the humidity, or the time difference as Boeing's airplane takes them somewhere new. "By the time you get there," he said, "we can trick your body to make you think you've already been there a long time." It was easy to forget he was referring to an airplane.

Article 3.3

WAL-MART MAKES THE CASE FOR AFFIRMATIVE ACTION
Lessons from the Supreme Court's ruling on sex discrimination.

BY JEANNETTE WICKS-LIM
September/October 2011

On June 20, 2011, the Supreme Court put an end to what would have been the largest class-action lawsuit in U.S. history. The lawsuit, filed on behalf of more than 1.5 million current and former female Wal-Mart employees, alleged that Wal-Mart supervisors routinely discriminated against female workers by promoting and paying them less than their male counterparts.

That's too bad, because the facts presented by the plaintiffs describe a situation that surely calls out for redress.

Wal-Mart has a bare-bones policy telling managers how to dole out promotions. Eligible workers need only meet three basic criteria: 1) an above-average performance rating, 2) at least one year of job tenure, and 3) a willingness to relocate. Among these candidates, local supervisors have full discretion over whom to promote.

With the door wide open for supervisors to act on their subjective preferences, it may be no surprise that men dominate the company's management team. In 2001 women made up only 33% of Wal-Mart's managers, according to labor economist Richard Drogin, even though they made up 70% of its hourly workforce. Compare that with Wal-Mart's peer companies, where 57% of managers were women.

Wal-Mart also gives its (mostly male) managers significant wiggle room in setting their supervisees' wages. The result? Drogin reported that in 2001, Wal-Mart women earned consistently less than their male counterparts even after controlling for such factors as job performance and job tenure. He concluded that "… there are statistically significant disparities between men and women at Wal-Mart … [and] these disparities … can be explained only by gender discrimination."

The trouble is that these disparities exist even though no part of Wal-Mart's wage or promotion policy directs managers to make biased decisions. In fact, Wal-Mart has an anti-discrimination policy on its books.

With no "smoking gun" corporate policy, the Supreme Court blocked the women of Wal-Mart from lodging a collective complaint against the company. In the majority opinion, Justice Antonin Scalia writes: "Other than the bare existence of delegated discretion, respondents have identified no 'specific employment practice' … Merely showing that Wal-Mart's policy of discretion has produced an overall sex-based disparity does not suffice."

In other words, the majority of Supreme Court justices intend to take a narrow view of which employment practices justify class-action discrimination lawsuits. Potential plaintiffs will have to show exactly how an employer discriminated. And as the Wal-Mart case demonstrates, this can boil down to the murky business of trying to expose employers' unspoken intentions.

What this means is that the traditional, complaint-driven approach to enforcing the 1964 Civil Rights Act cannot protect workers from discrimination. Deprived of class-action lawsuits as a tool, the women behind the Wal-Mart case and other workers in plainly discriminatory workplaces will now have to pursue their claims individually—at best putting them into a much weaker position with fewer resources.

To eliminate workplace discrimination and achieve true equality, policies have to focus squarely on the pattern of outcomes of employers' decisions. In a phrase, on the question of whether an employer discriminates, "the proof is in the pudding." President Lyndon Johnson recognized this more than 40 years ago when his administration first put such policies into action under the rubric of affirmative action.

What does affirmative action require? First, the employer keeps a record of whether the race and gender make-up of its workforce is proportional to the wider pool of eligible workers. If not, the employer develops a plan to act "affirmatively"—with goals and timetables—to improve female and minority representation.

Affirmative action plans may include sexual harassment awareness training for supervisors, for instance, or directing recruitment efforts toward minority and women's organizations. Rigid quotas—the most controversial aspect of affirmative action policies—can only be used in the context of a court-ordered or -approved plan in response to a discrimination suit.

The Wal-Mart case demonstrates why workers need affirmative action policies to eradicate discrimination. As President Johnson put it in 1965, affirmative action represents "… the next and more profound stage of the battle for civil rights. We seek … not just equality as a right and a theory, but equality as a fact and as a result." ❑

Sources: "Statistical analysis of gender patterns in Wal-Mart workforce," Expert testimony by Richard Drogin, Ph. D., February 2003 (walmartclass.com); "The representation of women in store management at Wal-Mart Stores, Inc.," Expert testimony by Marc Bendick, Jr., Ph.D., January 2003 (walmartclass.com); Supreme Court of the United States, Wal-Mart Stores, Inc., petitioner v. Betty Dukes et al. (No. 10–277) June 20, 2011.

Article 3.4

WHAT'S BEHIND UNION DECLINE IN THE UNITED STATES?

The role of the "employers' offensive" has been key.

BY ALEJANDRO REUSS
May/June 2011

The total number of union members in the United States peaked in the late 1970s and early 1980s, at over 20 million. As of 2010, it remained near 15 million. The story of union decline in the United States, however, does not begin in the 1980s, nor is it as modest as these figures would suggest.

Union density (or the "unionization rate"), the number of workers who are members of unions as a percentage of all employed workers, has been declining in the United States for over half a century. The share of U.S. workers in unions peaked in 1954, at just over 25%. For nonagricultural workers, the high-water mark—at more than one third of employed workers—came even earlier, in 1945. It would reach nearly the same percentage again in the early 1950s, before beginning a long and virtually uninterrupted decline.

By 2010, the U.S. unionization rate was less than 12%. It would be even lower were it not for the growth of public-sector unions since the 1960s. For private-sector workers, the unionization rate is now less than 7%.

There are multiple reasons for union decline, including shrinking employment in highly unionized industries, falling unionization rates within these traditional bastions of unionism, and failures to unionize in new, growing sectors.

Employers' determination to rid themselves of unions has certainly played a major role in declining unionization rates. Where employers could not break unions by frontal assault, they were determined to find ways around them. Unionized companies established parallel non-union operations, a practice sometimes known as "double breasting," gradually shifting production and employment away from their unionized facilities. Some employers began contracting out work formerly done by union employees to non-union subcontractors (the original meaning of "outsourcing"). Some established new operations far from their traditional production centers, especially in less unionized and lower-wage areas. Many companies based in the Northeast and Upper Midwest, for example, set up new production sites in the South and West, and eventually in other countries. (For a great historical account on one company, see Jefferson Cowie's Capital Moves: RCA's 70-Year Quest for Cheap Labor.) Finally, new employers entering highly unionized sectors usually remained non-union. The auto industry is a good example. So-called "transplants" (factories owned by non-U.S. headquartered companies) have accounted for an increasing share of the industry's shrinking labor force, and have remained largely non-union.

Historically, union growth has come primarily in short spurts when unions expand into new industries. Since the 1940s, however, U.S. unions have failed to organize in growing industries to compensate for the declines in employment and unionization rates in traditional union strongholds. The public sector represents the one major exception. Since the early 1970s, union density for public-sector workers

FIGURE 1: UNION MEMBERS AS A PERCENTAGE OF EMPLOYED WORKERS UNITED STATES, 1930-2003

Source: Gerald Mayer, Union Membership Trends in the United States, CRS Report for Congress, August 31, 2004, Table A1, Union Membership in the United States, 1930-2003 (digitalcommons.ilr.cornell.edu/key_workplace/174).

has increased from about 20% to over 35%. This has not been nearly enough, however, to counteract the decline among private-sector workers. To maintain the overall unionization rates of the 1950s or 1960s, unions would have had to enlist millions more workers in the private sector, especially in services.

Since the 1970s, employers have fought unions and unionization drives with increasing aggressiveness, as part of what labor historian Michael Goldfield calls the "employer offensive." Many employers facing unionization drives fire vocal union supporters, both eliminating pro-union campaigners and spreading fear among the other workers. Researchers at the Center for Economic and Policy Research (CEPR) have found that, between 2001 and 2005, pro-union workers were illegally fired in around one-fourth of all union election campaigns. Meanwhile, during many campaigns, employers threaten to shut down the facility (at least in part) if the union wins. Labor researcher Kate Bronfenbrenner reports, in a study from the mid 1990s, that employers threatened plant closings in more than half of all unionization campaigns, and that such threats cut the union victory rate (compared to those in which no such threat was made) by about 30%.

The employer offensive has unfolded, especially since the 1980s, against a backdrop of government hostility towards unions. The federal government has often turned a blind eye to illegal tactics (or "unfair labor practices") routinely used by employers to fight unionization drives. Employer retaliation against workers (by firing or otherwise) for union membership, union activity, or support for unionization is illegal. So is an employer threatening to close a specific plant in response to a unionization drive. However, since the 1980s, union supporters argue, the government agencies tasked with enforcing labor law have increasingly ignored such practices, imposed only "slap on the wrist" punishments, or delayed judgment, sometimes for years, long after the unionization drive is over and done with.

Many labor historians point to the Reagan administration's mass firing of striking air-traffic controllers (members of the Professional Air Traffic Controllers

FIGURE 2: WORK STOPPAGES INVOLVING 1,000 OR MORE WORKERS UNITED STATES, 1947-2010

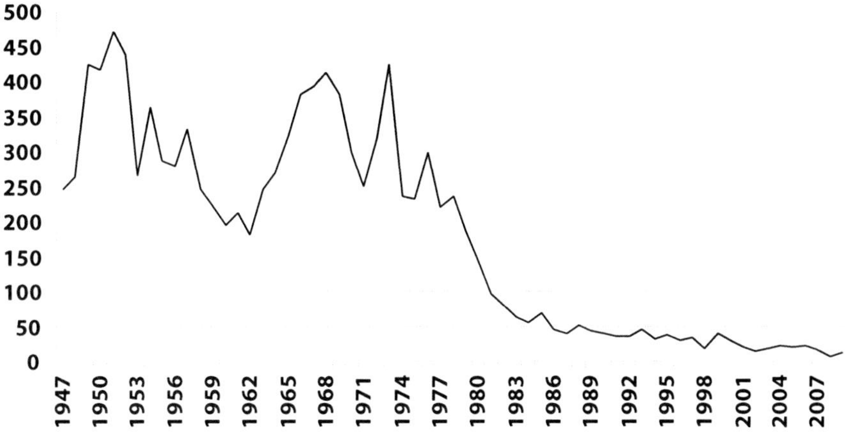

Source: Bureau of Labor Statistics, Work Stoppages Involving 1,000 or More Workers, 1947-2008 (bls.gov/news.release/wkstp.t01.htm).

Organization, or PATCO) in 1981 as a signal that the government approved of private employers' own union-busting activities. Before the PATCO strike, it was relatively rare for employers to fire striking workers and hire "permanent replacements." (Sometimes, employers would bring in replacements during a strike, but striking workers would get their jobs back after a settlement was reached.) After PATCO, private employers increasingly responded to strikes by firing the strikers and bringing in permanent replacements—a practice that is illegal in many countries, but not in the United States. The number of large strikes, already in sharp decline during the preceding few years (possibly due to the employer offensive, rising unemployment, and other factors), has since declined to microscopic proportions.

At this point, unions in the United States—including less than a tenth of private-sector workers—are almost back down to the level they were on the eve of the Great Depression. The 1930s turned out to be the greatest period of union growth in U.S. history, with substantial additional growth in the 1940s and 1950s largely an aftershock of that earlier explosion. There is no guarantee, however, that history will repeat itself, and that the weakness of organized labor today will give way to a new burst of energy. In the midst of a deep recession, and now the beginnings of a halting recovery, there have been few signs of a labor revival. Ironically, only the recent attacks on public-sector workers and unions have provoked a mass-movement fight-back. Labor supporters, however, should understand this, soberly, as coming from a very defensive position.

Sources: Michael Goldfield, "Labor in American Politics—Its Current Weakness," *The Journal of Politics*, Vol. 48, No. 1. (Feb., 1986), pp. 2-29; Kate Bronfenbrenner, "Final Report: The Effects of Plant Closing or Threat of Plant Closing on the Right of Workers to Organize," *International Publications,* Paper 1, 1996 (digitalcommons.ilr.cornell.edu/intl/1); Gerald Friedman, *Reigniting the Labor Movement: Restoring Means to Ends in a Democratic Labor Movement* (New York:

Routledge, 2008); Gerald Mayer, "Union Membership Trends in the United States," CRS Report for Congress, August 31, 2004, Table A1, Union Membership in the United States, 1930-2003 (digitalcommons.ilr.cornell.edu/key_workplace/174); Bureau of Labor Statistics, "Work Stoppages Involving 1,000 or More Workers," 1947-2008 (www.bls.gov/news.release/wkstp.t01.htm); John Schmitt and Ben Zipperer, "Dropping the Ax: Illegal Firings During Union Election Campaigns," Center for Economic and Policy Research, January 2007 (www.cepr.net/documents/publications/unions_2007_01.pdf).

Article 3.5

UNIONS AND ECONOMIC PERFORMANCE

BY ARTHUR MacEWAN
November/December 2011

Dear Dr. Dollar:
I know unions have shrunk in the United States, but by how much? And how best to respond to my right-wing friends who claim that unions are bad for the economy?   —*Rich Sanford, Hardwick, Mass.*

Take a look at the graph below. The two lines on the graph show for the period 1917 through 2007 (1) labor union membership as a percentage of the total U.S. work force and (2) the percentage of all income obtained by the highest 1% of income recipients. So the lines show, roughly, the strength of unions and the distribution of income for the past century. (John Miller and I developed this graph for our book *Economic Collapse, Economic Change.*)

The picture is pretty clear. In periods when unions have been strong, income distribution has been less unequal. In periods when unions have been weak, income distribution has been more unequal. In the post-World War II era, union members were about 25% of the labor force; today the figure is about 10%. In those postwar years, the highest-income 1% got 10% to 12% of all income; today they get about 25%.

The causation between union strength and income distribution is not simple. Nonetheless, there are some fairly direct connections. For example, when unions are

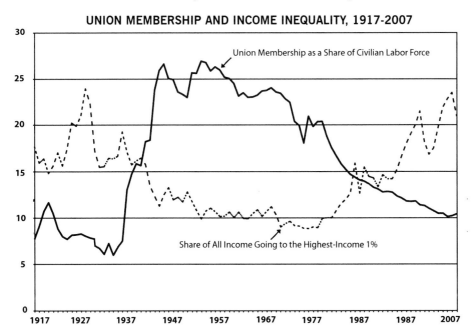

UNION MEMBERSHIP AND INCOME INEQUALITY, 1917-2007

Union Membership as a Share of Civilian Labor Force

Share of All Income Going to the Highest-Income 1%

Source: Arthur MacEwan and John A. Miller, *Economic Collapse, Economic Change: Getting to the Root of the Crisis* (M.E. Sharpe, 2011).

strong, they can push for higher wages and thus we see a more equal distribution of income. Also, strong unions can have an impact on the political process, bringing about policies that are more favorable to workers.

But causation can work in the other direction as well. Great income inequality puts more power in the hands of the rich, and they can use that power to get policies put in place that weaken unions—for example, getting people who are hostile to unions appointed to the National Labor Relations Board.

And then there are other factors that affect both union strength and income distribution—for example, the changing structure of the global economy, which places U.S. workers in competition with poorly paid workers elsewhere. Yet the structure of the global economy is itself affected by the distribution of political power. For example, the "free trade" agreements that the United States has established with other countries generally ignore workers' rights (to say nothing of the environment) and go to great lengths to protect the rights of corporations. So, again, causation works in complex ways, and there are certainly other factors that need to be taken account of to explain the relationship shown in the graph.

However one explains the relationship, it is hard to imagine that we can return to a more equal distribution of income while unions remain weak. This means, at the very least, that the interests of unions and of people at the bottom of the income distribution are bound up with one another. Building stronger unions is an important part of fighting poverty—and the hunger and homelessness that are the clear manifestations of poverty.

One important thing to notice in the graph: In the post-World War II years, economic growth was the best we have seen. Certainly no one can claim that it is impossible for strong unions and a more equal distribution of income to co-exist with fairly rapid economic growth. Indeed, we might even argue that strong unions and a more equal distribution of income create favorable conditions for economic growth!

Stronger unions, it turns out, could be good preventive medicine for much of what ails our economy.

Article 3.6

THE ASSAULT ON LABOR IN CANANEA, MEXICO

BY ANNE FISCHEL AND LIN NELSON
September/October 2010

> *The actions taken in collusion between Grupo México and the Mexican government are an outrage. And if they can crush this very effective, independent union ... all independent unions in Mexico are at risk. And then other countries that are watching can say, "Well, if they can do it there, we can do it here too." And so I think that ... a union that is fighting for safe working conditions, fighting for decent treatment of the ... workers in those mines, if we can't stand behind that as a global labor movement, we're in trouble.*
>
> —Leo Gerard, president, United Steelworkers Union

On the night of June 6, 2010, more than 3,000 federal and 500 state police descended on the city of Cananea, Mexico (population 32,000), 30 miles south of the Arizona-Mexico border, where Section 65 of the Union of Miners and Metallurgical Workers (the Mineros) has been on strike for three years. They drove workers out of the mine, pursued them to the union hall, and gassed all who took refuge inside, including women and children. Several people were injured in the melee and at least five miners were arrested.

The attack on the workers of Cananea was a bitter turn in the prolonged David-and-Goliath struggle between a proud union and a powerful transnational copper mining company, Grupo México, backed by a neoliberal Mexican government. The miners are striking to restore health and safety protections guaranteed by their union contract and to mitigate environmental damage to their region and community. More fundamentally, they are fighting for the survival of independent Mexican unions—for the power to organize, and protect workers and their communities from corporate abuse.

Fighting for the Right to Health and the Right to Strike

> *Grupo México doesn't respect the lives or the dignity of workers. It doesn't invest in safety or in reducing pollution. It is not interested in the hygiene of its worksites and it is not interested in rights or collective agreements.*
>
> —Napoleón Gómez Urrutia, general secretary, Union of Miners
> and Metallurgical Workers

The Mineros union is at the forefront of an international movement defending workers and communities against neoliberal incursions. Although the U.S. media has largely ignored the Mineros' struggle, the strike has drawn global support from unions, including the United Steelworkers, the main union at Grupo México's U.S. plants. Steelworkers president, Leo Gerard, was quick to denounce the Mexican government's action, calling it "a reign of terror for the workers."

Grupo México became notorious in 2006 for its role in the Pasta de Conchos mining disaster in Coahuila, Mexico, in which 65 members of the Mineros union were killed. In the months leading up to the massive explosion in the mine, workers repeatedly warned of dangerous conditions, including a build-up of explosive methane gas. They were ignored by the company and by regulating agencies charged with overseeing mine safety in Mexico. On February 19, 2006, the mine blew up. Napoleón Gómez Urrutia, general secretary of the Mineros, accused Grupo México of "industrial homicide," and called for an investigation. Gómez was already well known for his opposition to neoliberal labor reforms and his focus on international labor solidarity. Under his leadership the Mineros forged alliances with the Steelworkers (United States and Canada) and with Grupo's key union at its Peruvian mines, the Federation of Metal Workers of Peru.

After Gómez Urrutia denounced the state's complicity in the Pasta de Conchos explosion, Calderón's government removed him from his leadership post. Gómez was charged with mishandling union funds and forced to flee to Canada, where he now lives as a guest of the Steelworkers. After an independent audit by a Swiss accounting firm exonerated Gómez and the union, Mexican courts threw out the charges and Gómez was officially reinstated as general secretary. Despite this, the government continued to seek his extradition, but Canada repeatedly refused. The Mineros refused to accept government control of their union and have re-elected Gómez Urrutia six times. In the United States, the AFL-CIO denounced Gómez' ouster as part of "the continuing suppression of the independent labor movement … by the Mexican government."

In Cananea the Mineros have been on strike since July 2007, when 1,300 workers walked off their jobs citing dangerous health and safety conditions and contract violations that threaten the health and safety of the community. The violations were thoroughly documented by the Maquila Health and Safety Support Network (MHSSN), a bi-national group of occupational health experts who toured the mine in fall 2007. Among their findings: piles of silica dust, which can cause silicosis and lung cancer; dismantled dust collectors; and inadequate ventilation systems, respirators, and auditory equipment. MHSSN's report documents "a workplace being deliberately run into the ground" where workers are "exposed to high levels of toxic dusts and acid mists, operate malfunctioning and poorly maintained equipment, and work in … dangerous surroundings."

Since then Grupo México and the union have waged a prolonged legal battle, as the company sought repeatedly to have the strike declared invalid. Under Mexican constitutional law, strikes must be honored unless invalidated by the courts; as long as union workers are striking, companies cannot hire replacement workers or resume production. In January 2008, the courts briefly sided with the company, and police ousted the workers from the mine. Helicopters bombed strikers with tear gas; police beat them with clubs; 20 miners were injured. The next day the court reversed its position and upheld the strike, forcing Grupo México to withdraw from the mine.

In February 2010, two and a half years into the struggle, the Supreme Court again declared the strike invalid, and terminated the union's contract. Mexico's Political Coordination Board, a governing body of the National Chamber of Deputies, urged the government to "avoid the use of public force against the strike movement" and instead consider revoking Grupo México's ownership of the Cananea mine concession "given their persistent refusal to resolve, by means of dialogue and negotiation, the strike that this mine's workers maintain." The Board called for a 30-day cooling-off period followed by negotiations. Looking broadly at the struggles against Grupo México at all its mining sites in Mexico, it called for a "legal, comprehensive and fair solution to the Cananea, Sonora, Sombrerete, Zacatecas, and Taxco, Guerrero miners' striking conflicts, within a frame of respect to the rights of unions' autonomy, strike, collective hiring, safety and hygiene and all other labor rights." Hoping that the Political Coordination Board's recommendations would win out, the workers continued to press their demands.

Imposing a Company Union on a Community

In May 2010, we traveled to Cananea with a delegation of labor educators and activists to meet union members and the Women's Front (the Frente) that works in solidarity with them. We stayed in the homes of mining families, met with union and Frente leaders, and were taken on a tour of the vast open pit mine. During the tour we saw for ourselves some of the conditions that impelled the miners to strike. We talked with Cananea's mayor about the state of the city's economy and with the head of the local hospital about Grupo México's problematic health and safety record. We returned to the United States prepared to support the growing movement of global solidarity that has coalesced around the Mineros. Two weeks later the government sent in the police, rupturing the constitutional protections that undergird Mexican labor law.

In a 2008 report the International Metalworkers Federation wrote, "The line between the Mexican government and Grupo México has remained blurry since Calderón took office ... and the two have worked in concert to plan and execute the assault on los Mineros." In fact, Mexico's ruling party, the Partido del Acción Nacional (PAN), has long pursued an openly neoliberal agenda. One of President Calderón's legislative priorities was to fundamentally restructure the relationships between labor, capital, and the state. Since winning the presidency for the first time in 2000, the PAN has championed the dismantling of contractual protections for workers. In Mexico, the process is known as "flexibilization," which allows companies to hire temporary and part-time workers without benefits or job security, and subcontract out jobs previously held by unionized workers. Grupo México has played a leading role in implementing flexibilization; as the Mineros explained to us, all of the union locals at Grupo's mines have been under assault, and several have been replaced by a *sindicato blanco*, a company union. In the days following the police incursion at Cananea, Grupo announced that all the strikers were welcome to return to work, as long as they agreed to join the *sindicato blanco*. With the mine secured, Grupo México, Minister of Labor Javier Lozano, and Sonora Governor Guillermo Padres quickly unveiled a new partnership: Grupo México will invest $120 million to rebuild and expand the mine, while the state will invest almost $440 million in new infrastructure and aid for economic development in Cananea.

Cananea's Place in Mexican History

The struggle for workers' rights is not new to Cananea. The city holds a special place in Mexican history. In June 1906, Mexican miners walked off the job, demanding equal pay with their U.S. co-workers. Their U.S. employer sent for Arizona vigilantes who fired into a crowd of striking miners, killing 23. The massacre in Cananea created outrage throughout Mexico and helped start the Revolution of 1910. The city is proud of its revolutionary and working-class history. Visitors are welcomed by a sign, "Cananea: the Proletarian City," and in one of the older neighborhoods, the "Neighborhood of the Martyrs of Cananea," streets are named for miners who died in the 1906 struggle. To millions of Mexicans, Cananea symbolizes their nation's long and incomplete struggle for political and economic independence, while the union is a standard-bearer in the battle for workers' rights.

The rights to organize and strike were written into the Constitution of 1917 and codified into labor law in 1931. The Mexican Constitution also charges the government with safeguarding resources essential to national development. Mining is high on the list, as are railroads and oil. In the 1960s, the government purchased the Cananea mine from its U.S. owner in accordance with Constitutional law. But in 1988, facing a debt crisis and a rapidly devaluing currency, then-President Salinas agreed to privatize state-owned industry. The concession to operate Cananea was auctioned off to a group of wealthy cronies, who created what is now Grupo México. While Grupo México is a relatively young company, its origins lie with one of the oldest U.S. miners, the American Smelting and Refining Company, or ASARCO (see box).

Undermining Health, Wasting the Environment

> *Environment is the last thing that Grupo Mexico cares about. We see the destroyed mountains; we see the contamination; the acids in the atmosphere, the dust which is toxic to the people. [But] all GrupoMexico wants is the metal. To destroy, take the profits and leave the city in ruins, that is what they want.*
> —Dr. Luis Calderón, medical director, El Ronquillo Hospital, Cananea

When Grupo acquired the Cananea mine in 1989, it immediately began to dismantle the historic social contract with the workers and the community. It closed the Workers Clinic, a well-equipped hospital run by the union and subsidized by the company, where miners and their families received treatment, including maternity and pediatric care. This left only the Ronquillo Hospital, a tiny, aging medical center owned and administered by the company. In 2008, in the midst of the strike, company officials summoned hospital personnel and announced the closure of the hospital. The company refused to pay for gasoline to transport dialysis patients to Hermosillo, four hours away; instead, hospital employees had to ask passersby for donations to buy gasoline. The community was left without access to health care. Dr. Calderón, the hospital's medical director, said, "They are stingy. They are exploiting a very rich mineral and there are positive things they could do to support the people. Instead Grupo Mexico has taken away all the benefits we used to receive in Cananea." The state of Sonora has since reopened the hospital, though at a very basic level of service.

Grupo México and ASARCO: A Case Study of a Corporate Shape-shifter

Grupo México began as ASARCO Mexicana. From its 1880s beginnings ASARCO operated mines in Mexico. ASARCO helped open Mexico to U.S. investment and economic control. ASARCO's mines produced fabulous wealth for its U.S. owners, while ASARCO's railroads trekked Mexico's ore across the border to ASARCO's smelters and refineries. At one time ASARCO had over 95 U.S. mines, smelters, and refineries, as well as holdings in Mexico, Chile, Peru, Australia, the Philippines, and the Congo.

In 1998, plagued by aging plants, contaminated sites, and the plunging price of copper, ASARCO put itself on the market and was purchased by its former Mexican affiliate. In 2002 ASARCO sold its lucrative Peruvian subsidiary, Southern Peru Copper, to its new owner, shifting its most potent assets across the border to Mexico. In 2005, ASARCO filed for Chapter 11 bankruptcy, citing lack of assets and environmental liabilities as the primary causes. The most prolonged and complex environmental bankruptcy in U.S. history was finally concluded in late 2009, when the company settled its claims and Grupo México regained control, over the strenuous objections of the Steelworkers. This closely watched bankruptcy left many communities struggling to complete remediation projects with modest funds; Texas State Senator Eliot Shapleigh called it an environmental test case for corporate polluters, while the Government Accounting Office warned of a precedent that could encourage corporations to use bankruptcy to evade the public trust.

After ASARCO was sold to Grupo México, workers at the Hayden, Arizona, plant complained about inadequate training for employees working with industrial chemicals and hazardous equipment. Workers reported that stocks of safety equipment were consistently low, and even gloves and toilet paper were often unavailable. In interviews conducted in summer 2006, workers told of accidents caused by inadequate training, fingers lost because of poor lockout procedures, broken limbs, and a co-worker who was electrocuted when the power was improperly shut down. The local union's president, Tony Mesa, told us, "You're like a number; you can be replaced. That's not part of the agreement when you hired on that I'm going to leave part of my fingers here or I'm going to leave my arm or my leg or my life."

Grupo México now proposes to consolidate ASARCO and Southern Copper Corporation into a single entity. This Mexican-U.S.-Peruvian conglomerate is well-engineered for today's global economic landscape, able to shift assets and investments across borders, dedicated to eliminating obstacles to profits, and relying on international financial instruments and compliant governments for backup. It is this corporate shape-shifter, and the threat it represents to workers and communities, that the Mineros are fighting in Cananea.

During our visit the Mineros warned of the dangers that mine wastes pose to Cananea's air and water supply and to the region's watershed. The town is bordered on the northwest by the ever-expanding mine and on the east by a valley filling up with mine waste. Cananea maps show the valley area as a leachate lake, or reservoir, into which chemicals used to separate copper from its impurities are drained. Mountains of mine wastes, known as "halis" or tailings, loom on the outskirts of the city. When the winds blow, the top layers of the tailings drift through town, often ending up as a fine powder inside residents' homes. We were told that on windy days the sky is grey and thick, and waste materials blow as far north as the Arizona border. Local historian Arturo Rodriquez Aguero says, "On a bad day, you can't see the mountains at all." Increasingly the town is being swallowed up as the mine and the leachate lake continue to expand.

When Grupo took over the mine it promised to provide electricity and water to the community as the government and previous corporate owners had done. Instead, the company refused to pay the town's electrical bills and demanded exclusive use of the majority of town wells. This left the city with an inadequate water supply and distribution system. The city is building new wells, but this will take time; for now, the majority of residents use the Sonora River, which is contaminated by mine wastes, for their household needs, including drinking water—or purchase purified water, if they can afford it.

There is growing concern about the movement of mine wastes through the San Pedro River watershed, which begins in Cananea and flows 140 miles north to its confluence at Winkleman, Arizona, site of an ASARCO smelter. The San Pedro has one of the most diverse bird populations in the United States, including 100 species of breeding birds and 300 species of migrating birds. Agustín Gómez-Álverez reports, "Acid mining drainage from mine tailings is currently reaching a tributary of the San Pedro River with heavy metals and sulfates in water and sediments." Cadmium, copper, iron, manganese, lead and zinc have become fluid parts of the regional ecosystem.

"With the Support of Our Friends"

The Minero's strike has been broken, at least temporarily, but the struggle continues. The attack in Cananea is only the first wave in the corporate/state onslaught against workers' rights and unions in Mexico. Eleven days after the government sent in the police, Gammon Gold, a Canadian company, fired 397 union workers at its Mexican mine, citing the "relentless distractions of union labor disruptions." According to the *Financial Post*, the company said the Labor Ministry's support of Grupo México has "emboldened other miners to take decisive action against the union."

As Grupo's profits mount ($337 million in the last quarter), the Mineros continue to fight. They rely on the support of a growing international movement. The Steelworkers union has a steady presence in Cananea and is working with the Mineros to create an international alliance to strengthen workers' rights. The International Federation of Chemical, Energy and Mine Workers has sent delegations to Cananea. The International Metal Workers Foundation has published two white paper reports about the Mineros' struggle; the IMF supports the findings of the independent International Tribunal on Trade Union Rights, which met for over a year to consider the growing crisis of labor in Mexico. In its May 2010 report, the Tribunal questioned "the illegal sentence that has terminated the employment relationship ... between workers and the company." The Tribunal condemned the "partiality" of the Mexican government which appeared "as if acting on behalf of employers," and expressed concern about "the continuing use of force to end labor disputes." It concluded, "Repeated use of force and abuse of the law could lead to social upheaval and social unrest, and to the closure of legal avenues to resolve labor problems."

On July 9, the Superior Court of Justice of the Federal District of Mexico dismissed the arrest warrant against Napoleon Gómez Urrutia, removing any legal base for a case against him. And amidst the frenzy of the World Cup in South Africa, the National Congress of Mineworkers and the Coalition of South African Trade Unions mobilized an international demonstration of support for the Cananea miners. These signals of support give hope to the Mineros in their ongoing struggle. Sergio Lozano, secretary of the Cananea local told us, "You help us overcome the barrier of the border. In the past this didn't happen so much. It makes a big difference."

Just as in 1906, the miners of Cananea are standing against the abuses of unregulated corporate power backed by a compliant state. As a recent email from a union member stated, "We have lost a battle, but our struggle continues. We remain hopeful that with the international support of our friends and allies, we can persist and win."

Postscript

On August 11th, two months after the federal police seized the mine, the Ninth District Judge in Sonora ruled that the Mineros' strike was still in existence and once again legally recognized. The judge found that the federal Attorney General and Secretary of Public Security had the authority to send police to inspect mine installations, but not to remove the strikers. The judge has granted a temporary injunction barring Grupo Mexico's replacement workers and the police from the mine until a permanent court ruling can be made. At least one replacement worker died in a mining accident and an estimated 25 have been injured on the job. As this article goes to press 800 miners and their supporters are waiting outside the gates to once again take control of the mine. ❑

Sources: Judy Ancel, "Mexican Government Threatens to Open Mine by Force," *The Cross Border Network*, June 2010; Barr, Heather et. al., "Workplace Health and Safety Survey and Medical Screening of Miners at Grupo México's Copper Mine, Cananea, Sonora, Mexico, *Maquiladora Health and Safety Support Network*, www.igc.org/mhssn, October 5–8, 2007; Garrett Brown, "Genuine Worker Participation—An Indispensable Key to Effective Global OHS," *New Solutions: A Journal of Occupational and Environmental Health*, 2009; Garrett Brown, "International OHS Through the Looking Glass of the Global Economy," *EHS Today*, January 2008; Gómez-Álvarez, Augustín, et al. "Estimation of potential pollution from mine tailings in the San Pedro River (1993-2005), Mexico-U.S. border," *Environmental Geology*, vol. 57, #7, 2009; "Hasta La Victoria: Napoleon Gómez Speaks," speech to ITUC, June 29, 2010, www.mua.org.au; International Metalworkers' Federation, "Report of IMF Fact Finding Mission to Mexico," July 2006, www.solidaritycenter.org; International Metalworkers' Federation, "An Injury to One: The Mexican Miners' Struggle for Union Independence." March 2008, www. imfmetal.org; International Metalworkers' Federation, "International Tribunal on Freedom of Association condemns Mexican government policies," www.imfmetal.org; Interview with Dr. Calderón, El Ronquillo Hospital, Cananea, Mexico, May 2010; Interview with Tony Mesa, Phoenix, Arizona, July 2006; Mara Kardas-Nelson, Lin Nelson, and Anne Fischel, "Bankruptcy as Corporate Makeover: ASARCO demonstrates how to evade environmental responsibility," *Dollars & Sense*, May/June 2010; Gerald Markowitz and David Rosner, "Deceit and Denial: The Deadly Politics of Industrial Pollution," UC Press, 2002; Ingrid Zubieta, "Cananea Copper Mine: Is it Safe for Workers?" NIEHS presentation, 2009; Ingrig Zubieta et al., "Cananea Copper Mine: An International Effort to Improve Working Conditions in Mexico," *International Journal of Occupational and Environmental Health*, 2009.

Chapter 4

AUSTERITY AND ITS ALTERNATIVES

GOVERNMENT "LIVING WITHIN ITS MEANS"?
Claims about budget balancing are baloney.

BY JOHN MILLER
November/December 2011

> "Government has to start living within its means, just like families do.
> We have to cut the spending we can't afford so we can put the economy
> on sounder footing, and give our businesses the confidence they need to
> grow and create jobs."
> —President Barack Obama, weekly radio address, July 2, 2011

> "If the US was a business, it would be a failing business. That's the
> problem. You have to spend less than you make. Business 101."
> —Boston-area car dealer Ernie Boch, Jr., quoted in "From some of the
> richest, two cheers for higher taxes," *Boston Globe*, August 21, 2011

Turn on any of the television or radio gab shows and it won't be long before you hear someone proclaim that government must live within its means just as families do and businesses must.

Barack Obama gave this analogy the presidential seal of approval in a radio address in early July. In August, Ernie Boch, Jr., the Boston-based auto dealership magnate, added his two cents to Warren Buffett's call to hike taxes on the rich: he would pay more taxes only if the government balanced its budget just as his and every other business must do.

But the truth is neither families nor businesses balance their books in the sense of forgoing borrowing. And even if they did, to insist that government do the same would extinguish whatever remains of economic growth and job creation, not ignite them.

Family and Business Red Ink

Few families balance their budgets the way the guardians of financial rectitude are now demanding of government. Nearly all families spend more than they earn and borrow to do so. When a family takes out a car loan, a student loan, or a mortgage on a house, it's spending money it doesn't have.

Is borrowing the road to ruin? Not if the debt is affordable. That depends not just on the size of the debt relative to the income available to service that debt, but also on how the family spends the borrowed money. For instance, assuming the size of the debt is manageable, borrowing to pay for education is justified if the education improves the family's earning potential and so helps provide the income necessary to service the debt.

The same holds true of businesses. They borrow to invest and operate, especially in the United States where corporations finance the bulk of their investments by borrowing rather than by issuing stock. While exact numbers are not available about the privately held Boch auto dealerships, rest assured that Boch's company borrows to put the cars on his lot that he sells to the public or to build yet another dealership. That borrowing allows Boch's and other businesses to spend more than they are taking in—Business 101.

Families and businesses in the United States do quite a bit of borrowing and quite a bit more borrowing than they had in the past. Today families rely on credit to meet their needs—for everything from food to fuel, from education to entertainment, and especially housing. Total household debt stood at 92.5% of GDP in 2010, more than thirty percentage points higher than its level two decades earlier, 60.2% in 1990. And as their debt rose, families shelled out more and more of their income to make payments on that debt. In the first quarter of 2011, household payments on consumer and mortgage debt consumed 11.5% of disposable personal income.

Businesses, too, have increased their reliance on debt to finance their operations. Total debt of non-financial businesses was 53% as great as GDP in 1980, but reached 74.3% in 2010.

Those figures surely put the lie to the claim that families and businesses balance their budgets year in and out without relying on borrowing to spend beyond their income.

Government's Red Ink

Still it's true that federal government debt has increased steadily and rapidly over the last decade as the government has consistently run budget deficits. The ratio of the outstanding debt of the federal government to the country's GDP rose from 32.5% in 2001 to 62.1% in 2010.

However, payments on that rising debt are less of a burden on the federal government budget than debt payments are on family budgets. The U.S. government can perpetually refinance its debt in ways that are not open to the richest family or the largest business. Its debt burden, then, consists of the net interest payments on its debt, which will amount to 9.5% of federal revenues in 2011. That's two percentage points less than the proportion of their income that families devoted to making their debt payments—interest payments and payment on the principal—in the beginning of 2011.

Moreover, a good share of federal spending has gone to investments that are aimed at increasing its (and U.S. families') future income—similar to a household taking out an education loan or a business borrowing to expand its operation. A recent study conducted by the Brookings Institution, the Washington-based think tank, found that in 2008 the federal government spent $253.8 billion on non-defense investments in infrastructure, mostly transportation, research and development, and education and training, all expenditures that will boost the productivity of the economy and help to provide the tax revenue to service the debt. That investment spending equaled a little more than half of the $453.6 billion budget deficit in 2008.

Political Will

The aversion to the federal government deficits and borrowing fostered by pundits and politicians who pronounce that governments must balance their budgets like families and businesses do, even as the economy falters, is not only at odds with the facts. It has made us worse off by blocking government spending just when it is most needed. When family budgets are tight, and spending constrained with so many out of work and with the overhang of mortgage debt, it falls to government to provide the spending necessary to get the economy going. Government spending can put people to work and provide the income that will loosen tight family budgets, so they too can buy what businesses produce.

What's needed is to reverse the austerity budgets favored by conservative politicians in the United States and Europe today. More government spending and tax cuts targeted at working people, beyond what President Obama has proposed in his recent jobs bill, will surely make the budget deficit yet larger and drive up government debt. But that ratio of government debt to GDP, currently 62.1%, is still far below the 1946 record peak of 109% at the end of World War II, which was followed by the two of the strongest decades of economic growth in U.S. history.

It has happened before, and during even worse economic conditions than today's stagnation. In a Pittsburgh campaign speech in October 1932, some three years into the Great Depression, presidential candidate Franklin Delano Roosevelt promised that he would slash federal expenditures by 25% and balance the federal budget. But once in office, FDR reneged on his promise to balance the budget and initiated the New Deal. When he returned to Pittsburgh during his 1936 campaign for reelection, FDR declared, "to balance the budget in 1933, or 1934, or 1935 would be a crime against the American people."

Without massive government spending and without the political will to brand balancing the government budget as a "crime against the American people," today's crisis will likely drag on for a decade as economic hardship mounts for more and more of us. ❏

Sources: Barack Obama, Weekly Radio Address, July 2, 2011; Erin Ailworth, "From some of the richest, two cheers for higher taxes," *Boston Globe*, Aug. 21, 2011; Congressional Budget Office, *The Budget and Economic Outlook: Fiscal Years 2011 to 2021*, January 2011; Emilia Istrate and Robert Puentes, "Investing for Success," Metropolitan Policy Program at Brookings, Dec. 2009; Arthur MacEwan and John Miller, *Economic Collapse, Economic Change: Getting to the Roots of The Crisis*, M.E. Sharpe, 2011; Address of Gov. Franklin D. Roosevelt, Pittsburgh, Pa., Oct. 19, 1932; Franklin D. Roosevelt, "Address at Forbes Field, Pittsburgh, Pa.," Oct. 1, 1936, The American Presidency Project.

Article 4.2

FULL EMPLOYMENT AS THE ANSWER FOR EUROPE

BY ROBERT POLLIN
March/April 2011

The economic crisis in Western Europe today—including, most seriously, Greece, along with the other PIIGS economies, Portugal, Ireland, Italy, and Spain—is fundamentally a crisis of neoliberalism. Neoliberalism is the package of economic measures whose guiding principles include deregulation of financial markets and the displacement of full employment, in favor of inflation control, as the central concern of macroeconomic policy.

Financial market titans have always been the biggest cheerleaders for neoliberalism. Of course, they never appreciated having government regulators tell them how to run their businesses. Big-time financiers also know that inflation will almost always lower the value of the financial assets they own and manage for their clients. Even moderate inflation therefore cuts into their profits.

Neoliberal policies have been ascendant throughout the world since the mid-1970s, and especially since Margaret Thatcher took office in the United Kingdom in 1979 and Ronald Reagan became the U.S. president in 1980. Over this 35-year span, neoliberalism has produced persistent financial crises, along with greater unemployment and sharply rising inequality throughout the world. But there has also always been a solution to crises readily at hand within the neoliberal recipe book: to impose austerity on the majority of middle- and working-class families and the poor—squeezing their incomes and social services to find the funds to clean up the mess created by ruling elites.

The European crisis should be properly seen as marking yet another failure of neoliberalism. But this failure has not created a demand for a return to an economic policy framework centered around full employment. This is despite the fact that creating an economy with an abundance of decent employment opportunities—a "full-employment" economy, as we are using the term—is a matter of basic ethics. Without full employment, the fundamental notion of equal rights for everyone—the core idea emanating from the Enlightenment and elaborated upon in both the liberal and socialist traditions—faces insurmountable obstacles in practical implementation.

Rather, to date, the crisis has only elicited ever more severe variants on the standard neoliberal austerity policies, even with political parties in power that are socialist in name, as in Greece, Portugal, and Spain. The main justification for such measures is that—in the spirit of Margaret Thatcher's famous dictum of the late 1970s—"there is no alternative."

In fact, as the Greek experience is demonstrating every day, austerity policies are self-defeating. By imposing severe cuts in incomes for ordinary people, they reduce the ability of these people to spend money, which in turn means fewer sales for businesses. Without seeing strong market opportunities ahead of them, businesses then become less willing to invest in expanding their operations and, in particular, hiring new workers.

It is true that constructing a viable full-employment agenda is always a challenge, but most especially so out of the wreckage created by neoliberalism. To begin with, full employment is not simply a matter of everyone spending their days trying to scratch out a living. If that were our definition of full employment, austerity would work perfectly, by forcing people to become "employed"—doing anything to stave off destitution. A meaningful definition of full employment entails an abundance of decent jobs.

What kind of full-employment policy could work in Europe in the current globalized age? Such a policy should strive for an officially measured unemployment rate below 4%. To achieve this would entail channeling more public and private investments to those industries that both generate high levels of social benefit and also produce an abundance of jobs anchored to the domestic economy.

Two clear areas of interest here are energy and education. Building a clean-energy economy—i.e., an economy powered by solar power, wind, and other renewable energy sources and that achieves high levels of energy efficiency—is highly effective for generating jobs per euro of spending. And by a significant margin, education is the *most* effective source of domestic job-creation per euro of spending.

There are two reasons for this. The first is labor intensity, i.e. how much of the total increase in new spending is devoted to hiring workers as opposed to spending on buildings, machines, land, and energy itself. The second factor is relative domestic content per euro of overall spending—that is, how much of total spending remains within the Greek, Spanish, or other EU economies as opposed to leaking out of the domestic economy through imports and outsourcing. With education, by far the largest share of total spending is for people working directly in local communities.

With renewable energy and energy efficiency, the employment boost is not as high as with education, but it is far higher than spending the same amount of money on oil imports. Consider, for example, an economy-wide project to increase the energy efficiency of the country's existing stock of buildings. This would create major energy savings throughout each of the oil-importing EU economies, and each euro saved would be one that is not spent on imported oil.

Of course, investments in education and clean energy also deliver major social and environmental benefits. Spending on education is the foundation for building a productive economy over the long term. Investments in energy efficiency will both lower greenhouse gas emissions and save money for both businesses and consumers over time. These investments, along with those to build a renewable energy infrastructure, will also diminish the country's dependence on foreign oil.

Of course, one has to figure out how to pay for the full-employment economy. Technically speaking, the problem is actually simpler to solve than it appears. In the short term, the European Central Bank only has to emulate what Ben Bernanke has already undertaken at the Federal Reserve. Under the banner of "quantitative easing," the Fed is now buying up long-term U.S. Treasury bonds, as a way to lower long-term interest rates and stimulate private borrowing. If the ECB would undertake basically the same operation now on a scale similar to the Fed, the result would be a two-fold benefit. It would contribute toward lowering interest rates on long-term European government bonds. It would also remove a significant share of the toxic sovereign debt from the balance sheets of the private European banks.

This would allow the private banks to refocus on making loans for productive investments and job creation rather than obsessing over crisis management. But the banks would then also have to be prepared to make loans to support job creation, rather than hyper-speculation. This means that, along with full employment, Europe needs to establish a new, viable system of financial regulations, committed to supporting the productive economy and job creation. In short, the real solution to the crisis in Europe today is to abandon the failed policies of austerity and neoliberalism, and begin the long transition toward establishing full employment and financial stability as the centerpieces of economic renewal. ❑

Article 4.3

THE PEOPLE'S BUDGET

A plan to get deficit reduction off our backs.

BY JOHN MILLER
September/October 2011

Balance the budget and have the federal government do more for those with less? Impossible, according to a Washington consensus convinced that a lethal dose of budget austerity was the only solution to the manufactured crisis over lifting the federal debt ceiling.

But why not? Because corporate elites, corporate-financed politicians of both parties, and a compliant corporate media ruled out the very measures that could do the job: Tax the rich and corporations as they had been taxed three decades ago, end the wars in Afghanistan and Iraq, expand Medicare to all, and devote the savings to renewing U.S. infrastructure and creating jobs.

Thankfully, one group of D.C. politicians escaped the groupthink: the Congressional Progressive Caucus, comprising one senator and 75 members of the House of Representatives dedicated to promoting a progressive agenda based on the promise of "fairness for all." Last April the caucus released its budget proposal for fiscal year 2012. Dubbed the "People's Budget," the caucus's plan would eliminate the federal budget deficit within a decade and would fulfill President Obama's abandoned promise "not to balance the budget on the backs of the very people who have borne the biggest brunt of this recession."

The People's Budget increases the funding of Social Security, extends healthcare reform, seriously reduces military spending, and institutes progressive tax reforms. In addition, it preserves Medicare, Medicaid, and Social Security benefits, and devotes its savings and additional revenues to boosting public investment as well as eliminating the budget deficit. Those measures would protect low-income people while asking those who have benefited most from the pro-rich economic growth of recent decades to contribute the most to closing the budget deficit. The chart on the next page provides a closer look at the plan.

In addition to cuts in wasteful spending and tax changes to raise additional revenue and create a more progressive tax system, the People's Budget proposes $1.7 trillion worth of new spending on public investments over the coming decade. Specifically, it budgets $212.9 billion for a surface transportation reauthorization bill, including $30 billion as start-up costs for a national infrastructure bank that would leverage private financing to help rebuild America's public capital stock. General public investments of $1.45 trillion, including high-speed rail and port improvement projects, are front-loaded to put Americans back to work quickly; $1.2 trillion of the total would be spent over the next five years.

Adding up these policy changes, the People's Budget would reduce primary spending by $868.9 billion, reduce interest payments on government debt by $856 billion, increase general revenue by $2.8 trillion, and increase payroll tax receipts by $1.2 trillion over a decade, relative to the projections of the Congressional Budget

The People's Budget at a Glance

Spending Cuts		
War Fighting	· Ends wars in Iraq and Afghanistan by 2013	**$1.3 trillion**
Non-War Military Spending	· Reduces personnel in all branches · Eliminates Trident II missile · Reduces missile defense and space weapons programs	**$1 trillion**
Health Care	· Expands the public option offered by the insurance exchanges under the Obama health-care reform · Negotiates lower prices for government drug purchases	**$448 billion**
Revenue Increases		
Social Security	· Raises the cap on wages subject to payroll/FICA tax, which funds Social Security, so that just 10% of all wages exceed the cap (as was the case in 1983), versus 17% in 2009 · Eliminates the cap on the matching tax paid by employers, as is already the case with the Medicare payroll tax	**$1.2 trillion**
Corporate Income Taxes	· Closes several loopholes that have left U.S. corporations paying lower taxes on their profits than corporations in other industrialized countries · Taxes foreign income as it is earned (as opposed to when it is repatriated) · Repeals tax preferences on fossil fuels extended to oil, natural gas, and coal producers	**$155.2 billion**
Taxes on Finance	· Imposes a modest transactions tax (no more than one half of one percent) on the trading of several financial instruments · Taxes the liabilities of large financial institutions at a rate of 0.15%, which provides an incentive for large firms to decrease their liabilities and helps rectify the "too big to fail" problem	**$502.9 billion**
Individual Taxes	· Allows Bush tax cuts to expire for individuals earning more than $200,000/year ($250,000 for couples) · Continues certain provisions helping middle-class families: marriage-penalty relief, the expanded child tax credit, education incentives, and other incentives for children and families · Restores the estate tax, with $3.5 million exemption ($7 million for couples); nonetheless only one quarter of one percent of estates would be taxed · Creates new, higher tax brackets for those with taxable income over $1 million, with a top tax bracket of 49% for income over $1 billion · Raises the tax rate on capital gains and stock dividends to match the rate on wages. · Sets upper limit on itemized deductions for earners in top two income brackets.	**$2.3 trillion**

Office based on current policy adjusted for two credible assumptions (that the Alternative Minimum Tax exemption will continue to be adjusted upward for inflation and that the "doc fix," which prevents cuts in doctor reimbursements under Medicare, will continue, both of which add to the expected deficit).

In total, the People's Budget would reduce deficits by $5.6 trillion over 2012-21 relative to this adjusted CBO baseline and is projected to turn the budget deficit to a budget surplus by the year 2021. At that point, the deficit would be 3.1% of GDP under the CBO baseline, and 4.0% of GDP under the adjusted CBO baseline. The House Republican Budget, aka the Ryan plan, and the president's budget would also still be in the red in 2021.

We might prefer a budget proposal that did even more to tax the rich, made Medicare available to all, cut military spending by yet more, and expanded spending enough to close the jobs deficit even if it meant a larger federal budget deficit.

Still, the People's Budget is a stunning proposal. It is far more progressive than any other budget proposal before Congress, insists on budget changes that respond to the actual drivers of the deficit over the next decade (the Bush Tax Cuts, the wars overseas, and the causes and effects of the economic crisis), and rekindles hope that yet more fundamental changes are possible.

For all those interested in avoiding "the fundamental moral default" that Jim Wallis of Sojourners, the progressive Christian organization, says will result "if low-income people are not exempted from deficit reduction," the People's Budget is our ticket to salvation. ❑

Sources: "The People's Budget: Budget of the Congressional Progressive Caucus, Fiscal Year 2012: Executive Summary," U.S. House of Representatives (grijalva.house.gov); "The People's Budget: A Technical Analysis," EPI Working Paper #290, Economic Policy Institute, April 13, 2011 (epi.org).

Article 4.4

JOBS, DEFICITS, AND THE MISGUIDED SQUABBLE OVER THE DEBT CEILING

BY TIM KOECHLIN
August, 2011

These are obviously very grim economic times. One in six Americans who would like full-time work is unable to find a full-time job. Millions of Americans have lost their homes, and many millions more are "underwater"—they owe more than their homes are worth. The pain has been felt by nearly every household in the United States. Some have been hit harder than others. The unemployment rate for African Americans is double the rate for whites; since 2007, the median wealth of Black and Hispanic households has fallen by more than half. The distributions of wealth and income in the United States—the most unequal among industrialized countries before the crash of 2008—have become even more unequal.

In the midst of all of this suffering, U.S. corporate profits are at an all-time high. In 1980, the richest 1% of income earners in the United States claimed about 12% of all income; in 2008, they earned nearly one quarter of all income. The share of the top .1% has increased even faster. The U.S. economy and the human beings it ought to serve are suffering, first and foremost, from a *jobs deficit*. Closing this gap—creating and facilitating the creation of good jobs—should be the very top priority of Congress and the White House. At this point, it is not. Indeed, Republicans (enabled by President Obama) are currently doing what they can to make things worse.

The absurd squabble over the debt ceiling and the national debt is distracting, destructive, and almost entirely beside the point. The budget deficit is not the most pressing economic problem facing the United States—not by a long stretch. Whatever comes of these negotiations, it will not address the jobs deficit, and it will not improve the lives of the overwhelming majority of U.S. families. Indeed, it is likely to make things worse.

Let's be clear: the Republican approach to the economy and the budget is deeply misguided, wrong-headed, mean-spirited, and irresponsible. Their approach is as familiar as it is appalling: more tax cuts for the rich; more tax cuts for corporations; and cuts in social programs, including Medicare and Social Security. This tack is unconscionable. It is also bad economic policy, that is, it will not promote growth and it will not create jobs. Nobel Prize winner Paul Krugman is exactly correct when he concludes that "the G.O.P... has gone off the deep end."

President Obama's approach is less troubling for sure, and clearly preferable to the appalling Republican strategy. But this is a very low bar. President Obama has, unfortunately, embraced the faulty premise that deficit reduction should be a top priority. As a result, the President is prepared to make substantial spending cuts at precisely the wrong moment—when the economy needs demand, and people need help. And, alas, Mr. Obama has demonstrated a disturbing willingness to pursue cuts in Medicare and Social Security.

An intelligent response to this crisis has to reflect an understanding of its causes. Cutting spending during a recession is like blood-letting an anemic patient, or invading Iraq in an attempt to disempower Osama bin Laden.

Our best hope on this issue is that the president and Congress will be forced to "kick the can down the road." We can only hope that whenever we re-encounter the can, saner heads will prevail—or, more to the point, that the balance of political forces will have changed enough that we won't have to endure a repeat performance.

Some Good Ideas and Some Bad Ideas about the Economic Crisis, Economic Policy, and the Federal Budget

1. *Cutting spending in the middle of a recession is a terrible idea.* It will destroy jobs, and undermine the economy's already feeble momentum. Intelligent spending—extending unemployment benefits, block grants to states and municipalities, spending on green infrastructure, and keeping college affordable, for example—will create jobs today, lighten the load of those who are in the most economic trouble, and facilitate growth and competitiveness in the long run. Serious, enforceable, well-funded efforts to liberate homeowners from their enormous debt burden would help to re-ignite consumer spending and the housing market.

This is indeed the worst crisis since the Great Depression. How did and why did the Great Depression finally come to an end? After nearly a decade of mass unemployment (peaking at 25%), the U.S. government increased its *debt-financed spending* massively to pay for the war; that is, it ran enormous budget deficits. War spending put people to work; these newly employed workers spent their income, and this spending created jobs for others. In fact, during the war, the U.S. economy suffered from *labor shortages.* The U.S. government and corporations actively recruited women into professions and trades that had previously been off limits—women in large numbers "manned" the factories and shipyards.

An implication of this argument and this history is that *the primary problem facing the U.S. economy is not the budget deficit.* Indeed, in the short run, substantial *budget deficits are likely to accelerate the recovery.*

The National Debt is often characterized as "a burden to future generations." In fact, deficit spending—and the long-run growth and opportunities that it can facilitate—can be *a gift to our children* and grandchildren. Debt-financed investments today can leave them with a more prosperous, productive, sustainable economy, an economy that can provide them with educational, economic and personal opportunities that would not otherwise have been possible.

Notice, also, that, during a period of economic stagnation, budget deficits and government spending can be good for *business.* Rising demand means rising revenues, and this provides businesses with an incentive to hire workers. With adequate demand, it will be profitable for many businesses to increase hiring.

2. *The current debt ceiling "crisis" is utterly unnecessary; it is an irresponsible political maneuver by the Republicans.* Since 1962, the debt ceiling has been raised 74 times (including 18 times under President Reagan). With one exception—Newt Gingrich's government shut down in 1995—this has been trivial and routine. If Congress simply voted to raise the debt ceiling—allowing the Treasury to pay its

bills, as it is mandated to do by the Constitution—there would be no crisis. If the Republicans want to make changes in economic policy or shrink the federal government that is their prerogative. But this is not a reasonable or responsible way to make policy. It is an especially irresponsible way to make major decisions about the government's long-standing commitment to provide health coverage and minimal economic security to elderly Americans.

3. *The Republicans do not care about reducing the deficit.* Their objective is to cut taxes—especially for the rich—and dismantle what's left of the New Deal. Indeed, they have a long history of enthusiastically supporting enormous budget deficits and squandering surpluses (see the presidencies of Reagan and George W. Bush). Representative Paul Ryan's proposed ten-year budget—which got *unanimous* support from House Republicans in April—proposes trillions in tax cuts (over ten years), cuts which will overwhelmingly benefit corporations and the rich. Note: tax cuts do not reduce deficits! Ryan's plan also includes massive cuts to programs that benefit the poor and the middle class (most notably Medicare and Medicaid). According to the non-partisan Congressional Budget Office (CBO), Ryan's plan would reduce the deficit by $155 billion over 10 years—a meager $15 billion per year. The Republican plan is rooted in politics, ideology, and mendacity. There is no evidence at all that it is rooted in a commitment to "fiscal responsibility."

4. *Taxes in the United States are extraordinarily low.* Taxes in the United States are lower (as a share of GDP) than any other industrialized country. As a share of GDP, U.S. corporate taxes are lower than every industrialized country but Iceland. Tax rates for corporations and the wealthy have fallen substantially over the past 30 years. In the three decades following World War II—when taxes on the wealthy and corporate profits were considerably higher—the U.S. economy performed better: higher average growth rates, lower average rates of unemployment, and a much more equal distribution of income. Tax cuts for the rich are unfair, and trickle-down economics—the notion that giveaways to corporations and the rich will stimulate growth and employment—simply does not work.

5. If political pressures compel us to focus on the deficit at this moment, *our first step should be to tax the rich more heavily.* Refusing to extend President Bush's tax cuts (which will expire in 2013) for the top 5% income earners would raise government revenue by more than two trillion dollars over ten years. Spending cuts (if we must) should be back loaded—that is, they should occur disproportionately down the road, so that they do not undermine our efforts to get out of the current economic malaise.

6. *The U.S. federal budget deficit (and the national debt) is not analogous to overspending by a household.* The U.S. government—despite a national debt that is $14 trillion and growing—will not go bankrupt. Budget deficits can be problematic for sure; but at this moment, the benefits of debt financed government investment overwhelm the costs. (More on this below.)

7. *Republicans have been working diligently to disempower the Government's ability to regulate Wall Street's excesses, and protect consumers.* Their current target is the brand-new Consumer Financial Protection Bureau. If they are successful, another financial crisis is inevitable.

8. *This economic crisis is a devastating indictment of neoliberalism,* the free-market ideology that has framed economic policy debates since Ronald Reagan. The

financial meltdown of 2008 revealed (yet again!) that financial markets do not regulate themselves. The deep and ongoing recession that followed reflects the fact that depressed economies do not have a reliable mechanism for restoring full employment, prosperity and growth. The "invisible hand" cannot do it alone. In early 2009, many of us imagined that this ideology was on its last legs. Even Alan Greenspan—the once-legendary Federal Reserve Chairman, the "Maestro" of monetary policy, and a devoted protégé of the libertarian icon Ayn Rand—acknowledged before Congress that the model on which his worldview and policy recommendations had been premised—the view that unfettered markets (including financial markets) are efficient and stable—had failed. Of course it had! How could anyone continue to argue that *laissez faire* works? But bad ideas can be resilient—especially when they are promoted by well-funded think tanks.

The Logic of a Recession: What Happened to All of the Jobs?

The catalyst to this current economic disaster was an unregulated financial system that ran amok—as unregulated financial systems inevitably do. Financial panics and crises are a chronic part of let-it-rip capitalism. If financial markets are not regulated adequately, this tendency will eventually manifest itself. The historical record is overwhelmingly clear about this.

The financial system crashed in October, 2008—although the strains had been mounting for years. Major financial institutions failed; housing prices collapsed and foreclosures spiked; the Dow Jones Industrial Average fell by nearly half, and banks stopped lending money. Investors panicked—with good reason. Consumers, spooked by shrinking retirement accounts, plummeting home prices, layoffs, a pervasive sense of economic chaos and, of course, declining incomes, cut their spending. The U.S. economy shed nearly two million jobs over the last third of 2008, and another four million in 2009.

The essential logic of a recession is not terribly complicated. When businesses experience declining demand, they shed workers (or decelerate hiring). These laid-off workers in turn cut their spending, because they must. In some cases, their increasingly nervous neighbors begin to reduce their spending also—they put off buying a new car, taking a trip, or re-modeling the kitchen. Thus the process accelerates—car dealerships, airlines, hotels, and contractors (etc.) are forced to lay workers off. *These* newly unemployed workers spend less, and so on. Tax revenues fall, forcing state and local governments to fire teachers and cops and to cut social spending when it is needed most. At some point, apparently healthy businesses begin to worry that their demand projections are overly optimistic; many decide to put off investment in plant and equipment. Because of this "multiplier" process, "shocks" to the economy have the potential to accelerate. According to a recent *Wall Street Journal* article, "The main reason U.S. companies are reluctant to step up hiring is scant demand, rather than uncertainty over government policies, according to a majority of economists in a new *Wall Street Journal* survey."

Insufficient demand explains the jobs deficit, not "high" corporate taxes, not regulation, not immigration, not "uncertainty" about taxation and regulation, not President Obama's health-care plan, nor his allegedly flawed leadership. Spending by the private sector—consumers and businesses—is not, at this moment, up to the job of ensuring full employment. So the government needs to provide demand.

The Federal Reserve can facilitate private spending (demand) by keeping interest rates low. The federal government can generate demand by (a) spending (including grants to strapped state and municipal governments); (b) working to reduce the debt overhang constraining homeowners, and/or (c) lowering taxes on the middle class and extending unemployment benefits (the middle class and the poor spend a greater share of their income, and so tax cuts for the middle class are more effective than tax cuts for the rich).

Again, the U.S. economy emerged from the Great Depression because the Government spent like mad. "Future generations" (Baby Boomers, their kids, and their grandchildren) benefited enormously from this debt-financed spending, because they inherited a more prosperous, productive economy, an economy that provided them with educational, economic, and personal opportunities that would not otherwise have been possible. Deficit spending—and the long-run growth that it can facilitate—can be a *gift* to our children and grandchildren.

Let me be completely explicit: an intelligent response to this crisis will lead to *larger* budget deficits in the short term. Budget deficits and government debt are potentially problematic but, at this moment—as in 1939—the benefits of deficit-spending overwhelmingly exceed the costs.

Burdening Our Grandchildren?
Why a Smart Deficit is a Gift to Future Generations

The commonplace assertion that budget deficits are a "burden to our grand-children" is both vague and deceptive, in large part because it fails to acknowledge that deficit spending today can—if done wisely—provide enormous benefits to us, our neighbors, our children, and our grandchildren.

The U.S. government finances its deficits (the difference between revenue and spending) by borrowing. Generally speaking, it borrows by selling bonds—which are essentially IOUs (with interest) from the U.S. Treasury to bondholders (lenders). The government borrows from many sources—individuals, pension funds, banks, foreign governments—and it pays these lenders back with interest.

There is a tendency to think that borrowing is inherently problematic, that it implies that we are "living beyond our means." But this is a dangerously narrow understanding of debt. Individuals borrow money all the time—to finance homes, cars, appliances, and college educations. Businesses borrow money to finance investment in equipment, technology, and research and development; many businesses have lines of credit with their suppliers, and this often works for both parties. Municipalities commonly undertake "bond issues" to finance school construction and other "capital" projects.

Sometimes, of course, borrowing is a bad idea. But borrowing can also allow a family, a business, or a government to make useful and/or productive purchases that otherwise would not be possible. Is borrowing a problem? *It depends on what the borrowing is for, and it depends on the capacity of the borrower to repay the debt.*

Government spending can improve the quality of our lives. Government spending pays for schools, environmental protection, parks and other public spaces, food and drug safety, public colleges and universities, fire and police protection, infrastructure, consumer protection, and health and income security in old age, to name just a few. Beyond the provision of these beneficial services, the government can create (and facilitate the creation of) jobs. When the economy is stagnant, an important benefit of borrowing is that it can lead to job creation.

So, we have a choice. We can limit the growth of the national debt by firing school teachers, cops, firefighters, and mine inspectors; cutting health-care coverage for the poor and elderly; ignoring our long-run energy issues, defunding our public schools and forcing states to raise tuition at our public universities ...*and* destroying millions of jobs. Or we can borrow money to support these services while, at the same time, preserving and creating jobs. The Republicans pretend that cutting the budget is a magic bullet—more jobs, and less debt. But this is utterly wrong.

In 1939, the U.S. national debt was about $40 billion. By 1945, it had grown by a factor of six to $259 billion dollars. The benefits of this borrowing were enormous. First, it allowed the Allies to defeat the Nazis (something that would have been more complicated if Congress were constrained by a balanced budget amendment). Second, this debt-financed increase in government spending facilitated economic growth and employment. The U.S. economy was more productive by far in 1945 than it otherwise would have been. A rich country with a moderate debt burden is, by any reasonable measure, preferable to a moderately rich country with no debt. Deficit spending allowed the United States to avoid six more years of massive waste—that is, unemployment. This was undoubtedly a very wise investment.

This does not imply that budget deficits are always wise. Again, it depends on what the government does with the money. For example, budget deficits soared under President George W. Bush. This stunning increase in debt was a terrible mistake, because the borrowing was used to finance massive tax cuts for the rich, and two expensive, ill-advised wars. (President Bush's policies, by the way, have had a *much* larger effect on the deficit than President Obama's time-limited fiscal stimulus.) In contrast to Bush's folly, borrowing for job creation and mortgage relief during an historic economic downturn is a good idea.

Government debt can be problematic, for sure, but it is *not analogous* to household debt. The U.S. government will not go bankrupt—it has never missed a debt payment and, unless Congress impedes its ability to meet its obligations for political reasons, it never will. That is, the U.S. government's "capacity to repay" is enormous. No one who understands the basics of government finance believes that bankruptcy is an issue for the U.S. government (although deficit hawks often *suggest* that it is, sometimes disingenuously, sometimes out of ignorance). The U.S. government has run budget deficits in all but five years since 1961 (four of them under President Clinton). Sometimes it made sense, other times it did not.

Why are budget deficits problematic? Deficits can cause inflation. They can also put upward pressure on interest rates, and these higher interest rates, by making borrowing more expensive, can restrict the accessibility of capital to businesses and households, which can be a drag on investment and growth. Over the long term, this sort of chronic under-investment can be substantial, as can its effects on our living standards down the road. (For the wonks and/or economics majors among you, economists refer to this as "crowding out," as in government borrowing may *crowd out*, or displace, private borrowing and investment.) It is worth worrying about, for sure.

The "good news" is that, in this depressed economy, interest rates are extraordinarily low. Inflation is also a minor concern; indeed "deflation" is arguably a greater threat. At this moment in time, borrowing is especially easy and cheap because there are lots of potential investors sitting on big piles of cash and, further, in a depressed economy there are relatively few attractive alternatives—especially for risk averse investors.

All of this is to say that the potential benefits of deficit spending during a recession are great—it is by far the most effective way to address the jobs deficit; and borrowing can help us to deliver the goods and services on which many Americans depend, especially during a recession. And at this moment in history, the "costs" of the deficit—its potential effects on inflation and interest rates are all but non-existent.

When the economy recovers sufficiently—when the jobs deficit has been resolved—relatively large budget deficits will probably no longer make sense. But until then, cutting spending is a terrible idea. I repeat: cutting spending during a recession is like blood-letting an anemic patient. The Republican "jobs program" starts with massive dismissals of teachers and other public sector employees. That won't work.

The content of this spending is important, of course. A detailed proposal is beyond the scope of this short paper. This said, it is clear that Congress should pass another economic stimulus package—several hundreds of billions of dollars at least. This package ought to include generous grants to state and municipal governments, investments in green infrastructure, urban jobs programs, extended unemployment benefits, and more generous financial aid for poor and middle class college students.

The Republican Party, the neoliberals, the "efficient market" theorists and other fetishizers of "The Market" are wrong. In contrast, the great John Maynard Keynes was (and is) right: unregulated, let-it-rip capitalism is prone to financial crises; capitalism has no reliable mechanism for resolving a jobs deficit, and the free market generates intolerable levels of inequality. ❑

Sources: Center for American Progress, "Ten Charts that Prove the US is a Low Tax Country," June 10, 2011; Citizens for Tax Justice, "US is one of the least taxed countries," June 30, 2011; Emmanuel Saez, "Striking it Richer: The Evolution of Top Incomes in the US," July 10, 2010 (elsa.berkeley.edu/~saez/); Huffington Post, "Income Inequality is at an all-time high" (report on the work of UC-Berkeley Economist Emmanuel Saez); James Crotty, "The Great Austerity War: What Caused the Deficit Crisis and Who Should Pay to Fix It?" Political Economy Research Institute (PERI), June, 2011; James Fallows, "The Chart that Should Accompany all Discussions of the Debt Ceiling," June 25, 2011; James R. Horney, "Ryan Budget Plan Produces far Less Deficit Cutting than Reported" Center for Budget & Policy Priorities, April 11, 2011; Joseph Stiglitz, "Of the 1%, by the 1%, for the 1%,", May, 2011; Paul Krugman, "No, We Can't? Or Won't?," *New York Times*, July 11, 2011; Paul Krugman, *New York Times,* "The Death of Horatio Alger," January 5, 2004; Robert Pollin, "18 Million Jobs by 2012," *The Nation,* Feburary 18, 2010; Robert Pollin, "Austerity is not a solution: why the deficit hawks are wrong," Political Economy Research Institute, Nov/Dec, 2010 (peri.org); Sabrina Tavernise, "Recession Study Finds Hispanics are Hit the Hardest," *New York Times,* July 26, 2011; Phil Izzo, "Dearth of Demand Seen Behind Weak Hiring," *Wall Street Journal*, July 18, 2011.

Article 4.5

SAND IN THE WHEELS, NOT IN THE FACE
Why a transaction tax is a really good *idea.*

BY JOHN MILLER
March/April 2010

> WHY TAXING STOCK TRADES IS A REALLY BAD IDEA
>
> [S]urely it is "socially useful" to let free people transact freely, without regulators and legislators micromanaging them. ... It's Economics 101 that the free actions of market participants cause supply and demand to reach equilibrium. And isn't that what investors—indeed even speculators—do? Can they do it as well when facing the dead-weight costs of a transaction tax?
>
> If not, then trading volume in our stock markets will fall. Beyond the tax, everyone—investors and speculator, great and small—who buys or sells stocks will pay more to transact in markets that are less liquid. In such a world, markets would necessarily be more risky, and the cost of capital for business would necessarily rise. The consequence of that is that innovation, growth, and jobs would necessarily fall. That would be the full and true cost of the trading tax.
>
> —Donald L. Luskin and Chris Hynes, "Why Taxing Stock Trades Is a Really Bad Idea," *Wall Street Journal*, January 5, 2010

"**S**ome financial activities which proliferated over the last 10 years were socially useless," Britain's Finance Service Authority Chairman Adiar Turner told a black-tie gathering of financial executives in London in September 2009. That is why he had proposed a transaction tax for the United Kingdom and why British Prime Minister Gordon Brown would propose an international transaction tax at the November G-20 summit.

The gathered bankers "saw red," as one report described their reaction. Investment bankers Donald L. Luskin and Chris Hynes are still irate.

In some ways their reaction is surprising. A financial transaction tax is nothing other than a sales tax on trading stocks and other securities. Transaction taxes are already in place in about 30 countries, and a transaction tax applied to the sale of stock in the United States from 1914 to 1964.

In addition, the transaction tax rates on a single trade are typically quite low. For instance, the "Let Wall Street Pay for the Restoration of Main Street Act of 2009," proposed by U.S. Representative Peter DeFazio (D-Ore.), would assess a one quarter of one percent (.25%) tax on the value of stock transactions, and two one hundredths of one percent (.02%) tax on the sale on a variety of derivative assets—including credit default swaps, which played such a large role in the mortgage crisis. To target speculators, the bill exempts retirement accounts, mutual funds, education and health savings accounts, and the first $100,000 of transactions annually.

In other ways, Luskin's and Hynes's reaction is not surprising at all. At its heart, a transaction tax is a radical measure. Its premise is that faster-acting financial markets driven by speculation don't bring relief to the economy—instead, they loot the economy. Its purpose, as Nobel Prize-winning economist James Tobin put it when he proposed his original transaction tax on international money markets during the 1970s, is to "throw sand in the wheels" of our financial markets.

Also, while its tax rate is low, the burden of a transaction tax adds up as securities are repeatedly traded, as is the practice on Wall Street today. For instance, even after accounting for its exemptions and allowing for a sizable decline in trading, the DeFazio bill would still raise $63.5 billion annually, according to the estimates of Dean Baker, co-director of the Center for Economic Policy Research.

Luskin and Hynes have two main objections to the transaction tax. The first is that a transaction tax would affect every single person who owns and invests in stocks, not just speculators. Customers would not have to pay a tax to buy or sell mutual funds, but, as Luskin and Hynes emphasize, the mutual funds themselves would have to pay a tax every time they trade stocks. So everyone holding mutual funds would still end up paying the tax.

What Luskin and Hynes don't say is this: Mutual funds that actively trade stocks would pay three times the transaction taxes of an average fund, as the Investment Company Institute, the fund industry trade group, reports. And stock index funds, which hold a sample of all stocks but seldom trade them, are taxed the least. Those funds have historically outperformed other mutual funds. So a transaction tax would work to push mutual fund customers to invest their savings more wisely, providing some with higher rates of return with a transaction tax than their previous funds provided without it. And that would mean fewer broker fees and lower profits for the fund industry.

But what really sticks in Luskin's and Hynes's craw is the assertion that financial trading is not socially useful. That claim flies in face of the long-held contention, buttressed by much of finance theory, that the equilibrium outcomes of financial markets are efficient. And if financial markets are efficient, there is no need for a tax that will reduce trading.

But much of what Luskin and Hynes have to say is not right. First, as anyone who *paid attention* in Economics 101 would know, reaching an equilibrium is not in and of itself desirable. To endorse the outcomes of today's speculative financial markets as desirable because they reach an equilibrium is the equivalent of describing a gambler in a poker game raking in a big pot as desirable because it clears the table. And the gamblers in our financial markets did rake in some awfully big pots betting that subprime borrowers would default on their loans. The last few years show us just how undesirable that equilibrium turned out to be.

Second, speculation dwarfs financing investment in U.S. stock markets. During the 1970s, for every dollar of new investment in plants and equipment, $1.30 in stocks were traded on the U.S. exchanges, reports Robert Pollin, co-director of the Political Economy Research Institute. But from 1998 to 2007, $27 in stocks were traded on the U.S. exchanges for every dollar of corporate investment in plant equipment. Such a rapid stock turnover has diverted the attention of managers of enterprises from long-term planning. Whatever damage that churning caused on Main Street, it paid off handsomely on Wall Street. From 1973 to 2007, the size of the financial (and insurance) sector relative to the economy doubled, financial sector profits went from one-quarter to two-fifths of domestic profits, and compensation in the finance industry went from just about average to 180% of the private industry average.

By counteracting these trends, a transactions tax can actually enhance, not diminish, the efficiency of financial markets. If it forces the financial sector to fulfill its function of transferring savings to investment with less short-term churning, then the tax will have freed up resources for more productive uses.

A transaction tax would surely be a step in the right direction toward reducing the bloat of the finance industry, righting the balance of speculation over enterprise, and restoring the focus on long-term planning and job-creation in the economy.

None of that will happen unless every last grain of the decades' worth of sand the bullies on Wall Street have kicked in our faces gets thrown into the wheels of finance. That is a tall order. But as DeFazio's and Turner's example shows, some of today's policymakers are up to the task. ❑

Sources: "The Benefits of a Financial Transaction Tax," by Dean Baker, Center For Economic and Policy Research, December 2008; ""Public Investment, Industrial Policy, and U.S. Economic Renewal," by Robert Pollin and Dean Baker, Political Economy Research Institute, December 2009; "Turner Plan on 'Socially Useless' Trades Make Bankers See Red," by Caroline Binham, Bloomberg.com; "Taxing Wall Street Today Wins Support for Keynes Idea (Update 1)," by Yaiman Onaran, Bloomberg.com; "The Potential Revenue from Financial Transactions Taxes, by Dean Baker, Robert Pollin, Travis McArthur, and Matt Sherman, Political Economy Research Institute, Working paper no. 212, December 2009; "Why Taxing Stock Trades Is a Really Bad Idea," by Donald L. Luskin and Chris Hynes, *Wall Street Journal*, January 5, 2010; "Lawmakers Weigh A Wall Street Tax," by John McKinnon, *Wall Street Journal*, December 19, 2009; Tobin Tax, freerisk. org/wiki/index.php/Tobin_tax; text of HR 4191—"Let Wall Street Pay for the Restoration of Main Street Act of 2009," www.govtrack.us.

Chapter 5

GLOBAL RESISTANCE TO NEOLIBERALISM

Article 5.1

GREECE AS A DEMONSTRATION PROJECT

Will the Black Sheep Bite Back? Will the PIIGS? What about US?

BY MIKE-FRANK EPITROPOULOS
May/June 2010

There has been an avalanche of coverage on Greece's economic situation in the past few months. Most of the coverage rightly attempts to diagnose the underlying problems ofGreece's government deficit and national debt, and how they might affect the value of the euro and the integrity of the eurozone. But, as anyone who has followed this story knows, Greece is not alone in this precarious situation. It is lumped into a group of EU countries that have been labeled the "PIIGS"—Portugal, Ireland, Italy, Greece, and Spain. Additionally, it is known that some of the other countries in this group have worse problems and are larger than Greece, which could have an even greater negative impact on the EU and the value of the euro. So, why the focus on Greece?

The Greek situation is both complicated and simple.

Greece has long had a bloated public sector that has employed disproportionate numbers of the population. This system has not operated on market or even traditional public sector principles, but rather on *rousféti*, or patronage. This means that there have typically been more civil servants employed than necessary, with shorter working hours and more lax conditions of service. All of these things have become targets for neoliberal reform around the world, as we are seeing harsh, IMF-style austerity measures once again being pushed as conditions on countries that find themselves in a bind.

Next, the Greek state has long been known as a bastion of corruption. In the financial press, Greece is often described as a leader in black-market economic activity. In 2006, under the conservative New Democracy (ND) government (recently voted out of office), Finance Minister Giorgos Alogoskoufis "redefined" the always-problematic measure of social and economic well-being, Gross Domestic Product (GDP), by essentially adding an estimate of Greece's well-known "black market" activities. In doing so, the government proudly announced that Greece and Greeks were 25% wealthier overnight! More importantly, the Greek government got on board with the global neoliberal program, catering to both domestic and foreign capital, and Washington.

Beyond this, Greece is at the top of the list in military spending as a percentage of GDP in the EU. At the same time, Greek teachers are next to last in salaries in the EU. In the past few years, riot police have beaten and tear-gassed teachers and students more frequently than any other groups. Both the ND and their competitors in Greece's two-party stranglehold, the Pan-Hellenic Socialist Movement (PASOK), have consistently been more in line with the neoliberal economic agenda and tougher in the social arena than their reputation in the West as the "black sheep" of Europe would suggest.

In December 2008, a police officer shot and killed 15-year-old Alexis Grigoropoulos in Athens. Since the shooting occurred in the Exarchia neighborhood of the capital, many identified the incident with the anarchists, for whom Exarchia is a traditional center of activity. The police's claims that the youth had attacked them, however, did not jibe with eyewitness accounts of the event. Greek society was outraged by the incident, and protests ensued across the country, lasting for weeks. The murder of Alexi was the spark that triggered the demonstrations and riots, but the causes were many and had been simmering under the surface of Greek daily life for a long time. Among those were the neoliberal policies of the ND government, such as the privatization of public services and cuts in social spending, in addition to police brutality, overt corruption and scandals, and poor job prospects and working conditions for youth, to name just a few.

While youth and students from universities down through the elementary schools took the lead in organizing and conducting the demonstrations—many of which caused significant property damage, leading to a backlash against the protesters in some circles—a broad spectrum of Athenian society, including left political parties, unions, parents, and immigrant groups also joined in. It was this broad-based anti-government and anti-brutality outpouring that acted as a check against abuse and misrepresentation of events by the mainstream media in Greece. When the media portrayals of events didn't correlate with what the people in the streets and their families directly experienced, the media's credibility suffered. Mainstream news organizations were forced to modify or retract earlier reports of events. The legitimacy of both the media and the government suffered as parents listened to their kids, and as people from all walks of life and classes condemned the killing of Alexi, the government crackdown on dissent, and the sensationalized and inaccurate media depictions of the protests.

In the past few years, Europe has faced serious riots not just in Greece, but also in France, England, and Italy. Government elites in both Europe and the United States have expressed overt concern about these uprisings, especially with the backdrop of the greatest economic downturn since the Great Depression. In France, President Nicolas Sarkozy backed down on education reforms, saying that, "We don't want a European May '68 in the middle of Christmas." Alluding to the increasing number of Greek youth who are relegated to low-wage, part-time, no-benefit jobs, he added, "...The slogan of the Greek students about 'the 600 euro generation' could easily catch on here."

For U.S. intelligence and security officials, Greece has long been a focus of attention, going back to the U.S. government's *de facto* support for Greece's military junta (1967-1974). Today, the United States views Greece as a centerpiece of "counterinsurgency" doctrine, especially with regard to suppressing leftist and anarchist forces. Among the more familiar tactics employed in such counterinsurgency efforts is infiltrating opposition groups with provocateurs. In the context of the December 2008 riots in Greece, Paul J. Watson of Prison Planet reported that

> police masquerading as anarchists were committing acts of wanton violence to inflame tensions and provide a pretext for a brutal crackdown on legitimate demonstrators protesting against police brutality and the mishandling of the economic crisis.

These are the kinds of tactics that lie at the heart of manycounterinsurgency strategies, and can be expected as government responses to anti-authoritarian dissent, especially during a period of economic crisis. Recently, José Trabanco, an independent writer based in Mexico, reported in an article on the website of the Centre for Research on Globalization on official concerns about potential civil unrest in the United States, as elites begin to grasp the magnitude of the economic crisis. This may not square with recent positive economic news, but we should be just as wary of numbers and projections from the White House as we are from credit-rating agencies.

And this is the crux of why Greece is in the spotlight now.

Greeks, like other Europeans, have a history of bold protest, direct action, and civil disobedience. They have shown willingness to fight for their own class interests, time and again. And this current crisis is no different. It is fine that Greek Prime Minister George Papandreou, German Chancellor Angela Merkel, and even President Barack Obama pay lip service to cracking down on financial speculators and the big banks. But none of them has moved seriously to regulate, restrict, or punish them. In the United States, we bailed the banks out with taxpayer money. In Greece, the government is introducing punitive austerity measures on the working and middle classes to pay for the "accounting magic" that Wall Street consultants, like Goldman Sachs and JP Morgan, provided to the previous government.

Americans should arguably be *more* angry about the bailout of Wall Street than they already are. U.S. taxpayers are funding not only TARP and other corporate bailouts, but even the largesse of the Greek business and political elite. How? It was Goldman Sachs and J.P. Morgan that were hired to hide the magnitude of the Greek debt. Meanwhile, the executives on Wall Street continue to get paid spectacularly generous bonuses and serious financial regulatory reform is not currently on the radar in Washington. So it should also be clear is that these global bankers' actions have global consequences.

Why *shouldn't* we Americans feel slighted? Barack Obama won the presidency on the slogans of "Hope" and "Change," but the system continues to work for elites at the expense of ordinary people, here and abroad. On recent TV panel discussions in Greece, the mainstream political parties present the austerity measures as "necessary" and "responsible" solutions to a national problem. The government has even characterized the austerity drive as a "war effort," arguing that Greeks should rally together to help pay for the crisis and return to traditional, hard-working Greek ways. Some are even resorting to invoking Barack Obama's slogan of "Hope"!

Yet the government is trying to impose the costs of the crisis squarely on the worse-off. The Bank of Greece recently admitted that the lion's share of public revenues is collected from working- and middle-class households, while the rich and super-rich evade taxes. Meanwhile, it is precisely the working and middle classes that are targeted by the austerity measures. Besides that, austerity measures are arguably the *opposite* of what is needed during recessions and looming depressions.

The real issue, then, is *resistance*. The Greek unions and public have been striking and demonstrating against the austerity measures by stating in clear class terms that, "We are not sacrificing to pay interest to the leaders!" The mainstream and business media analyses of the crisis in Greece and the PIIGS have focused on the potential impact on the euro. Given the choice, however, between the currency (and the perpetrators that created the crisis) bearing the adjustment costs and pain, or the Greek people paying for those costs in prolonged unemployment and poverty, who can reasonably argue for the latter? There are indications that mainstream union leadership will compromise with the government on austerity measures that cut wages and benefits. The question is whether the traditionally protest-oriented and militant Greek people will meekly accept what they see as an unjust solution to this difficult problem.

The global banks, corrupt politicians, and financial speculators are engaging in real economic warfare by betting against Greece and the euro. As one PASOK parliamentarian, Mimis Androulakis, pointed out, "…the often-used casino analogy is faulty because a problem gambler at a casino is betting *his own* money, while these guys are using *other people's* money!"

Mainstream apologists argue that "there is no alternative" but for the working and middle classes to pay for the damage the banks and politicians have left. Greeks, however, are giving a class-conscious response. It's not that they don't want to deal with the crisis, but that many insist on taking it out of the hides of the perpetrators.

So why has the focus been on Greece? To see if public-relations media blitzes, calls to national unity and patriotism, along with fear and repression, can squelch a traditionally militant and class-conscious working class. The Greek workers have historically been willing to take to the streets to defend their own material interests—their pay, their education, their healthcare, and their pensions. They know that saying "Hope!" is not enough, especially when the perpetrators of the current global economic catastrophe continue to operate unencumbered and unscathed.

If the Greeks do not quietly accept the austerity measures, as the American public seems to be doing once again, there may have to be a more forceful *demonstration effect* in the form of violent confrontation between the people and the state. Whose state is it after all? And whose "mess" is this? The working people of Greece—or anywhere in the world, for that matter—should not have to pay and/or suffer for the crimes and risks of global financial speculators.

Big business does not desire and will not stand for insubordination at this juncture. The non-productive paper economy that has taken control of the global economy is not sustainable for people or governments. There is frustration across the ideological spectrum around the world. The selfish interests that global financial capital is pursuing are naked. We must demand that these people be reined in. It is time for the "black sheep" to bite back. But then there are the PIIGS of Europe and us, here, in the United States. Let us recall the late Howard Zinn and ask: Which is worse at this moment in history—civil disobedience or civil *obedience*? ❏

Sources: Peter Boone and Simon Johnson, "Greece Saved For Now—Is Portugal Next?" Huffington Post, April 11, 2010, co-posted on BaselineScenario.com; Peter Boone and Simon Johnson, "Standing at Thermopylae: Greek Economic Situation Worsening Fast," Huffington Post, April 8, 2010; Peter Boone and Simon Johnson, "Greece And The Fatal Flaw In An IMF Rescue," Huffington Post, April 8, 2010; Kevin Gallagher, "The Tyranny of Bond Markets: Credit rating agencies helped cause the financial crisis—and as they rear their heads again, it's time for Obama to get tough." *The Guardian*, April 9, 2010; Diana Johnstone, "The Fall of Greece: Yes, It Really is a Capitalist Plot," CounterPunch, March 10, 2010; Paul Krugman, "Learning from Greece," *New York Times*, April 10, 2010; Landon Thomas, Jr., "As Greek Bond Rates Soar, Bankruptcy Looms," *New York Times,* April 6, 2010; Paul J. Watson, "CIA Preparing To Install Military Government In Greece?" PrisonPlanet.org; Robert Wielaard, "Europe Offers Greece 30 Billion Euros in Loans to Deal With Debt Crisis" Associated Press, April 11, 2010.

Article 5.2

ON THE JASMINE REVOLUTION
Tunisia's political economy exemplifies a region in transition.

BY FADHEL KABOUB
March/April 2011

The success of the revolutions in Tunisia and Egypt, which put an end to two of the most oppressive police states in the Middle East, continues to spark similar popular uprisings across the region. Despite the different institutional structures, geopolitical roles, and military capabilities across the region, the experience in Tunisia, whose uprising sparked the rest, exemplifies what most countries in the region have experienced since their independence from European colonialism, and can shed some light onto their likely post-revolution paths.

In January, Tunisia succeeded in toppling the 23-year Ben Ali regime via a popular grassroots revolt against injustice, corruption, and oppression. The protesters' demands in what has been dubbed the "Jasmine Revolution" were very straightforward: jobs, freedom, and dignity. Like all revolutions, the Tunisian revolution was not an overnight event but rather a long process that can be dissected into four distinct phases with important economic consequences: the neoliberal phase that started in the 1980s with the introduction of World Bank-sponsored economic policies; the plutocracy phase which began in the early 2000s with the rise of the Trabelsi-Ben Ali business empire; the uprising phase which began after the self-immolation of Mohammed Bouazizi on December 17, 2010; and finally the ongoing reconstruction phase which began after the departure of Zine El Abidine Ben Ali on January 14, 2011.

The 1980s neoliberal phase began as Tunisia's external debt soared. Its economy faced high unemployment, low currency reserves, bad harvests, decline in oil revenues, and closure of European labor market outlets for Tunisian immigrants. Like many developing countries, Tunisia was subjected to the World Bank and IMF structural adjustment program: in 1985, aggressive austerity measures led to food riots killing at least 100 people. As the crisis intensified, Ben Ali was appointed interior minister in 1986 and later prime minister in 1987. He then took over as president in a bloodless coup d'état on November 7, 1987. His immediate agenda was two-fold: crush the opposition and forge ahead with structural adjustment policies. Opposition party leaders were arrested, tortured, jailed, killed, or exiled. On the economic front, the government began privatizing state-owned enterprises, promoting free-trade zones, supporting export-oriented industries, and capitalizing on the growth of the tourism industry. Despite robust economic growth rates in the 1990s, unemployment remained stubbornly high, and socioeconomic indicators began to show signs of rising income inequality and deterioration of the economic status of the middle class.

The plutocracy phase began in the early 2000s. While the Trabelsi-Ben Ali clan was amassing billions of dollars in business deals, corruption ravaged the economy, and the Tunisian middle class slid further down the income ladder.

Highly educated youth were facing humiliating life conditions and long-term unemployment with little to no hope for a better future. After more than a decade of clearing all opposition forces from the political arena and affirming Ben Ali's grip on the political and security apparatus, Leila Trabelsi, Ben Ali's second wife, expanded her First Lady duties to include securing business deals for her family. The Trabelsi-Ben Ali clan built a gigantic business empire in less than a decade. They secured quasi-monopoly deals in industries such as banking, telecommunications, media, real estate, and retail. Their aggressive and violent approach alienated even the traditional business class, which was forced to sell to or work for the Trabelsi-Ben Ali clan or face serious consequences. Banks were coerced into extending more than $1.7 billion in credit to the Trabelsi-Ben Ali clan without any repayment guarantees.

The uprising phase that followed was intense, well focused, and effective, taking only 23 days to put an end to 23 years of Ben Ali's rule. The leaderless youth movement was spontaneous, secular, fearless, and determined to put an end to an era of repression, theft, and humiliation. In a day-long general strike on January 14, the Tunisian economy was brought to a complete standstill, and men and women from all walks of life joined the protesters to unseat Ben Ali.

The reconstruction phase began as soon as Ben Ali fled the country. It is the most labor-intensive phase and it requires active participation from all facets of Tunisian society. Tunisians have faced the challenge of institutionalizing democracy head-on with popular demands to dissolve Ben Ali's RCD ruling party, free all political prisoners, rewrite the constitution, seize all the Trabelsi-Ben Ali assets, and most importantly, cleanse all socio-economic and government institutions of corrupt RCD loyalists.

While Tunisians are forging ahead with radical constitutional, judicial, and democratic reforms, they will still face a major economic challenge: unemployment among the highly educated youth. The Jasmine Revolution's achievements thus far are commendable, but the revolution will be incomplete without full employment as a means of achieving true social justice.

The challenges after Egypt's revolution are more serious than Tunisia's. The Egyptian military is very large and owns much of the country's industrial and business infrastructure; it also plays a significant role in protecting the American and Israeli interests in the region. A truly democratic civilian government in Egypt will very likely want a military that is more disengaged from the political and economic arena. Egypt is also facing a more serious economic challenge, with mass unemployment and poverty in a population that is eight times larger than that of Tunisia.

While watching events unfold in Libya, Yemen, Bahrain, and beyond, one cannot help but wonder about the extent to which a revolutionary domino effect is likely to sweep the entire region, and its significance for the political economy of the Middle East and its relationship with the United States and Europe. It is clear that there is a critical mass of empowered and fearless youth whose movements are supported by labor advocates, human rights activists, and democratic voices. The challenge, however, is to create lasting radical economic and political changes that will ensure a successful post-revolution reconstruction phase.

Western powers must also recognize that a double-standard policy cannot be an effective way of promoting peace and security in the region. The threat of an Iranian-like anti-Western Islamic revolution is simply not plausible today, so one cannot use the anti-terrorism Bush-Cheney rhetoric to justify Western support for oppressive regimes. It is the actions taken by post-revolution movements in conjunction with the reaction of the West to these events that will determine whether the Jasmine Revolution was a turning point in world history or just a footnote in the history of the region. ❑

Article 5.3

THE MIDDLE EAST'S NEOLIBERALISM-CORRUPTION NEXUS

BY FADHEL KABOUB
March/April 2011

Many observers in the West view microfinance institutions and grassroots non-governmental organizations (NGOs) as progressive forces aimed at counter-ing the negative effects of neoliberal economic policies. In the Middle East, however, corrupt regimes have hijacked NGOs and grassroots movements to serve the inter-ests of the ruling party at the cost of corrupting the entire socio-economic fabric. Such organizations are technically not part of the government, but in effect they are controlled by members of the ruling party and infiltrated by the secret police. Truly independent NGOs generally cannot even obtain a license to operate, since govern-ment ministries only grant such licenses with secret-police approval.

Of all the autocratic governments in the Middle East, Tunisia's Ben Ali regime (1987-2011) mastered the art of GONGOs—government-organized non-governmental organizations—especially well. In the 1990s, the regime created the so-called "Solidarity Network," which is comprised of three key institutions: the National Solidarity Fund (NSF), the National Solidarity Bank (NSB), and the National Employment Fund (NEF). Each one of these institutions was created with seed money from the government and was financially sustained through fundraising and "charitable donations."

The NSF was established in 1992 with the professed aim of eradicating extreme poverty in the most economically disenfranchised areas. The NSB was established in 1997 to promote entrepreneurship, self-employment, and small business through microcredit. The NEF was introduced in 1999 to promote youth employment with a special emphasis on those with college degrees and vocational training.

The Solidarity Network was Ben Ali's magic trick: it was supposed to remedy the negative socio-economic consequences of neoliberal structural adjustment programs without increasing government spending. Technically speaking, the network was (for the most part) not funded by the government. So it was con-sistent with austerity measures, promoted market-based solutions, and gave the illusion of the existence of a grassroots movement. In reality, however, the Solidarity Network, like all other NGOs in Tunisia, was under the control of the ruling-party elite to ensure that all civil-society movements were funneled under Ben Ali's leadership to prevent the emergence of a real opposition party. The charitable donations that funded the Solidarity Network were in fact forced contributions from businesses and individuals throughout the country. The ruling party rewarded contributors with easy access to government resources, scholarships, employment opportunities for family members, government con-tracts, commercial licences, and export subsidies.

When the Trabelsi-Ben Ali business empire emerged in the 2000s, it capitalized on the role of the RCD ruling party in policing the economy through GONGOs, quickly transforming this culture of patronage into widespread corruption across all aspects of society. Their mafia-style business model forced many businesses either to join them as business partners (and enjoy the perks), sell their businesses to the Trabelsi family, or face harassment or intimidation. This corrupt business environment forced many entrepreneurs to divest from the real economy and invest in real estate and financial markets.

In addition to the urgent constitutional and democratic reforms that Tunisia is undertaking today, the most significant challenge now is on the economic front. True solidarity cannot coexist with corruption and racketeering. Effective anti-corruption measures have to be quickly implemented to take advantage of the revolutionary momentum, especially after the dissolution of the secret police agency and the RCD ruling party. In the post-Ben Ali era, Tunisians are reclaiming the true meaning of solidarity and creating a genuine grassroots movement that will question the validity of the neoliberal economic model.

Transforming GONGOs into NGOs in the post-revolutionary Middle East is one step toward building a support network for democracy and social justice, but the real challenge is to roll back the neoliberal policies that have dominated the region since the 1980s, and to rid the system of the habits of corruption that GONGOs wove into the social fabric of the Middle East. ❑

Article 5.4

LABOR RADICALISM AND POPULAR EMANCIPATION
The Egyptian uprising continues.

BY STEPHEN MAHER
November/December 2011

In mid-August, the eminent Marxist philosopher Slavoj Žižek wrote, "Unfortunately, the Egyptian summer of 2011 will be remembered as marking the end of revolution, a time when its emancipatory potential was suffocated." Indeed, the forcible clearing of protestors from Tahrir Square, the outlawing of labor strikes, and the imprisonment of thousands by the military that was taking place as Žižek wrote did not bode well for the revolution. In the months since his words were published, things have not gotten much better: the military has reinstated Mubarak's Emergency Law, the International Monetary Fund has issued grim predictions for Egypt's economic performance as interest rates soar, and Moody's has again downgraded Egypt's bond rating and that of several of its major banks. Meanwhile, the Islamists, marginalized in the earlier days of the revolutionary uprising, have returned, well organized and poised to play a significant part in the constitution-writing process that will commence following the upcoming elections.

Yet since the overthrow of Mubarak, industrial actions against low wages and poor working conditions have persisted, and a multitude of new, independent labor unions have been formed. In recent weeks, a new wave of labor strikes has exploded across the country on a scale "not seen since the earliest weeks of the revolution," as the *Washington Post* put it. But in view of the monumental challenges they face, what can these ongoing labor and leftist popular political movements still hope to accomplish? Is the revolution doomed, as Žižek suggests, or is a brighter future, and a truly radical social transformation, away from the domination of Egyptian society by capital, still within reach for Egypt?

Rise to Rebellion

The years leading up to the overthrow of Hosni Mubarak saw the development of a democratic social movement unprecedented in the history of the modern Middle East. This movement developed partly in resistance to the neoliberal policies imposed after a 1991 debt restructuring by the Egyptian state in collaboration with the International Monetary Fund (IMF) and the World Bank. The "reforms" consisted of the familiar neoliberal package: liberalized capital flows, deregulation and privatization of industries, and the gutting of the national health care and education systems along with the retreat of the state from other areas of social provision. As Marxist theorist David Harvey has argued, "the evidence strongly suggests that the neoliberal turn is in some way and in some degree associated with the restoration or reconstruction of the power of economic elites." Egypt's neoliberal transformation was no exception, with the breakdown of the powerful nationalist solidarity that held sway during the presidency of Gamal Abdel Nasser, followed by the ascendance of a powerful bourgeoisie linked to global capitalism. Despite increased production and strong GDP growth—between 4% and 7% per year—much of the new wealth was concentrated into the hands of Egypt's ruling class, while workers were left with barely enough to eat and social services for the poor were degraded or eliminated outright.

These programs were accelerated after 2004 with the inauguration of the "reform cabinet" of Ahmad Nazif. But alongside this push grew fierce resistance: between 2004 and 2010, there were more than 3,000 labor actions in Egypt, as workers exercised leverage from within the labor process against the ruling class and an authoritarian, unresponsive state apparatus. A sudden spike in inflation (which doubled in 2009), partly spurred by the liquidity that flooded the market as a result of the U.S. Federal Reserve's $2 trillion Quantitative Easing program, exacerbated the social crisis as the pitifully low wages paid out to Egyptian workers proved inadequate to meet basic needs. Egyptian society—beginning with the workers in the factories—was increasingly pushed toward revolutionary social transformation. The spread of high technology linked together workers in the industrial towns and an urban youth movement chafing under the authoritarian state apparatus, expanding conceptions of the revolutionary potential for the future. An 18-day popular uprising, which eventually saw millions gather in Cairo's central Tahrir Square, led on February 11 to the resignation of Hosni Mubarak, the suspension of the constitution, the repeal of the dreaded Emergency Law (which effectively circumvented all constitutional protections) and the transfer of power to the Egyptian army under the auspices of the Supreme Council of the Armed Forces (SCAF).

Reaction and Normalization

Despite Mubarak's resignation, large-scale protests and labor actions continued across Egypt. Such ongoing actions have made clear that the uprising is fundamentally social: it seeks to challenge not just the leadership of one individual, but rather an entire social-institutional order. Concern that the movement could turn explicitly anti-capitalist and lead to a more radical transformation of Egyptian society led the IMF to cloak its proposed post-revolution loan programs—negotiated in secret with Mubarak-appointed finance minister Samir Radwan—behind claims of "social justice" and an "orderly transition" to democratic rule. Meanwhile, after supporting Mubarak until his final days in office, the United States hurriedly expressed its support for the revolutionary movement, which it claimed had achieved its goals and urged the activists to return home and get back to work.

But soon after Mubarak's resignation, 5,000 employees from the Tawhid wa-Nur department store chain descended on Cairo, winning a 12-hour workday and a significant pay increase. Then, on March 3, planned protests against newly appointed Prime Minister Ahmad Shafiq, widely viewed to be a member of Mubarak's old guard, caused him to resign, replaced by Essam Sharaf. Ongoing industrial actions also forced the army to permit the organization of independent labor unions. But by the end of March, ongoing mass demonstrations across the country led the Egyptian cabinet to order a law criminalizing all strikes and protests, which were made punishable by huge fines or imprisonment.

Still, the revolutionaries were not deterred. On April 1, "Save the Revolution Day," tens of thousands again filled Tahrir in defiance of the new measures. Massive protests continued on May 27 in opposition to the repression of SCAF, in particular the practice of subjecting civilians to military trials. The ongoing demonstrations forced SCAF to hastily announce on June 30 that it would reject all loans from the IMF and World Bank, which had been negotiated by Finance Minister Radwan just three weeks previously. This powerful mass movement was able to retain its momentum throughout July, before the military forcibly cleared Tahrir in early August. After arresting thousands of demonstrators, by September SCAF had reinstated the despised Emergency Law, one of the primary targets of the revolution.

Slowly but surely, the U.S.-backed Egyptian military and the ruling elite to which it is intimately connected seemed to consolidate their grip on power, ensuring that Egypt would remain closely linked to global capitalism and stay within the U.S. imperial system. Harsh repression, aimed at stifling a democratic social transformation and solidifying the hegemony of the army and the bourgeoisie, proceeded even as the show trial of Mubarak and a few of his closest associates got underway. Designed to demobilize the population and create the impression that justice has been achieved and "the system is working," the trial of Mubarak is perhaps the most effective measure the SCAF has taken so far toward the goal of preserving the existing social order.

Dark Clouds

Thorough the maintenance of a debt cycle, international capital keeps Egypt on a short leash. The establishment of a self-reinforcing cycle of debt means that as Egypt needs constant access to new credit in order to service its long-term obligations, the government will have to do whatever is necessary to keep new loans coming in. The result is a net *outflow* of capital from Egypt to international lenders. Between 2000 and 2009, net transfers on Egypt's long-term debt (the difference between received loans and debt payments) reached $3.4 billion. In the same period, Egypt's debt *grew* by 15%, despite the fact that it repaid a total of $24.6 billion in loans. This self-reinforcing cycle of dependency, which redistributes billions from Egypt's poor to Western financiers, gives these institutions tremendous leverage over Egypt's government. This, despite the fact that much of this debt is what is referred to as "odious" debt, contracted by an unelected dictatorship with the encouragement of the IMF, World Bank, and others. Mubarak's inner circle and the capitalist class were enriched to the tune of billions of dollars, while millions of Egyptians were kept in desperate poverty.

Keeping the economy open to foreign investment by eliminating trade barriers and capital controls is another way Egyptian dependence on foreign capital is maintained, establishing what is often referred to as a "virtual parliament." If the Egyptian government does not serve the interests of capital, Western investors can literally defund the country by rapidly withdrawing capital, thereby driving up interest rates and destroying the Egyptian currency. Not surprisingly, the maintenance of liberalized capital flows is a key demand made on the new Egyptian government, likewise tied to the continued extension of aid and credit, as the Egyptian business class warns the ongoing revolutionary movement of the dangers of capital flight. Ominously, Moody's

Investor Service downgraded its rating for five major Egyptian banks, a move certain to provoke a reaction in international markets. Further liberalization and privatization, on the other hand, would almost certainly improve such ratings.

The downgrades bode ill for Egypt's ability to borrow on international markets. With Egypt in danger of bankruptcy, Egyptian finance minister Hazem el Beblawi has suggested that Egypt would again consider returning to the IMF for a loan, regardless of the popular outrage sparked by the deal made by his predecessor. Beblawi has already concluded a deal for $400 million from the World Bank to finance various public works projects, and Saudi Arabia and the United Arab Emirates have sought to preserve the rule of Egypt's capitalist class by lending Egypt $5 billion in budget support, and to finance new infrastructure projects. By soaking up unemployment through the implementation of Keynesian programs and making financing available for capitalistic activities, these loans seek to stabilize an Egyptian capitalism whose future—in the face of a massive new labor uprising—seems uncertain at best.

An IMF report on the Egyptian economy issued in late September further clarified the dark clouds on Egypt's horizon, projecting just 1.5% growth in 2011, mildly recovering to 2.5% in 2012. Gaping budget deficits, as the state seeks to buy off dissent and agitation for a more radical transformation by increasing the wages of public sector workers, are meeting with soaring interest rates that led the Cairo Central Bank to halt the sale of two- and three-year bonds on September 19. On September 22, Egypt gained $1.3 billion through the sale of six-month and one-year bonds, but at an average interest rate of 13.9%. Even at this astronomical interest rate, government borrowing risked crowding out private investment, according to the IMF report, which suggested that Egypt might have to return to the IMF after all in order to meet its budgetary shortfall.

A New Explosion

During Mubarak's rule, the only labor organization permitted to operate was the regime-dominated General Federation of Trade Unions, which supported the neoliberal agenda and worked to keep labor in line with state and ruling-class objectives. Before the uprising, labor organizers risked arrest, imprisonment, and torture to organize workers underground, but since the resignation of Mubarak labor organization has exploded: 130 new unions have been formed in the past seven months. In recent weeks, laborers from a broad swath of Egyptian society have taken advantage of the gains of the revolution, with a tidal wave of strikes engulfing the country on an unprecedented scale. While Mubarak never hesitated to obstruct labor action by deploying brute force, today's empowered strikers confront the state and the bourgeoisie with demands to reverse many of the neoliberal measures and redistribute the vast wealth that was concentrated in the hands of the upper classes in the neoliberal era.

Doctors staging sit-ins at hospitals are demanding better pay and insisting on a trebling of health spending in order to reverse the neoliberal gutting of what was once a strong public-health system. Striking teachers demanding the restructuring of the educational system to include classes on democracy and human rights, pay increases, and the firing of the education minister have forced the total or partial shutdown of 85% of Egyptian schools. Transit workers, demanding better pay, have brought the Cairo metro system to a screeching halt. Dockworkers at the port of Ain Al Sokhna are also refusing to work, disrupting trade with the Far East. This growing class consciousness, and willingness to confront the authorities, is taking hold of ever-wider segments of Egyptian society, and now, according to a *Washington Post* report, "appears to be spreading to private factories and farms, fueled by the breaking of a barrier of fear that served to curb union activity here for decades." As Abdel Aziz El Bialy, deputy director of the Independent Teachers' Union, put it: "This is a social revolution to complete the political revolution."

The Road Ahead

Given the organizational head start of the Islamists, the upcoming parliamentary elections are likely to bring victories to such conservative social forces, which will give them a tremendous hand in the constitution-writing process that will follow. The Islamists, who were an integral component of social stability during the Mubarak regime, are likely to accept the privilege of the army and the ruling class in exchange for increased ideological dominance. But as this tremendous labor uprising makes clear, the Egyptian people do not want the restoration of economic growth based on the gross exploitation of poorly paid workers by the owners of capital. Egypt has already been through that, with much of the vast wealth produced by workers in the neoliberal period simply concentrated in the hands of the bourgeoisie. Indeed, the IMF and World Bank issued one glowing assessment after another on Egypt's economic performance during the period of its neoliberal transformation (including one issued just days before the beginning of the uprising), which saw social inequalities grow to unprecedented heights amid severe state repression of labor and other dissent.

The purpose of the revolution was not to preserve market stability and assuage global capitalism; on the contrary, capitalist exploitation of labor in factory towns like Mahalla was the target of the uprising in the first place. A true, democratic social transformation is possible for Egypt, but this means discarding the advice and interests of capitalists, local and international, and their affiliates and agents. It means the democratic management of production and social life, the construction of a society in which despair and unemployment are impossible and true human flourishing is the foremost social goal, not the senseless accumulation of capital. In other words, the revolution must seek a true social transformation: one that puts an end to the exploitation of the workers and the violent deprivation of the poor and brings about genuine democratic management of social and political life. Such a radical social transformation will not be looked upon kindly by global capitalism and those at its head. But, again in the words of Slavoj Žižek, "liberation hurts." ❑

Sources: Slavoj Žižek. "Shoplifters of the World Unite," *London Review of Books*, August 19, 2011; Slavoj Žižek and Eric Dean Rasmussen, "Liberation Hurts: An Interview with Slavoj Žižek," *Electronic Book Review*, July 1, 2004; Anthony Faiola, "Egypt's Labor Movement Blooms in Arab Spring," *Washington Post*, September 25, 2009; David Harvey, *A Brief History of Neoliberalism*, Oxford University Press, 2005; Ismail Arslan, World Bank Independent Evaluation Group, *Egypt, Positive Results From Knowledge Sharing and Modest Lending: An IEG Country Assistance Evaluation, 1999-2007*, World Bank

Publications, 2009; Adam Morrow and Khaled Moussa al-Omrani "Economists Blame 'Neo-liberalism' for Region's Woes," *Inter Press Service*, January 18, 2010; Walter Armbrust, "A Revolution Against Neoliberalism?" Al-Jazeera English, February 24, 2011; "The Struggle For Worker Rights in Egypt," The Solidarity Center, February, 2010 (www.solidaritycenter.org/files/pubs_egypt_wr.pdf); "IMF agrees to $3bn Egypt loan for post-Mubarak transition," Bloomberg, June 5, 2011; Anand Gopal, "Egypt's Cauldron of Revolt," *Foreign Policy*, February 16, 2011; Steve Hendrix and William Wan, "Egyptian prime minister Ahmed Shafiq resigns ahead of protests," *Washington Post*, March 3, 2011; Yassin Gaber, "Egypt workers lay down demands at new trade union conference," *Al-Ahram,* March 3, 2011; Klaus Enders, "Egypt: Reforms Trigger Economic Growth," IMF Middle East and Central Asia Department, February 13, 2008; Abigail Hauslohner, "Has the Revolution Left Egypt's Workers Behind?" Time Magazine, June 23, 2011; "Tens of Thousands attend 'Save the Revolution' Day," Al-Ahram, April 1, 2011; "Tens of thousands of Tahrir protesters demans swift justice in 'Second Friday of Anger'," *The Daily News Egypt*, May 27, 2011; Edmund Blair, "Egypt says will not need IMF, World Bank funds," Reuters, June 25, 2011; Malika Bilal, "Egypt: An incomplete revolution," *Al-Jazeera English*, August 19, 2011; Shahira Amin, "Activists fight revival of emergency law," *CNN*, September 19, 2011; "IMF: Egypt economy to grow just 1.5 per cent in 2011," *Al Ahram*, September 21, 2011; Alaa Shahine, "Arabs May Buy Egypt Debt to Cut Highest Yield Since 2008," *Bloomberg Businessweek*, September 23, 2011; Tim Falconer, "Moody's Downgrades Egypt's Ratings," *Wall Street Journal*, March 16, 2011; "Standard & Poor's Downgrades Egypt Debt Rating," CBS/AP, February 1, 2011; Tarek El-Tablawy, "Moody's downgrades five Egyptian banks," *The Daily News Egypt*, February 3, 2011; Sharif Abdel Kouddous, "Hot Teachers," *Foreign Policy*, September 21, 2011; Michael Robbins and Mark Tessler, "What Egyptians mean by democracy," *Foreign Policy*, September 20, 2011; International Monetary Fund, "Arab Republic of Egypt—2010 Article IV Consultation Mission, Concluding Statement," Cairo, February 16, 2010.

Article 5.5

WOUNDED TIGER
Ireland submits to the IMF.

BY DAN READ
July/August 2011

Guinness is, apparently, now good for public relations. President Barack Obama, in his recent visit to Ireland, seemed to develop a fondness for the drink, or at least put on a brave face when he posed for the cameras with a pint in his hand. Less than twenty-four hours later, though, he had departed the country, after promising to do "everything that we can to be helpful" on Ireland's economic woes that have led to not just one, but potentially two bailouts by the International Monetary Fund (IMF).

The initial three-year Extended Fund Facility granted by the IMF in December 2010 amounted to a loan of over 22.5 billion euros (roughly $32 billion). Coupled with loans from the European Union and state intervention from Dublin, the grand total comes to around $121 billion. The extraordinary price tag came with conditions: Ireland has had to make structural adjustments to its economy that align with IMF goals.

On the surface there is a lot of financial jargon involving "debt restructuring" that will ostensibly render the Irish economy "solvent" once again. The practical implications of these vague and somewhat strange phrases are spelled out in a National Recovery Plan enacted by the government and endorsed by the IMF.

The plan aims to cut government spending by over $21 billion within three years, with $8.5 billion being taken out of the public sector in 2011 alone.

Government pay and staffing levels are thus being downscaled, with the state payroll having already been slashed in 2010 to the tune of over $2 billion. Wages for "new entrants" have also been hit with a blanket 10% reduction, with recruitment to the state sector limited to 3,300 new personnel each year. In conjunction with measures to fire existing staff, the government hopes to have a leaner, less well-paid public sector, with fewer than 294,000 employees by 2014. Taking public-sector employment figures for late 2008, this entails a decline of 75,100 employees.

Downgrading for Growth

In their online press releases, the IMF has lauded the plan for laying the foundations for recovery while still paying "due regard to a social safety net." The safety net is looking a little worn, however. Some measures proposed by the plan involved the withdrawal of $144 million from state pension funds, as well as raising the retirement age to 66 in 2014, to 67 in 2021, and to 68 in 2028. Furthermore, for 2011 alone $1.1 billion is to be taken from Social Protection (welfare), which will see a total cut of $4.3 billion by 2014.

The plan paves new ground for political institutions worldwide in that it openly admits the measures "will negatively affect the living standards of citizens," but claims that this is necessary to "to return [the Irish] economy to a sustainable medium-term economic growth path."

The state sector employs workers from a diverse set of industries, ranging from hospital nurses to postmen to police officers. Policies threatening these workers' jobs have prompted renewed militancy on the part of trade unions and leftist political organizations.

"We have had several huge workers demonstrations in the past couple of years," Macdara Doyle, a spokesman for the Irish Congress of Trade Unions (ICTU), told *Dollars & Sense*. "These were some of the largest in Europe—I mean, if you factor in the overall size of the population of Ireland, one hundred

---

THE WRONG MEDICINE: WHY FISCAL AUSTERITY IS A BAD IDEA FOR A SLUMPING ECONOMY

As protesters take to the streets in Europe to oppose government spending cuts, proponents of austerity in the United States and Europe claim that immediate moves to reduce government deficits are the way to renewed economic growth. Accepting a little pain now, they argue, will reduce the pain in the long run.

Those familiar with Keynesian economic theory will find the austerity-to-growth claims surprising. Fiscal austerity, or a "contractionary fiscal policy," means either spending cuts or tax increases, or a combination of the two. Reductions in government spending reduce total demand directly. Government spending on real goods and services is just as much a part of total demand as private consumption or investment spending. Spending cuts can also reduce demand indirectly, as those who would have received income as a result of government spending cut back on their spending as well. Tax increases reduce demand by reducing the disposable incomes of private individuals, who then spend less. Either way, lower demand for goods and services can translate into less output and employment.

How, then, is fiscal contraction supposed to lead to growth? Austerity proponents argue that balancing government budgets and reducing public debt will boost private-sector "confidence." As public debt increases, the argument goes, people may become wary about spending, since they will be on the hook (through taxes) to pay down that debt in the future. Individuals and firms will spend more freely now if they do not have future taxes hanging over their heads.

The pro-austerity faction has relied heavily on a few recent studies, especially one by Harvard economists Alberto Alesina and Silvia Ardagna claiming to have identified 26 cases in which fiscal contraction led to renewed growth. This conclusion, however, has not stood up to careful scrutiny. Economists Arjun Jayadev and Mike Konczal, after studying the cases that Alesina and Ardagna describe, find that "in virtually none did the country a) reduce the deficit when the economy was in a slump and b) increase growth rates while reducing the debt-to-GDP ratio."

In 20 of the 26 cases, Jayadev and Konczal argue, the government did not carry out a fiscal contraction during the low (or "slump") phase of a business cycle. (Budgets are much easier to balance, and debt easier to pay down, during the "boom" phase of a business cycle. With output and incomes high,

thousand or so people on the streets of Dublin is like several million in London and Paris."

The ICTU has not been slow to note a mounting pressure on working families. Speaking to a meeting of trade unionists in April, the congress's economic advisor, Paul Sweeney, took note of a deteriorating economic situation made worse by a global rise in food and oil prices.

Coupled with a recent rise in interest rates for Ireland's existing consumer debts, Sweeney cited "extra hardship for people all over the country" due to people

total tax revenue is bound to be high as well, while expenditures on things like unemployment insurance are bound to be low.) Out of the six remaining cases, they find, the rate of economic growth actually declined in five. Looking at a broader sample of countries engaging in austerity, Jayadev and Konczal find that, in most cases, deficit cutting during a slump results in lower growth. Even in most of the cases where the growth rate did increase, the ratio of debt to gross domestic product actually increased as well. This suggests that, even if fiscal austerity had some effect in reducing the growth of total debt, it also resulted in such weak overall economic growth that the debt burden (relative to GDP) continued to rise.

Austerity can actually undermine a country's ability to reduce its government deficit and debt, and increase the interest rates a government is forced to pay on its debt. A government's ability to borrow depends on the size and stability of the economy that it has the power to tax. By cutting demand, a government may prolong a slump. The longer the slump goes on, the longer tax revenues will remain below normal, and the longer the government will have above-normal expenditures on items like unemployment insurance. If investors conclude that the slump is bound to go on for a long time, and that the government will therefore be a bad credit risk for the foreseeable future, they will demand a higher interest rate (to compensate them for that risk). This, too, will tend to increase the government's debt burden.

Austerity advocates present themselves as tough-minded and pragmatic— not flinching from the painful sacrifices necessary for a better future. The facts might suggest, instead, that fiscal austerity during a slump amounts to cutting off one's nose to spite one's face. Except that, as the protests raging in Europe show, it is other people's noses that the pro-austerity faction aims to lop off.

—*Alejandro Reuss*

Sources: Arjun Jayadev and Mike Konczal, "The Boom Not the Slump: Not the Right Time for Austerity," The Roosevelt Institute, August 23, 2010; Alberto Alesina and Silvia Ardagna, "Large Changes in Fiscal Policy: Taxes Versus Spending," NBER Working Paper No. 15438, 2009; Andrew G. Biggs, Kevin A. Hassett, and Matthew Jensen, "A Guide for Deficit Reduction in the United States Based on Historical Consolidations That Worked," American Enterprise Institute, December 2010; International Monetary Fund, "Will It Hurt? Macroeconomic Effects of Fiscal Consolidation," World Economic Outlook, Chapter 3, October 2010; Paul Krugman, "Does Fiscal Austerity Reassure Markets?" June 13, 2010 (krugman.blogs.nytimes.com).

"being squeezed on too many fronts. There is a limit to the burden of austerity that any society, or household, can tolerate."

Yet the Dail, the principal house of Ireland's parliament, seemed more than willing to engage in economic austerity measures even before the IMF received its not-so-warm welcome last December. The national budget for 2010 detailed "savings" on expenditure to the tune of $4.3 billion. Of this sizeable sum, $1.1 billion was taken from "Social and Family Affairs"—in part welfare measures such as benefit payments to the unemployed—alongside $576 million from child care and health services.

"We have actually had four austerity budgets in this country," says Doyle of the ICTU, "December's bailout was actually triggered by the European Central Bank [ECB] in response to a broken and busted banking system that has brought down the whole country. We were in debt to the ECB to the tune of around 130 billion euros [$187 billion], and the government just kept going to them for aid until the ECB just said 'No, we can't do this anymore, this debt needs to be restructured.'"

IMF spokesmen are in agreement with Doyle on this point. In a document released shortly after the December bailout, the IMF emphasized the flaws of "an oversized banking system" that had become "overly dependent on financing from the European Central Bank."

The paradox here is that the ECB is still intimately involved in the recovery process and remains an important participant in the Extended Fund Facility. What has changed, however, is that the IMF intervention seems to have mollified the ECB into acting as creditors to what they might otherwise have viewed as a lost cause.

Fewer Resources

The case of Ireland's banks is similar to the British or American experience—except that the Irish government does not have the capital reserves to implement extensive banking bailouts. Figures compiled by the World Bank during the height of the recession in 2009 show Irish GDP sitting at just over $227 billion. The corresponding figure for the UK showed British GDP leagues ahead at over $2.1 trillion. Unsurprisingly, the United States won first with a GDP of well over $14 trillion. If the response to the crisis has been somewhat similar in these countries, the facts on the ground show that the Irish economy, despite its reputation as a "Celtic Tiger" in the 1990s, is simply unable to cope with the aftershocks of recession.

What prompted the crisis is, again, a somewhat familiar story: Ireland's former prosperity has been attributed to a housing bubble that lifted the country from depression in the late 1980s into the lofty heights of financial stardom less than ten years later. This claim is further substantiated by a 6.5% annual GDP growth rate between 1991 and 2007. *The Economist* had this to say in May 1997: "just yesterday, it seems, Ireland was one of Europe's poorest countries. Today it is about as prosperous as the European average and getting richer all the time."

Yet *The Economist* in its optimism overlooked some important facts. At the time of the article, house prices were already soaring dramatically; between 1992 and 2006 they rose by around 300%. In a story that is no doubt familiar, Irish banks were all too willing to lend at low interest rates while believing it safe to imitate the behavior of their American and British counterparts. But the property boom— and with it the banks' reckless lending and low interest rates—was not to last, and despite its former prosperity, Dublin is not the financial hub that London or New York can claim to be.

If the Dail cannot match Westminster in financial prosperity, however, it can match it in how it handles recession, and that's by passing the burden onto ordinary people. The Value Added Tax (VAT) has been hiked in both countries, despite the fact that, in Ireland in particular, a burden on the spending of the individual consumer is also an extra weight on small businesses, which are typically more dependent on the internal market than larger franchises with potential holdings overseas. "Obviously, it depends on what kind of small business we are talking about," said Sean Murphy, deputy chief executive for Chambers Ireland, Ireland's largest business advocacy organization, "but on the domestic side we are seeing a lowering of consumer confidence which is going to be affecting them. Outside of that, we can see that Irish exports are growing, but when dealing with the internal market and VAT rises and so on, things are not going so well."

A Second Bailout?

So far, talk of a second bailout in 2013 has been confined to supposition that the government will be forced to default on existing debts despite the implementation of the recovery plan. An additional bailout has therefore been raised as a possibility for boosting revenue, although the economic "adjustments" involved may differ in severity from those contained in the National Recovery Plan.

The possible additional bailout comes recommended by former IMF deputy director Donal Donovan. Donovan claimed last March that the country would need assistance until at least 2015, with further "debt restructuring" on the agenda should the economy prove "insolvent."

The Irish people themselves appear to disagree. The United Left Alliance (ULA), an umbrella organization of leftist groups founded last November, has already started to make waves on the political scene after winning five seats in the Dail in March.

"The only people who are in denial about a second bailout actually happening are the main political parties," Michael O'Brien, a member of the ULA's national interim steering committee, told *Dollars & Sense*. "It could be said that the reason why the original terms brought in last December were so harsh is that the IMF knew there would be a default, but not an immediate one, it's just that in the three-year period the first bailout is in effect foreign investors will be able to get more of a hold over the Irish banking sector before a second bailout becomes necessary."

"Both the left and the right don't seem to want to talk about this, but unless we reject these harsh terms we will certainly default, and that's when a second bailout becomes likely. Even if we reduce ourselves to serfdom there will be a default."

O'Brien is also a believer in Irish economist Richard Douthwait's theory that duplicity is integral to the IMF's strategy. If the IMF apparently believes a default will occur, then why have they bothered with a bailout in the first place? Douthwait believes, as does O'Brien, that the secret lies in the interests of foreign depositors in Irish banks. Writing in the magazine *Construct Ireland*, Douthwait poses the question: "If a default is inevitable, why is Ireland being paid, via the bailout money, not to default now? The answer is clear. A default now would mean that the foreign banks and other institutions which have lent to Ireland would suffer massive losses and might need to be rescued by the governments of the countries in which they are based. Big firms with deposits in Irish banks in excess of the l00,000 euros [$145,000] state guarantee would suffer big losses too. Indeed, if the two major banks collapsed, the government could find itself unable to honour its deposit guarantees at all."

Donovan, Douthwait, and O'Brien seem set on the belief that a second bailout will therefore be necessary, although they clearly have differing opinions as to why. Douthwait and O'Brien believe the priority of the IMF and ECB is to safeguard foreign deposits, or permit them to withdraw in time in order to avert further losses while adopting a wait-and-see approach to the Irish recovery. The IMF's Donovan, however, is slightly more optimistic. The British newspaper The Guardian quotes Donovan as being amenable to the notion of writing off some of Ireland's debt, provided that the nation continues to follow the measures prescribed by the National Recovery Plan. Once this is done, he argues, the ECB may be more willing to let Ireland off the hook, at least to a degree.

PIIGS

But talk of partial relief at some point in the future does little for those already facing unemployment and falling living standards. Moreover, economists at the IMF and elsewhere seem to have developed a contemptuous attitude towards Ireland and other countries still reeling from the economic crisis—an attitude that hardly endears them to the populations they claim to be helping.

Over the years, economists have referred to the weaker economies of Europe, such as Italy, as being "sick" or otherwise suffering some kind of ailment. The acronym "PIIGS" (as in Portugal, Ireland, Italy, Greece, and Spain) is now in use by economists and pundits to describe the economically troubled parts of the continent.

Being referred to as a pig is hardly likely to prompt a positive reaction, yet hardship and the contempt of powerful foreigners is not something that is new to Ireland. In the past, the Irish have often dealt with economic woes by moving abroad; almost a million Irish headed to the United States during the Potato Famine of the late 1840s. Although the Irish are now in different straits, their tried-and-tested method of seeking greener pastures abroad has resurfaced.

The ICTU has estimated that perhaps a thousand citizens leave the country each week, although according to Doyle "some of them are immigrants anyway." According to the Economic and Social Research Institute, a Dublin-based research organization, 60,000 people left the country in the twelve months leading up to April 2010 alone. Over the course of 2010 and 2011 this trend has only continued.

"The problem," said Doyle, "is that we are losing a lot of people who are very qualified and very skilled; the kind of people you need to help an economy recover."

Economic Freedom

The Irish socialist James Connelly once said that half-measures on the road to independence would ensure "England will still rule" through "the whole array of commercial institutions she has planted in this country and watered with the tears of our mothers and the blood of our martyrs."

Prophetic words, yet Connelly could not have envisaged the future scale of the problem. What Ireland now faces is not so much a single foreign aggressor but multiple economic ties to a globe-spanning organization imposing privation through financial means.

With the National Recovery Plan viewed more as a National Austerity Plan by large segments of the population, unemployment at over 13%, and discontent on the rise, the days of Irish prosperity appear to be over. The demand for a politically and economically free Ireland, as put forth by the likes of Connelly before his execution by the British in 1916, still remains valid. ❑

Sources: Irish Congress of Trade Unions (www.ictu.ie); International Monetary Fund (imf.org); "National Recovery Plan 2010-2014," An Roinn Airgeadais Department of Finance (www.budget. gov.ie); United Left Alliance (unitedleftalliance.org); Chambers Ireland (www.chambers.ie); Dáil Éireann (www.oireachtas.ie); Central Statistics Office Ireland (www.cso.ie); Economic and Social Research Institute (www.esri.ie); Richard Douthwait, "Ireland's inevitable default," Construct Ireland, May 9, 2011 (www.constructireland.ie); Lisa O'Carroll, "Ireland will need another bailout, says former IMF director," *The Guardian*, April 7, 2011 (www.guardian.co.uk); "Ireland Shines," *The Economist*, May 15, 1997 (economist.com).

Article 5.6

THE 99%, THE 1%, AND CLASS STRUGGLE

BY ALEJANDRO REUSS
November/December 2011

Between 1979 and 2007, the income share of the top 1% of U.S. households (by income rank) more than doubled, to over 17% of total U.S. income. Meanwhile, the income share of the bottom 80% dropped from 57% to 48% of total income. "We are the 99%," the rallying cry of the #OccupyWallStreet movement, does a good job at calling attention to the dramatic increase of incomes for those at the very top—and the stagnation of incomes for the majority.

This way of looking at income distribution, however, does not explicitly focus on the different *sources* of people's incomes. Most people get nearly all of their incomes— wages and salaries, as well as employment benefits—by working for someone else. A few people, on the other hand, get much of their income not from work but from ownership of property—profits from a business, dividends from stock, interest income from bonds, rents on land or structures, and so on. People with large property incomes may also draw large salaries or bonuses, especially from managerial jobs. Executive pay, though treated in official government statistics as labor income, derives from control over business firms and really should be counted as property income.

Over the last forty years, the distribution of income in the United States has tilted in favor of capitalists (including business owners, stock- and bond-holders, and corporate executives) and against workers. Between the 1940s and 1960s, U.S. workers' hourly output ("average labor productivity") and workers' real hourly compensation both grew at about 3% per year, so the distribution of income between workers and capitalists changed relatively little. (If the size of a pie doubles and the size of your slice also doubles, your share of the pie does not change.) Since the 1970s,

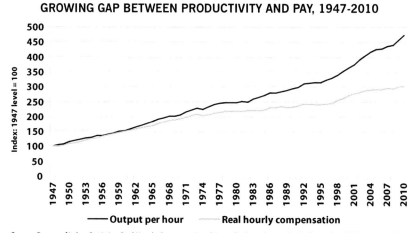

GROWING GAP BETWEEN PRODUCTIVITY AND PAY, 1947-2010

Index: 1947 level = 100

——— **Output per hour**   ·········· **Real hourly compensation**

Source: Bureau of Labor Statistics, Real Hourly Compensation, Private Business Sector, Series ID number: PRS84006153; Bureau of Labor Statistics, Output Per Hour, Private Business Sector, Series ID number: PRS84006093.

productivity has kept growing at over 2% per year. Average hourly compensation, however, has stagnated—growing only about 1% per year (see figure below). As the gap between what workers produce and what they get paid has increased, workers' share of total income has fallen, and capitalists' share has increased. Since income from property is overwhelmingly concentrated at the top of the income scale, this has helped fuel the rising income share of "the 1%."

The spectacular rise in some types of income—like bank profits or executive compensation—has provoked widespread outrage. Lower financial profits or CEO pay, however, will not reverse the trend toward greater inequality if the result is only to swell, say, profits for nonfinancial corporations or dividends for wealthy shareholders. Focusing too much on one or another kind of property income distracts from the fact that the overall property-income share has been growing at workers' expense.

Workers and employers—whether they like it or not, recognize it or not, prepare for it or not—are locked in a class struggle. Employers in the United States and other countries, over the last few decades, have recognized that they were in a war and prepared for it. They have been fighting and winning. Workers will only regain what they have lost if they can rebuild their collective fighting strength. In the era of globalized capitalism, this means not only building up labor movements in individual countries, but also creating practical solidarity between workers around the world.

A labor resurgence could end workers' decades-long losing streak at the hands of employers and help reverse the tide of rising inequality. Ultimately, though, this struggle should be about more than just getting a better deal. It should be—and can be—about the possibility of building a new kind of society. The monstrous inequalities of capitalism are plain to see. The need for an appealing alternative—a vision of a cooperative, democratic, and egalitarian way of life—is equally stark. ❏

Sources: Bureau of Labor Statistics, Real Hourly Compensation, Private Business Sector, Series ID number: PRS84006153; Bureau of Labor Statistics, Output Per Hour, Private Business Sector, Series ID number: PRS84006093; Congressional Budget Office, Trends in the Distribution of Household Income Between 1979 and 2007 (October 2011) (www.cbo.gov); James Heintz, "Unpacking the U.S. Labor Share," *Capitalism on Trial: A Conference in Honor of Thomas A. Weisskopf*, Political Economy Research Institute, University of Massachusetts-Amherst (September 2011).

Chapter 6

STIMULUS AND DEFICITS

Article 6.1

MYTHS OF THE DEFICIT

BY MARTY WOLFSON
May/June 2010

N early 15 million people are officially counted as unemployed in the United States, and more than 6 million of these have been unemployed for more than 26 weeks. Another 11 million are the "hidden" unemployed: jobless workers who have given up looking for work and part-time workers who want full-time jobs. Unemployment has especially affected minority communities; the official black teenage unemployment rate, for example, stands at 42%.

The *moral* case for urgently addressing the unemployment issue is clear. The costs of unemployment, especially prolonged unemployment, are devastating. Self-worth is questioned, homes are lost, families stressed, communities disrupted. Across the land, the number one issue is jobs, jobs, jobs.

The *economic* case for how to address the jobs issue is also clear. As Keynes argued during the Great Depression, federal government spending can directly create jobs. And the $787 billion stimulus package approved by Congress in February 2009 did help pull the economy back from disaster, when it was shedding 20,000 jobs *a day* in late 2008 and early 2009.

But we still have a long way to go. To get back just to where we were when the recession began in December 2007, the economy would need to create 11.1 million jobs: 8.4 million to replace the jobs lost and 2.7 million to absorb new workers who have entered the labor market since then.

Despite a pickup of economic activity recently, long-term projections are that the unemployment rate will fall only gradually over the next several years. The Congressional Budget Office forecast for the unemployment rate for 2012 is a stubbornly high 8%. So why are we not moving more aggressively to reduce unemployment?

The *ideological* opposition to government spending remains a major obstacle. There are those who see an increase in the role of government as something to be avoided at all costs—even if the cost is the jobs of the unemployed.

Even among those who are not subject to such ideological blinders, there is still a *political* argument that resonates strongly. The argument is that government spending to create jobs will create large budget deficits, which will have terrible consequences for the American people. Politicians, pundits, and other commentators—in a frenzied drumbeat of speeches, op-eds, and articles—have asserted that the most urgent priority *now* is to reduce the budget deficit.

It is important to note that this argument is focused on current policy, not just the long-term budgetary situation. There is room for debate about long-term budget deficits, but these are affected more by the explosive growth of health-care costs than by government discretionary spending to create jobs.

Why, then, are people taken in by an argument that says it is more important to reduce the budget deficit now than for the government to spend money to create jobs? Two myths constantly repeated in the public debate have contributed to this situation:

1) Families can't spend more than they have; neither should the government.

It seems to be common sense that a family can't spend more than it has. But of course that is exactly what the family does when it takes out a car loan or a student loan, or does any other kind of borrowing. The government, just like families, should be able to borrow. The real issue is whether or not the debt is affordable. For families, and for the government, that depends on the size of the debt relative to the income available to service the debt; it also depends on the nature of the borrowing.

For the federal government, the relevant debt-income measure is the ratio of outstanding debt of the federal government to gross domestic product. (*Outstanding debt* is the total amount owed at a particular time, roughly the result of debt accumulated over time by annual budget deficits; GDP, the value of goods and services produced, is equal to total income.) In 2009, this ratio was 53%. Although higher than the recent low point of 33% at the end of the 1990s expansion, the ratio in 2009 was still far lower than the record peak of 109% in 1946—after which the U.S. economy in the post-World War II period experienced the strongest economic growth in its history.

The U.S. ratio of 53% actually compares favorably to those of other advanced industrial countries. For example, IMF data indicate the following debt-to-GDP ratios for 2009: France (67%), Germany (70%), Japan (105%), and Italy (113%).

The nature of the borrowing also affects affordability. If a family runs up credit-card debt to finance a lavish lifestyle, after the fancy dinners are eaten the family still needs to figure out how to pay its debt. But if a family member borrows to buy a car to get to work, presumably the job will help provide the income to service the debt.

Likewise for the federal government: If the government borrows to finance tax cuts for the rich, and the rich use their tax cuts to purchase imported luxury goods, then the government still needs to figure out how to pay its debt. On the other hand, if the government borrows to put people to work creating long-term investments that increase the productivity of the U.S. economy, like infrastructure and education, then it is in a much better situation. The income generated by the more productive economy, as well as by the newly employed workers, can help to provide the tax revenue to service the debt.

So it is a myth to say that families can't spend more than they have. They can, and so can the government. And both are justified in borrowing if the size of the debt is manageable and if so doing helps to provide the income necessary to service the debt.

2) Large budget deficits create a burden for our grandchildren.

This is the issue that probably resonates most forcefully with public opinion. If we in the current generation run up a big debt, it may be left to our grandchildren to repay. The only difficulty with this reasoning is that the grandchildren who may be asked to repay the debt are paying it to other grandchildren. When the government incurs a debt, it issues a bond, an obligation to repay the debt to the holder of the bond. If the holders of the bond are U.S. residents, then paying off the debt means paying money to U.S. residents. In other words, debt that is an obligation of future U.S. taxpayers is also a source of income to the U.S. holders of that debt. Thus there is not a generational burden that we today are imposing on "our grandchildren" as a collective entity.

Of course, the obvious exception to this reasoning is the debt held by non-U.S. residents. In that case, it is indeed true that future generations of Americans will need to pay interest to foreign holders of U.S. debt. But the basic reason for this situation is the trade deficit, not the budget deficit. When we pay more for imports than we receive from exports, and when U.S. multinational companies ship production abroad to take advantage of low-cost labor, foreigners are provided with dollars that they can use to invest in U.S. assets. And the real burden that this causes is the same whether foreigners invest in U.S. government debt or whether they invest in U.S. companies, real estate, the U.S. stock market, etc.

Borrowing by the federal government can in some situations create a real burden, but it has less to do with generational transfers and more to do with distributional issues and the nature of economic growth (discussed above). If the grandchildren who are taxed in the future to pay off government debt are poorer than the grandchildren who are paid, the distribution of income becomes more unequal.

Also, cutting taxes for the rich and spending money on wars in Iraq and Afghanistan do not lead to the kind of productive economic growth that generates strong tax revenue. So financing these by debt *does* create a real distributional burden: The rich and military contractors benefit, but the losers are those who might be taxed, or those whose government programs might be squeezed out of the budget, because of the need to pay interest on the debt.

Borrowing money to put people back to work does make sense. It helps people most in need, the unemployed. It provides them with income that they can use to pay taxes and to buy goods and services that create more jobs, more income, and more tax revenue. Indeed, our inability thus far to seriously tackle the unemployment problem is what has worsened the budget problem, as tax receipts have fallen and spending for unemployment benefits and food stamps have risen. An analysis by the Economic Policy Institute reveals that the largest source of the 2009 budget deficit (42%) was actually the recession itself.

We *will* leave a burden for our grandchildren if we don't address the urgent problem of unemployment, if we let parents and grandparents suffer the indignities and financial hardships of lost jobs. We *will* leave a burden for our grandchildren if we don't rebuild our aging infrastructure, break our reliance on fossil fuels, and provide all our children with an excellent education. It makes perfect sense to borrow money now to address these problems, and we shouldn't let myths about budget deficits get in the way of meeting these real needs. ❑

Sources: Congressional Budget Office, "The Budget and Economic Outlook: Fiscal Years 2010 to 2020," January 2010; John Irons, Kathryn Edwards, and Anna Turner, "The 2009 Budget Deficit: How Did We Get Here?" Economic Policy Institute, August 20, 2009; Dean Baker, "The Budget Deficit Scare Story and the Great Recession," Center for Economic and Policy Research, February 2010; Office of Management and Budget, "The President's Budget For Fiscal Year 2011, Historical Tables: Table 7.1, Federal Debt at the End of Year: 1940-2015," February 2010.

Article 6.2

DEFICITS: REAL ISSUE, PHONY DEBATES
What's at Stake on Either Side of the Class Divide

BY RICHARD D. WOLFF
November/December 2010

Deficits have now risen, yet again, to headline status. Conservatives inside and right of the Republican Party frame the national debates by attacking deficits. They want to reduce them by cutting government spending. Liberals respond, as usual, by insisting that overcoming the crisis requires big government spending ("stimulus") and hence big deficits. Most Americans watch the politicians' conflicts with mixtures of confusion, disinterest, and disdain. Yet deficits pose a real issue for all citizens, even though the debates among politicians and their economist advisors miss, ignore, or hide that issue.

When the federal government raises less in taxes than it spends, it must borrow the difference. Such annual borrowing is each year's deficit. The U.S. Treasury borrows that money by selling bonds, federal IOUs, to the lenders. The accumulation of annual deficits comprises the national debt, the total of outstanding U.S. treasury bonds. So the first and simplest questions about deficits are (1) why does the federal government choose to borrow rather than to raise taxes? and (2) why does it borrow rather than cut its expenditures? The twin answers are profoundly political. Elected officials are afraid to raise taxes on business and the rich because their profits and great personal wealth can then finance the defeat of officials who do that. Cutting government spending that benefits business and the rich is avoided for the same reason. As the tax burden shifted increasingly onto middle- and lower-income citizens for decades, elected officials have faced rising tax revolts over recent years coupled with demands for more government services and supports.

In the United States—as in most capitalist countries—business and the rich, on one side, and the middle-income and poor on the other, have placed the same demands on the government budget. Each side has wanted *more* government spending on what it needs and *less* taxes on its incomes. Both parties thus fear raising taxes or cutting spending on the masses because that risks electoral defeats. This has been a very real, basic, and socially disruptive contradiction built into capitalist systems.

These days, business and the rich want *both* massive government supports to overcome the current crisis *as well as* their usual government benefits. The latter include government activities abroad—including wars—that secure export markets and access to crucial imports (e.g., the needed quantities and prices of business inputs and means of consumption not domestically available). They also demand the subsidies typically provided to agricultural enterprises, transport companies, defense producers, and so on, as well as tax reductions offered for various kinds of investments. Businesses press government to maintain or expand roads, harbors, airports, schools, mass transportation systems, and research institutes crucial for their enterprises' profits. Wealthy individuals want government spending on the police and judicial systems that protect their wealth.

Business and the rich likewise want the government not to raise their taxes. Businesses seek to keep in place their legal opportunities to evade taxes on profits (by means of offshore operations, internal transfer invoicing, etc.). Business and the rich in the United States want donations to their own foundations, to rich universities, art institutions, and their favorite charities to remain subsidized by generous federal tax reductions granted for such donations. They also currently demand the continuation of Bush-era tax exemptions and reductions on taxes on their incomes and on the estates they leave.

Middle-income and poorer Americans demand government spending for their unemployment insurance, to prevent or soften the blow of home foreclosures, to provide low-interest mortgage money for their home purchases or refinancing, and to guarantee low-interest educational loans for their children. They want public schools well financed to function as means of advancement for their children. They support government regulation to guarantee safe and honestly labeled consumer goods and services and likewise health and safety on their jobs. They demand Social Security retirement benefits and Medicare. There is broad support even for Medicaid, food stamps, and welfare despite some demonization of those programs and their poor recipients. The middle-income and poor alike demand no more taxes nor higher Medicare and Social Security deductions from their incomes.

In all capitalist countries, more or less, the contradiction between these conflicting financial demands on the government's budget has shaped politics. Elected officials have neither raised taxes nor cut spending enough to bring them into balance. Instead they have increasingly resorted to borrowing, running budget deficits. The officials like deficits because they reap immediate political benefits—"satisfying" business, the rich, and all the rest by holding down taxes and maintaining spending—while shifting the political costs of repaying rising national debt and its rising interest costs onto office-holders coming after them (today's equivalent of Louis XV's remark, "*après moi le deluge*").

Government borrowing also benefits businesses and the rich by offering them an attractive investment. They lend money to the government, which then repays those sums with interest. Instead of losing a portion of their wealth by paying taxes, those groups keep that portion (in the form of a purchased government bond) and earn more with it. Businesses and the rich are usually major lenders to their governments; workers rarely are. The same U.S. business leaders who advise governments to "live within their means" simultaneously fill their business and personal portfolios with government bonds.

Each country's unique history, culture, and politics determine how much its government borrows. In the United States, as elsewhere, successive governments (usually of both left and right) have borrowed so much that further borrowing is becoming increasingly difficult. One obstacle looms, because the more a government pays in interest and debt repayment, the less funds it has to undertake the spending business and the public demand. Over the last five years, annual interest payments on the United States' national debt have averaged over $400 billion. Political opposition to continuing those interest payments, and perhaps anger directed against lenders, may arise. Since lenders to governments are overwhelmingly businesses, rich individuals, and various government entities (foreign and domestic), such opposition may draw on deep resentments. Rising national indebtedness therefore builds its own opposition. Where and when that happens or even threatens to happen, major lenders stop risking further purchases of government bonds. Unable to borrow as before, governments return to face the original problem: which social groups are going to be taxed more and/or which will suffer government spending cuts.

Greece, Ireland, Hungary, and Spain are among countries whose people have already felt the impacts of their combinations of tax increases and spending cuts. In those countries, businesses and rich citizens have been able to impose their preferred response to the problem of deficits, what politicians call "austerity." When government borrowing must be reduced or stopped, "austerity" means sharply cut government spending on public sector jobs and services for the mass of people. Across Europe, government after government is being pressed by its businesses and its richest citizens to impose austerity on its people. However, also across Europe, slowly but steadily—because they are less well organized and financed—labor unions, left parties, and left political formations are mobilizing against austerity and for alternative plans. These involve raising taxes on business and the rich and/or reducing the government spending benefiting them.

Because the United States is the world's richest country and can borrow more and more easily than other countries, the federal government has not yet reached the limits of its borrowing capacity. However, states and municipalities are forbidden to borrow for their operating budgets, so they have already imposed austerities across the United States (especially visible in the massive spending cuts on public services in California and New York). Yet in the United States, too, there are the beginnings of signs of anti-austerity movement. For example, in January 2010, Oregon voters ratified their state's decision to respond to the economic crisis neither by borrowing nor by cutting state expenditures, but rather by raising over $ 700 million in taxes on businesses and on households earning over $250,000 per year.

Consider an illustrative example of this kind of alternative to austerity programs. Every year, two companies catering to rich investors survey their clients. Capgemini and Merrill Lynch Wealth Management's World Wealth Report for 2010 counts as High Net Worth Individuals (HNWIs) everyone with at least $1 million of "investible assets" *in addition to* the values of their primary residence, art works, collectibles, etc. HNWIs in the United States numbered 2.9 million in 2009: well *under 1 % of U.S. citizens*. The HNWIs' investible assets totaled $12.09 trillion. For 2009, the total U.S. budget deficit was $1.7 trillion. Had the U.S. government levied an economic emergency tax of 15% on only the HNWIs' investible assets, no government borrowing would have been necessary in 2009. Obama's stimulus program would have required no deficit, no borrowing, and no additional taxes for 99% of U.S. citizens.

The real debates all along should have been—and now ought to be—about *who* pays how much in taxes and *who* benefits in what ways from government spending. Deficits are neither necessary in normal economic times nor when crises hit and require government stimulus. That business and the rich prefer lending to finance government deficits over being their taxed instead is just their understandable self-interest. The rest of us have not only the right to a very different preference, but also a clear basis in economic theory and available empirical studies not to abandon our preference for theirs.We only have deficits because of who pays and who does not pay how much in taxes and who gets how much in government spending.

We should be debating the social acceptability of a capitalist class division between employers and employees that places dangerously contradictory pressures on government budgets. Had we had such debates and a democratic process of deciding them in the United States, deficits and their consequences might have been avoided or at least drastically reduced. But that never happened. Instead, the mainstream debates about deficits have simply assumed their necessity. Those debates then focus narrowly on the size of deficits—whether larger versus smaller is better—rather than on why they exist and who benefits from them. No wonder those debates never solved the deficit problem; they functioned rather to obscure the underlying issue about who pays for and who benefits from government budgets in capitalist societies.

A brief look at the two major current debates about deficits in the United States can show how they hide or obscure why we have deficits, who benefits from them, and who stands to lose now that further deficits become increasingly difficult for government budgets. The first debate rages in the world of electoral politics where the chief contenders are Republicans and Democrats. The second debate rages among professional economists (who include major advisors to both parties and their major candidates), where the chief contenders are the neoclassical and Keynesian camps.

In the United States, politicians take the blame for economic troubles more than those most clearly and directly responsible for those troubles. For example, high unemployment is *not* often blamed on the private corporations and their boards of directors who actually fire, lay off, or refuse to hire workers. Similarly, foreclosures are blamed more on politicians than on the banks and other lenders who actually choose to file the court papers ejecting families from their homes. Republican politicians therefore seek electoral gains chiefly by saying other politicians—Obama and the Democrats—caused and/or failed to overcome the economic crisis. Republicans stress how government is bad, deficit-financed big government is worse, and Democrats are worst because they favor both big government and big deficits. The Democrats counter that Bush caused or failed to overcome the crisis leaving an awful mess for Obama to fix and that Republicans keep obstructing Obama's programs that would otherwise overcome the crisis. Each side aims to channel anger, resentment, and anxiety about economic suffering (high unemployment and foreclosures, job insecurities, etc.) by blaming the other side. Neither side dares to criticize, let alone blame, the economic system and its class divisions. Neither side proposes (so neither side needs to oppose) avoiding deficits by taxing business and the rich. That option and the basic, underlying issue of who pays the taxes and who gets the government services drops out of the debates altogether.

Professional mainstream U.S. economists also debate deficits. The "left" among them (e.g., Keynesians such as *New York Times* columnist Paul Krugman) argues that ending the crisis requires more/larger government stimulus—deficit spending— than Obama undertook. Such economists want more spending on public works, greening the economy, etc. without offsetting the resulting economic stimulus by any similar rise in taxes. The resulting deficits, they insist, will only be temporary. This is because boosting government spending will increase production and employment (reducing mortgage defaults, bankruptcies, foreclosures, etc.) and that will generate more government tax revenue. The crisis will therefore pass, allowing government stimulus spending to be cut back. The temporary deficits necessitated *now* during the crisis can *then* be erased by using rising tax revenues and reduced government spending to pare down the government's outstanding debt.

The right (e.g. John B. Taylor of Stanford University's Hoover Institute) attacks bigger stimulus policies as ineffective: they cannot and will not overcome the crisis, which only the private sector can do. Moreover, higher government borrowing resulting from stimulus spending imposes increases on future taxpayers to cover the interest and repayment of mounting government debt. That, they insist, will undermine economic growth, not lift it. So they prefer minimal government intervention, tax cuts, and reliance on private enterprises to lift us out of crisis.

Like the mainstream politicians, the mainstream economists debate larger versus smaller deficits. They keep off the agenda for public discussion debate over why deficits exist, who benefits from them, and what alternative mechanisms exist (including basic changes in the economic system) to avoid their real social costs. ❑

Article 6.3

THE CASE FOR A NATIONAL INFRASTRUCTURE BANK

A bank could be a recession-proof source of jobs.

BY HEIDI GARRETT-PELTIER

November/December 2010

Tragic events in recent years, such as the Minnesota bridge collapse or New Orleans' failed levees, combined with the daily aggravations of pot holes and power failures, underscore the need for improved infrastructure across the United States. The American Society of Civil Engineers gave the United States a "D" on its most recent *Report Card for America's Infrastructure*; the organization estimates that it will cost $2.2 trillion over the next five years to bring our infrastructure up to "good" condition.

Besides helping prevent disasters, infrastructure improvements create jobs. Maintenance, repair, and new construction of roads, buildings, water, and energy systems create jobs for engineers, construction crews, machinery manufacturers, and bookkeepers, among others.

Infrastructure improvements also have so-called positive externalities: their social benefits are greater than the financial gains earned by the parties who fund them. Improving roads, bridges, and transit systems can increase productivity, lower the cost of maintaining cars and buses, and reduce carbon emissions. Energy investments can increase productivity, and if directed toward energy efficiency and renewables, can also promote environmental sustainability. Investments in water systems lead to better health and lower health care costs.

Private companies cannot reap financial rewards from all of these indirect benefits. For instance, a private rail company could not feasibly charge a fee to everyone who enjoys less-congested roads or cleaner air thanks to a new rail line. So infrastructure projects have traditionally been publicly funded, primarily at the local level with some state and federal assistance.

Public infrastructure funding often falls short, however. In a recession, state and local tax revenues fall, making it harder to fund infrastructure projects precisely at a time when they could help the economy recover. Another problem is that during downturns and recoveries alike, higher-income localities are better able to fund their own roads or water systems than poorer ones. So available funds do not necessarily go to the projects providing the greatest benefits.

Today the United States invests in infrastructure at only half the level the ASCE recommends. One proposal for an innovative method to finance infrastructure is currently garnering bipartisan interest—a national infrastructure bank (NIB). An NIB would be a quasi-public agency whose function would be to use some federal funds to leverage a much larger amount of state, local, and private money which it would then provide to infrastructure projects.

An NIB could use various tools to finance infrastructure. It could sell bonds to private investors. It could be set up as a revolving loan fund, whereby an initial pool of funds is lent, and future loans made only once the earlier ones are repaid. It could even make grants for certain projects.

There are merits and drawbacks to any of these financing models. Some would make the NIB entirely self-sustaining, and so compel it to prioritize projects with a revenue stream, for instance from tolls, that would go to paying back the loan. Such a model would limit the bank's ability to choose projects with greater social benefits but less ability to repay funds quickly: it might fund construction of a toll road to a wealthy suburb rather than an upgrade to a municipal water system despite the latter's greater benefit. Other models would require more federal spending, but would give the bank greater flexibility to fund projects with less revenue potential.

In any case, a national infrastructure bank would make an important contribution to upgrading and expanding the country's infrastructure. It would boost the overall level of infrastructure spending. By leveraging private investment, it could continue to fund infrastructure projects even during recessions. Plus, it would make infrastructure spending more equitable since it would raise funds from a geographically distributed population, then target those funds toward the areas of greatest need. ❑

Article 6.4

WHY DO THEY OPPOSE MORE STIMULUS?

BY ARTHUR MacEWAN
January/February 2011

Dear Dr. Dollar:
Why are conservatives, especially wealthy conservatives, against stimulating the economy through the government's deficit spending? Don't businesses' profits and the incomes of the wealthy depend on economic growth?
—*Andy Druding, Richmond, Calif.*

As it turns out, business profits are already doing pretty well in spite of—or perhaps because of—the poor economic conditions for most people. Corporate profits have been expanding at a good clip since the beginning of 2009. In the third quarter of 2010, profits of domestic corporations were running at an annual rate of $1.27 trillion—not back up to their peak of $1.40 trillion four years earlier, but well on the way to that high mark. Even after an adjustment for inflation, current profits are in relatively good shape.

So it is not too hard to see why the people whose incomes are tied to profits are not eager to see a dramatic shift of policy. Still, you might think that more economic growth would provide even more profits.

Profits, however, depend on two things: the amount of value that gets created (output) and the share of that value that goes to profits. With a high level of unemployment, workers are in a poor position to demand higher wages—i.e., a larger share of that value. So businesses, and the wealthy who get their income from owning businesses, do not want unemployment to fall too low—low enough to give workers more bargaining power.

The weak position of workers in the current economic situation affects more than wages. While a recession lasts, businesses are able to implement changes more readily than in "normal" times. For example, they can change work rules, get rid of older workers, and bring in new technology more easily, as workers are in a poorer position to resist change. Also, the "shock" imposed on society by bad economic conditions can be used in the political sphere, making it possible for businesses and the wealthy to obtain concessions from government—the tax incentives state governments offer, for example, in the hope of generating some local growth. (However, an economic crisis also opens up possibilities for changes in the other direction. Consider, for example, the progressive changes in the United States that came out of the Great Depression of the 1930s.)

From the perspective of the wealthy, then, perhaps a bit more growth would be better, but not so much as to weaken their positions. Most important, if that growth required the government to spend a lot more by running deficits, the wealthy are not interested. They fear that high deficits now mean more taxes down the line. In part, higher taxes could be needed to pay off the debt the government would incur when it ran those deficits. Perhaps more important, upping government spending today threatens to entrench a long-run higher level of government activity, which would require higher taxes on a permanent basis. The wealthy might be able to push the tax obligations onto lower income groups. Yet, with income inequality as great as it is, it's hard to get much more out of anyone but the wealthy. You can't get blood from a stone.

These concerns about higher taxes generate a strong anti-big-government ideology, and the ideology can trump common sense. There are plenty of people who because they oppose "big government" oppose the spending that would be involved in any program that would provide significant economic stimulus through deficit spending. Of course not all of these people are among the wealthy, but they share the anti-government, anti-tax ideology. After all, they cannot improve their incomes by voting for higher wages, but they can—or think they can—improve their incomes by voting against taxes, which means voting against "big government," which means voting against deficits.

All this said, most of today's large federal budget deficit is not the result of spending designed to stimulate the economy. In fiscal year 2009, the budget deficit was about $1.4 trillion. Yet the February 2009 "stimulus package" accounted for a small share of that deficit. In 2001, the Congressional Budget Office (CBO) estimated the government was on course for a 2009 surplus of $700 billion. Why this $2.1 trillion difference between the CBO estimate and reality?

Slow economic growth in the early 2000s followed by severe downturn in 2008 and 2009 accounted for over 40% of the difference, as tax income declined sharply and some spending automatically increased (e.g., unemployment compensation). About 50% of the difference resulted from legislation enacted in the Bush years— over half of which was war spending, tax breaks for the wealthy, and the bank bailout. The stimulus package of the Obama administration accounted for only about 8% of the difference, a pretty small share.

Businesses and the wealthy who rail against the deficit do have real interests that they are protecting. But they are also using the deficit issue to attack the Obama administration's stimulus efforts, which turn out not to have been all that big. ❑

Article 6.5

FED UP

The Federal Reserve's Balance Sheet Is Exploding on Both Ends

BY ROBERT LARSON

March/April 2011

After suffering for years from a dizzyingly high unemployment rate, Americans are eager for meaningful increases in hiring. In the past, the government jump-started economic growth with fiscal policy—increasing spending in order to create new demand for goods and services, which companies could fulfill only by hiring. After the nation languished through a decade of depression in the 1930s, the monumental fiscal outlays for World War II created an enormous "stimulus" to total demand and hiring. The massive spending for the war effort, financed in large part by aggressive 80%-plus tax rates on the richest households, created demand that gave employers reason to create millions of jobs.

Most people regard social spending, such as on education or public health, as a more acceptable form of stimulus than military spending. But apart from government programs started in the 1960s due to popular demand, stimulus has proven "politically difficult" unless it takes the form of military adventure or tax cuts that are typically skewed toward the richest households. Unfortunately, tax cuts for the wealthy are the weakest form of stimulus and have relatively little job-creating impact; and non-military stimulus plans, including the inadequate 2009 stimulus bill, are targets for deficit hawks.

Yet in this climate of public-spending cutbacks, policymakers recognize that some new government response to the desperate job-market situation is clearly needed. The traditional alternative to fiscal policy is monetary policy—encouraging growth by lowering short-term interest rates through the Federal Reserve Bank's interventions. But traditional monetary policy has failed—short-term rates remain near zero while the economy continues to show little response. So attention has turned to the Fed's new alternative, "quantitative easing," an enormous program of purchases of financial assets. Fed policymakers hope to make long-term borrowing cheaper and therefore spur hiring, but the result so far has been to load up the Fed's balance sheet while enriching bond investors and rescuing more banks, with little effect on interest rates.

Balancing Act

All companies have balance sheets, listing a company's "liabilities"—what the company owes—and "assets"—what the company owns. Assets and liabilities always balance (as long as the company owner's equity is included with the liabilities), due to how they are counted. For example, on the balance sheet of a typical commercial bank, the main assets are bank loans extended to consumers and businesses, because they provide the bank with interest income. The main liabilities are the depositors' account balances, which the bank is obliged to produce at any time. The Federal

Reserve is different, however, because it can essentially print money by electronically increasing the account balances it owes other banks. With the government's current refusal to run sensible fiscal deficits targeted at creating jobs, the Fed's ability to massively expand its balance sheet (and to even run a profit doing so) has attracted new attention.

Historically, the Fed's main assets have been U.S. Treasury bonds, which are pieces of government debt. This is because the Fed's usual role is to influence interest rates in order to moderate the business cycle. It does this by buying and selling large numbers of Treasury bonds from the largest U.S. banks, which influences interest rates across the economy, as money is pulled in and out of the banking system. This means the Fed generally has large volumes of these interest-bearing government bonds among its assets.

The Fed has historically held a number of liabilities, including the reserve accounts of the many private banks in the Federal Reserve system, held as cushions against losses. The U.S. Treasury Department's own "general account," used for government payments, also falls on this side of the balance sheet. But Fed liabilities also include the U.S. paper currency used across the economy, hence the "Federal Reserve Note" on bills. So the Fed is "liable" for the balances of the rest of the government, the private banks' reserve accounts it maintains, and for U.S. cash, which can be exchanged for other assets.

Throwing Money at the Problem

Over the course of the 2008 financial crisis and the ensuing weak recovery, the Fed's balance sheet has taken on a very different look. It has swollen with "quantitative easing" asset purchases: first, the Fed bought devalued "toxic assets" from the banks in the 2008 bank rescue, and more recently in a large "QE2" program of buying long-term U.S. government bonds. The Fed's current large-scale buying tends to push bond prices up, which lowers long-term interest rates. The Fed is buying great volumes of such assets, with its balance sheet rocketing from $800 billion in 2007 to $2.6 trillion in February 2011, and with QE2 still underway.

The mountain of new Fed assets is composed of three broad asset categories. The first is the extension of short-term credit to financial firms—lending on favorable terms to banks that are in dire need of immediate lending. This is an extension of the Fed's original role of "banker of last resort," lending cheaply to banks in need of money overnight or even facing a "run" of panicking depositors. This role included lending through both the Fed's normal "discount window" and the "Term Auction Facility," set up to allow staggering banks to borrow with more anonymity. "Currency swaps" to foreign central banks, in which the Fed bought foreign currency from banks needing U.S. dollars, were also part of the program. This category of Fed assets reached its high point during and immediately after the 2008 financial crisis, when the short-run lending markets dried up among fears of borrower insolvency, leaving many enormous banks, insurers, and other financial companies on the edge of failure. As the financial industry has recovered its footing, this category has declined as a share of the Fed's balance sheet.

The second category of the Fed's new asset pile is loans to broader borrowers in the economy, primarily short-term corporate bonds, or "commercial paper," from many U.S. corporations. Companies often rely on short-term borrowing to cover regular operating costs, like payroll or supplier bills, while waiting for receivables to come in. During the 2008 crisis, struggling investment groups like money market funds faced huge withdrawals, leaving them without the cash to continue investing in these short-term bonds. Therefore the commercial paper market "locked up": rates spiked and borrowing became almost impossible. The Fed stepped in to supply the market with emergency short-term credit, and its program earned headlines for the "bedrock" corporations—including Caterpillar, GE, McDonald's, Toyota, and Verizon—revealed to have relied heavily on the program. This category of assets also includes the TALF program, which sought to restart "securitization"—the packaging of loans into assets that may be bought and sold. Car loans, credit card debt, and student loans are among the forms of packaged debt the Fed invested in. As these short-term markets have returned to somewhat normal functioning, this component has also diminished as a proportion of the Fed's total assets.

TALF and its related programs have become particularly notorious for being "gamed" by financial firms and what the *New York Times* called "a cross-section of America's wealthy." The super-low interest rates provided by the Fed for desperate and important corporations were also used by canny investors to make enormous sums off

A Fed Balance Sheet Glossary

Assets: Tangible or intangible items of value owned by a firm, such as cash or interest-paying loans.

Liabilities: An obligation of a firm to another party, such as a bank depositor; equal to assets minus net equity.

Balance sheet: A financial statement indicating a firm's assets and liabilities at some point in time.

Bond: A tradable piece of an institution's debt. Bond interest rates decrease as prices increase, lowering funding costs.

Liquidity: An institution's access to cash or close equivalents

Reserve account: Deposit accounts kept by private banks with their regional Fed bank, holding the capital the Fed obliges them to maintain.

Open market operations: The Fed's normal practice of influencing interest rates by buying or selling large volumes of government bonds, which tends to decrease/increase short-term rates.

Quantitative easing: The Fed's recent program to lower long-term interest rates by buying massive amounts of Treasury bonds and mortgage-backed securities.

Securities: A general term for a financial asset, such as stocks and bonds.

Term Auction Facility: The Fed's program to extend cheap, short-term credit to financial institutions through a more anonymous process than the discount window, mostly during the 2008 financial crisis.

TALF: Term Asset-Backed Securities Loan Facility, set up by the Fed in 2008 to restart securitization markets, which package existing loans into tradable assets and have become a major source of U.S. credit.

the public aid. One investor, having seen impressive returns of up to 10%, referred to getting "a gift from the Fed." In this connection, it is notable that at every stage the Fed's policy has been to pursue options that preferentially benefit the rich. Bond ownership is skewed toward upper-income households, so supporting bond market conditions is of disproportionate benefit to them. Likewise, the Fed's actions during and after the 2008 financial crisis meant few losses for the well-off creditors of banks and insurers, with their institutions rescued at taxpayer expense. The Fed richly deserves its reputation as a "captured" regulator, being predominantly run by former Wall Street bankers who often return to the finance industry after leaving the Fed.

The third main category of the Fed's asset purchases is what the Fed calls "high-quality" securities, meaning debt instruments with relatively low risk. This

The Federal Reserve System: Left vs. Right Views

The Federal Reserve retains a strong reputation in mainstream circles. Its chairs, like Paul Volcker or Ben Bernanke, are treated with the reverence of high priests, even if their images are later tarnished by their disastrous policy decisions, as with Alan Greenspan.

The left position, however, begins with the recognition that the Fed's policymaking bodies are visibly controlled by Wall Street. From regular staffers to senior policymakers, there is a standard practice of Fed staff working for large commercial or investment banks before joining the Fed, and an expectation that they will likely return to the financial industry later in their careers. Further indicators that the Fed is to a large extent a pawn of Wall Street include its recent surrender of a significant part of its influence, as government deregulation has allowed huge "shadow banking" institutions to grow outside the Fed system, weakening the Fed's monetary policy effectiveness. Despite complaints from Fed leaders, the central bank generally accepted these changes since they were demanded by Wall Street, which is the center of economic power and where many Fed figures hope to return for employment.

So the left picture is of a "captured regulator," a government body run by the industries it's supposed to regulate. From this point of view, moves to reform the Fed would include greater transparency and replacing banking industry influence with democratic governance, along with an increased emphasis on creating jobs instead of treating inflation as the main threat to the economy.

Right-wing criticisms of the Fed, in contrast, are grounded in the traditional conservative insistence on reduced government intervention in the economy, at least for interventions that regulate investment or reduce profit. In this view, the Fed is another government intervention in markets that would operate better if left alone, despite the clear association between financial deregulation and bubbles/crashes over the last thirty years. More recently, the advent of QE1 and 2 have driven the right to decry the "hyperinflation" it will bring about, overcoming the strong deflationary pressures of our slack job market. Conservative efforts to reform the Fed range from demands for more transparency up to Ron Paul's demand to abolish the bank entirely, returning to the era of free-floating interest rates (and presumably the greater volatility that accompanied them).

is the component that has taken on enormous proportions as part of the Fed's QE program. This program of asset purchases, which could reach $3 trillion in total, has made massive purchases of U.S. Treasury bonds, "agency debt" issued by the government mortgage agencies Freddie Mac and Fannie Mae, and mortgage-backed securities.

While these colossal buys were meant to lower long-term interest rates, the bond market has seen rate increases instead, defying Fed policy. Bond investors evidently expect borrowers to have difficulty repaying loans in today's weak recovery, and may also be "spooked" at the huge supply of public and private bonds for purchase today. Higher interest rates, of course, act as a drag on the economic recovery, such as it is. This "overruling" of the Fed by the bond market is parallel to the recent reduction in the Fed's power, as more "shadow" banking among unregulated finance firms has taken the place of the commercial banks the Fed regulates, reducing its ability to influence the economy through interest rate changes for the banks in its system. The Fed's separate QE programs, although not themselves limited to Fed system banks, have also been so far unable to lower the price of in-demand credit.

Notably, the QE program is having a secondary effect as a semi-bailout for America's mid-size banks, which are still failing at a rate on course to swamp the FDIC, which insures their deposits. Since these second-tier banks received relatively little bailout money, the Fed is propping many up by buying their bad mortgage debt. QE is presumably also executed with the expectation that it will contribute to driving down the value of the U.S. dollar relative to other world currencies, as the Fed's buying spree effectively dumps the currency into world markets. This may have a positive effect in encouraging U.S. exports, which are cheaper for foreign buyers when the dollar loses value, but it also risks setting off a global currency war as other nations strive to weaken their own currencies in order to boost exports. Competition among trading blocks to deflate currencies was a prominent feature of the Great Depression and not an encouraging model for world economic recovery.

In the shadow of this still-growing mountain of Federal Reserve asset purchases, the Fed's liabilities have grown in parallel, but with less public attention. This is because most of the Fed's new assets are purchased from banks in the Federal Reserve regulatory system, which maintain their own reserve accounts with the Fed. So when the Fed buys some of a private bank's assets, like U.S. Treasury bills or mortgage-backed debt, rather than mail a check it simply increases the banks' deposit account balance. The Fed may be called on to give the bank the money in its Fed account, so these payments are a liability for the Fed, and have grown as a mirror image of the assets bought in the QE purchase program.

Quantitative Unease

The QE gambit—and its effects on the Fed's balance sheet—is by no means unanimously popular at the Fed. It is widely reported that QE is a contentious move among members of the Federal Reserve Open Market Committee, which decides monetary policy. Prominent Fed members, including the presidents of the Dallas,

Philadelphia, and Minneapolis Federal Reserve Banks, have stated discomfort with QE. Dissenters also include Kansas City Federal Reserve Bank President Thomas Hoenig, who has described QE as "risky," and prefers breaking up the "too-big-to-fail" banks. And in language rather unusual for a Fed bank president, he openly discusses the "Wall Street-Washington axis of influence" and decries the "enormous power" of the "oligarchy" of powerful banks.

But most of QE's critics are inflation "hawks"—investors and FOMC members who advocate an aggressively anti-inflationary posture. They oppose QE for two reasons. The first is a fear of runaway inflation caused by injecting so much money into the economy. However, this concern seems remote in an economy with a double-digit real unemployment rate and usage of manufacturing capacity at an embarrassing 72%. Also, the inflation rate itself has not reached 3% since the financial crisis, although significant inflation could originate in imported products should the dollar fall quickly. The hawks' second concern about QE is that the Fed will become unwilling to raise interest rates in the future. Increasing interest rates would reduce the value of the Fed's own large bond investments, when investors sell them for higher-yielding assets. Furthermore, higher rates would mean the Fed would have to pay more in interest to banks with deposits at the Fed. For these twin reasons the hawks fear a loss of the Fed's willingness to raise rates later, thus damaging its inflation-fighting "credibility."

Conservative critics also fear that QE jeopardizes the large payments the Fed makes to the government. By law, any profit the Federal Reserve Bank makes on its now-large investments must be paid to the U.S. Treasury, after covering the Fed's own costs. In 2009 the Fed made $78 billion from its huge investments, politically valuable income in a time of widening budget deficits. A Fed rate increase could eliminate that payment, and indeed the Fed could ultimately lose money on its investment—as the bond market has declined, the Fed's portfolio was recently down a few percent.

Whatever the long-term impact on the Fed of its asset-purchasing campaign, it is difficult to see significant positive effects on the broader economy. Even if the Fed ultimately succeeds in pushing down long-term interest rates, cheap borrowing won't boost the economy the way a targeted spending program would. Companies may appreciate cheap borrowing, but they still won't create jobs when there is not sufficient demand for goods: who would buy new workers' output? Likewise, while cash-strapped and indebted consumers will benefit from low interest rates, they're unlikely to increase spending again without the feeling of security that comes from a steady job. Aggressive fiscal outlays in energy and infrastructure would create far more jobs than quantitative easing is likely to do. No wonder popular discontent with the Fed has reached the point that it's a featured villain in many Tea Party and progressive protests (see sidebar), and now even faces limited audits. Now that the Fed has been disbursing literally trillions in aid to the rich and their institutions for years, with a pitiful trickle going to the majority, the public is getting fed up with the Federal Reserve.

So as the economy staggers on, instead of asking your neighborhood employer for a stimulus-driven job consider asking your neighborhood bank if you can borrow a cup of money. ❏

Sources: Binyamin Applebaum, "Mortatge Securities It Holds Pose Sticky Problem for Fed," *New York Times*, July 22, 2010; Agnes Crane and Robert Cyran, "Rising Interest Rates and the Fed's Red Ink," *New York Times*, December 15, 2010; Michael Derby, "Treasury Fall Poses Long-Term Dilemma for Fed Balance Sheet," *Wall Street Journal*, December 10, 2011; Peter Goodman, "Policy Options Dwindle as Economic Fears Grow," *New York Times*, August 28, 2010; Sewell Chan, "Fed Pays a Record $78.4 Billion to Treasury," *New York Times*, January 10, 2011; "Fed's Fisher: Bond Buying Likely to Run Its Course," *Wall Street Journal*, January 10, 2011; Luca Di Leo, "Yellen Staunchly Defends Fed's Bond Program," *Wall Street Journal*, January 8, 2011; Jon Hilsenrath, "Fed Chief Gets a Likely Backer," *Wall Street Journal*, January 10, 2011; Sewell Chan, "Fed's Contrarian Has a Wary Eye on the Past," *New York Times*, December 13, 2010; Christine Hauser, "A Bond Rush as Treasury Prices Fall," *New York Times*, December 8, 2010; Mark Gongloff, "Bond Market Defies Fed," *Wall Street Journal*, November 16, 2010; Sewell Chan and Jo Craven McGinty, "Fed Papers Show Breadth of Emergency Measures," *New York Times*, December 1, 2010; Jon Hilsenrath, "Fed Fires $600 Billion Stimulus Shot," *Wall Street Journal*, November 4, 2010; Sewell Chan and Ben Protess, "Cross Section of Rich Invested With the Fed," *New York Times*, December 2, 2010.

Chapter 7

THE ENVIRONMENT

Article 7.1

SAVING ENERGY CREATES JOBS

BY HEIDI GARRETT-PELTIER

May/June 2009

Improving energy efficiency—using less energy to do the same amount of work—saves money and cuts pollution. But today, the other benefit of investing in energy efficiency may be the best draw: saving energy creates jobs.

Let's look at energy use in residential and commercial buildings. In the United States, buildings account for 40% of all energy use and are responsible for 38% of U.S. carbon emissions. Homes and other buildings lose energy through wasted heat, air-conditioning, and electricity. Following Jimmy Carter's suddenly fashionable example, we can turn down the thermostat in the winter and put on a sweater. We can unplug appliances that aren't used and save "phantom" power.

Beyond these personal changes, though, lie massive opportunities for systematic energy efficiency gains. These include insulating buildings, replacing old windows, and updating appliances and lighting. All of these generate new economic opportunities—read, jobs—in construction, manufacturing, and other sectors.

For instance, retrofitting existing homes, offices, and schools to reduce heating- and cooling-related energy waste (also known as weatherization) creates jobs of many kinds. Recent media attention has spotlighted "green jobs" programs that are hiring construction workers to add insulation, replace windows, and install more efficient heating systems. Perhaps less visible, retrofitting buildings also creates jobs for the engineers who design the new windows and furnaces, the factory workers who build them, and the office workers who make the appointments and handle the bookkeeping.

In fact, retrofitting creates more than twice as many jobs per dollar spent than oil or coal production, according to a detailed study that my colleagues and I at the Political Economy Research Institute conducted in 2008. For each $1 million spent, retrofitting creates about 19 jobs while spending on coal creates nine jobs and oil only six. Retrofitting also creates more jobs per dollar spent than personal consumption on typical items such as food, clothing, and electronics. Personal consumption does better than fossil fuels, but not as well as retrofitting, generating about 15 jobs per $1 million spent.

Why does retrofitting create more jobs? First, retrofitting is more labor-intensive than fossil-fuel production, meaning that more of each dollar spent goes to labor and less to machinery and equipment. Retrofitting also has higher domestic content than either fossil fuels or consumer goods; in other words, more of the supplies used to retrofit buildings are produced in the United States. In fact, about 95% of spending on retrofits stays in the domestic economy, versus only 80% of spending on oil (including refining and other related activities). Since more of its inputs are produced in the United States, retrofitting employs more U.S. workers. And this raises its multiplier effect: when those workers spend their earnings, each retrofitting dollar leads to yet more demand for goods and services.

To be fair, not all energy efficiency improvements will create jobs. When a more energy-efficient appliance or window design is widely adopted, the manufacturing worker who produced a less efficient good yesterday is simply producing a more efficient good today, with no net increase in employment. On the other hand, many retrofitting activities are pure job creators. Insulating attics and caulking leaky windows are activities that necessitate new workers—not just a shift from producing one good to another. With the collapse of the housing bubble and the huge rise in construction industry unemployment, retrofitting is an activity that could put tens of thousands of people back to work.

The Obama administration's stimulus package contains a wide variety of energy efficiency incentives, from 30% rebates for home insulation and for installing efficient windows, to rebates for builders of energy-efficient new homes and commercial buildings. These provisions will drive energy-saving improvements, accelerating the transition to a low-carbon economy while also creating jobs. ❑

Sources: U.S. Department of Energy, EERE Building Technologies Program; Robert Pollin, Heidi Garrett-Peltier, James Heintz, and Helen Scharber, "Green Recovery," Political Economy Research Institute, September 2008.

Article 7.2

KEEP IT IN THE GROUND

An alternative vision for petroleum emerges in Ecuador. But will Big Oil win the day?

BY ELISSA DENNIS
July/August 2010

In the far eastern reaches of Ecuador, in the Amazon basin rain forest, lies a land of incredible beauty and biological diversity. More than 2,200 varieties of trees reach for the sky, providing a habitat for more species of birds, bats, insects, frogs, and fish than can be found almost anywhere else in the world. Indigenous Waorani people have made the land their home for millennia, including the last two tribes living in voluntary isolation in the country. The land was established as Yasuní National Park in 1979, and recognized as a UNESCO World Biosphere Reserve in 1989.

Underneath this landscape lies a different type of natural resource: petroleum. Since 1972, oil has been Ecuador's primary export, representing 57% of the country's exports in 2008; oil revenues comprised on average 26% of the government's revenue between 2000 and 2007. More than 1.1 billion barrels of heavy crude oil have been extracted from Yasuní, about one quarter of the nation's production to date.

At this economic, environmental, and political intersection lie two distinct visions for Yasuní's, and Ecuador's, next 25 years. Petroecuador, the state-owned oil company, has concluded that 846 million barrels of oil could be extracted from proven reserves at the Ishpingo, Tambococha, and Tiputini (ITT) wells in an approximately 200,000 hectare area covering about 20% of the parkland. Extracting this petroleum, either alone or in partnership with interested oil companies in Brazil, Venezuela, or China, would generate approximately $7 billion, primarily in the first 13 years of extraction and continuing with declining productivity for another 12 years.

The alternative vision is the simple but profound choice to leave the oil in the ground.

Environmentalists and indigenous communities have been organizing for years to restrict drilling in Yasuní. But the vision became much more real when President Rafael Correa presented a challenge to the world community at a September 24, 2007 meeting of the United Nations General Assembly: if governments, companies, international organizations, and individuals pledge a total of $350 million per year for 10 years, equal to half of the forgone revenues from ITT, then Ecuador will chip in the other half and keep the oil underground indefinitely, as this nation's contribution to halting global climate change.

The Yasuní-ITT Initiative would preserve the fragile environment, leave the voluntarily isolated tribes in peace, and prevent the emission of an estimated 407 million metric tons of carbon dioxide into the atmosphere. This "big idea from a small country" has even broader implications, as Alberto Acosta, former Energy Minister and one of the architects of the proposal, notes in his new book, *La Maldición de la Abundancia* (*The Curse of Abundance*). The Initiative is a "*punto de ruptura*," he writes, a turning point in environmental history which "questions the logic of extractive (exporter of raw material) development," while introducing the possibility of global "*sumak kawsay*," the indigenous Kichwa concept of "good living" in harmony with nature.

Ecuador, like much of Latin America, has long been an exporter of raw materials: cacao in the 19th century, bananas in the 20th century, and now petroleum. The nation dove into the oil boom of the 1970s, investing in infrastructure and building up external debt. When oil prices plummeted in the 1980s while interest rates on that debt ballooned, Ecuador was trapped in the debt crisis that affected much of the region. Thus began what Correa calls "the long night of neoliberalism:" IMF-mandated privatizations of utilities and mining sectors, with a concomitant decline of revenues from the nation's natural resources to the Ecuadorian people. By 1986, all of the nation's petroleum revenues were going to pay external debt.

Close to 40 years of oil production has failed to improve the living standards of the majority of Ecuadorians. "Petroleum has not helped this country," notes Ana Cecilia Salazar, director of the Department of Social Sciences in the College of Economics of the University of Cuenca. "It has been corrupt. It has not diminished poverty. It has not industrialized this country. It has just made a few people rich."

Currently 38% of the population lives in poverty, with 13% in extreme poverty. The nation's per capita income growth between 1982 and 2007 was only .7% per year. And although the unemployment rate of 10% may seem moderate, an estimated 53% of the population is considered "underemployed."

Petroleum extraction has brought significant environmental damage. Each year 198,000 hectares of land in the Amazon are deforested for oil production. A verdict is expected this year in an Ecuadorian court in the 17-year-old class action suit brought by 30,000 victims of Texaco/Chevron's drilling operations in the area northwest of Yasuní between 1964 and 1990. The unprecedented $27 billion lawsuit alleges that thousands of cancers and other health problems were caused by Texaco's use of outdated and dangerous practices, including the dumping of 18 billion gallons of toxic wastewater into local water supplies.

Regardless of its economic or environmental impacts, the oil is running out. With 4.16 billion barrels in proven reserves nationwide, and another half billion "probable" barrels, best-case projections, including the discovery of new reserves, indicate the nation will stop exporting oil within 28 years, and stop producing oil within 35 years.

"At this moment we have an opportunity to rethink the extractive economy that for many years has constrained the economy and politics in the country," says Esperanza Martinez, a biologist, environmental activist, and author of the book *Yasuní: El tortuoso camino de Kioto a Quito*. "This proposal intends to change the terms of the North-South relationship in climate change negotiations."

As such, the Initiative fits into the emerging idea of "climate debt." The North's voracious energy consumption in the past has destroyed natural resources in the South; the South is currently bearing the brunt of global warming effects like floods and drought; and the South needs to adapt expensive new energy technology for the future instead of industrializing with the cheap fossil fuels that built the North. Bolivian president Evo Morales proposed at the Copenhagen climate talks last December that developed nations pay 1% of GDP, totaling $700 billion/year, into a compensation fund that poor nations could use to adapt their energy systems.

"Clearly in the future, it will not be possible to extract all the petroleum in the world because that would create a very serious world problem, so we need to create measures of compensation to pay the ecological debt to the countries," says Malki Sáenz, formerly Coordinator of the Yasuní-ITT Initiative within the Ministry of Foreign Relations. The Initiative "is a way to show the international community that real compensation mechanisms exist for not extracting petroleum."

Indigenous and environmental movements in Latin America and Africa are raising possibilities of leaving oil in the ground elsewhere. But the Yasuni-ITT proposal is the furthest along in detail, government sponsorship, and ongoing negotiations. The Initiative proposes that governments, international institutions, civil associations, companies, and individuals contribute to a fund administered through an international organization such as the United Nations Development Program (UNDP). Contributions could include swaps of Ecuador's external debt, as well as resources generated from emissions auctions in the European Union and carbon emission taxes such as those implemented in Sweden and Slovakia.

Contributors of at least $10,000 would receive a Yasuní Guarantee Certificate (CGY), redeemable only in the event that a future government decides to extract the oil. The total dollar value of the CGYs issued would equal the calculated value of the 407 million metric tons of non-emitted carbon dioxide.

The money would be invested in fixed income shares of renewable energy projects with a guaranteed yield, such as hydroelectric, geothermal, wind, and solar power, thus helping to reduce the country's dependence on fossil fuels. The interest payments generated by these investments would be designated for: 1) conservation projects, preventing deforestation of almost 10 million hectares in 40 protected areas covering 38% of Ecuador's territory; 2) reforestation and natural regeneration projects on another one million hectares of forest land; 3) national energy efficiency improvements; and 4) education, health, employment, and training programs in sustainable activities like ecotourism and agro forestry in the affected areas. The first three activities could prevent an additional 820 million metric tons of carbon dioxide emissions, tripling the Initiative's effectiveness.

These nationwide conservation efforts, as well as the proposal's mention of "monitoring" throughout Yasuní and possibly shutting down existing oil production, are particularly disconcerting to Ecuadorian and international oil and wood interests. Many speculate that political pressure from these economic powerhouses was behind a major blow to the Initiative this past January, when Correa, in one of his regular Saturday radio broadcasts, suddenly blasted the negotiations as "shameful," and a threat to the nation's "sovereignty" and "dignity." He threatened that if the full package of international commitments was not in place by this June, he would begin extracting oil from ITT.

Correa's comments spurred the resignations of four critical members of the negotiating commission, including Chancellor Fander Falconí, a longtime ally in Correa's PAIS party, and Roque Sevilla, an ecologist, businessman, and ex-Mayor of Quito whom Correa had picked to lead the commission. Ecuador's Ambassador to the UN Francisco Carrion also resigned from the commission, as did World Wildlife Fund president Yolanda Kakabadse.

Correa has been clear from the outset that the government has a Plan B, to extract the oil, and that the non-extraction "first option" is contingent on the mandated monetary commitments. But oddly his outburst came as the negotiating team's efforts were bearing fruit. Sevilla told the press in January of commitments in various stages of approval from Germany, Spain, Belgium, France, and Switzerland, totaling at least $1.5 billion. The team was poised to sign an agreement with UNDP last December in Copenhagen to administer the fund. Correa called off the signing at the last minute, questioning the breadth of the Initiative's conservation efforts and UNDP's proposed six-person administrative body, three appointed by Ecuador, two by contributing nations, and one by UNDP. This joint control structure apparently sparked Correa's tirade about shame and dignity.

Within a couple of weeks of the blowup, the government had backpedaled, withdrawing the June deadline, appointing a new negotiating team, and reasserting the position that the government's "first option" is to leave the oil in the ground. At the same time, Petroecuador began work on a new pipeline near Yasuní, part of the infrastructure needed for ITT production, pursuant to a 2007 Memorandum of Understanding with several foreign oil companies.

Amid the doubts and mixed messages, proponents are fighting to save the Initiative as a cornerstone in the creation of a post-petroleum Ecuador and ultimately a post-petroleum world. In media interviews after his resignation, Sevilla stressed that he would keep working to ensure that the Initiative would not fail. The Constitution provides for a public referendum prior to extracting oil from protected areas like Yasuní, he noted. "If the president doesn't want to assume his responsibility as leader…let's pass the responsibility to the public." In fact, 75% of respondents in a January poll in Quito and Guayaquil, the country's two largest cities, indicated that they would vote to not extract the ITT oil.

Martinez and Sáenz concur that just as the Initiative emerged from widespread organizing efforts, its success will come from the people. "This is the moment to define ourselves and develop an economic model not based on petroleum," Salazar says. "We have other knowledge, we have minerals, water. We need to change our consciousness and end the economic dependence on one resource." ❑

Resources: Live Yasuni, Finding Species, Inc., liveyasuni.org; "S.O.S. Yasuni" sosyasuni.org; "Yasuni-ITT: An Initiative to Change History," Government of Ecuador, yasuni-itt.gov.ec.

Article 7.3

THE PHANTOM MENACE
Environmental regulations are not "job-killers" after all.

BY HEIDI GARRETT-PELTIER
July/August 2011

Polluting industries, along with the legislators who are in their pockets, consistently claim that environmental regulation will be a "job killer." They counter efforts to control pollution and to protect the environment by claiming that any such measures would increase costs and destroy jobs. But these are empty threats. In fact, the bulk of the evidence shows that environmental regulations do not hinder economic growth or employment and may actually stimulate both.

One recent example of this, the Northeast Regional Greenhouse Gas Initiative (RGGI), is an emissions-allowance program that caps and reduces emissions in ten northeast and mid-Atlantic states. Under RGGI, allowances are auctioned to power companies and the majority of the revenues are used to offset increases in consumer energy bills and to invest in energy efficiency and renewable energy. A report released in February of this year shows that RGGI has created an economic return of $3 to $4 for every $1 invested, and has created jobs throughout the region. Yet this successful program has come under attack by right-wing ideologues, including the Koch brothers-funded "Americans for Prosperity"; as a result, the state of New Hampshire recently pulled out of the program.

The allegation that environmental regulation is a job-killer is based on a mischaracterization of costs, both by firms and by economists. Firms often frame spending on environmental controls or energy-efficient machinery as a pure cost—wasted spending that reduces profitability. But such expenses should instead be seen as investments that enhance productivity and in turn promote economic development. Not only can these investments lead to lower costs for energy use and waste disposal, they may also direct innovations in the production process itself that could increase the firm's long-run profits. This is the Porter Hypothesis, named after Harvard Business School professor Michael Porter. According to studies conducted by Porter, properly and flexibly designed environmental regulation can trigger innovation that partly or completely offsets the costs of complying with the regulation.

The positive aspects of environmental regulation are overlooked not only by firms, but also by economists who model the costs of compliance without including its widespread benefits. These include reduced mortality, fewer sick days for workers and school children, reduced health-care costs, increased biodiversity, and mitigation of climate change. But most mainstream models leave these benefits out of their calculations. The Environmental Protection Agency, which recently released a study of the impacts of the Clean Air Act from 1990 to 2020, compared the effects of a "cost-only" model with those of a more complete model. In the version which only incorporated the costs of compliance, both GDP and overall economic welfare were expected to decline by 2020 due to Clean Air Act regulations. However, once the costs of compliance were coupled with the benefits, the model showed that both GDP and economic welfare would increase over time, and that by 2020 the economic benefits would outweigh the costs. Likewise, the Office of Management and Budget found that to date the benefits of the law have far exceeded the cost, with an economic return of between $4 and $8 for every $1 invested in compliance.

Environmental regulations do affect jobs. But contrary to claims by polluting industries and congressional Republicans, efforts to protect our environment can actually create jobs. In order to reduce harmful pollution from power plants, for example, an electric company would have to equip plants with scrubbers and other technologies. These technologies would need to be manufactured and installed, creating jobs for people in the manufacturing and construction industries.

The official unemployment rate in the United States is still quite high, hovering around 9%. In this economic climate, politicians are more sensitive than ever to claims that environmental regulation could be a job-killer. By framing investments as wasted costs and relying on incomplete economic models, polluting industries have consistently tried to fight environmental standards. It's time to change the terms of the debate. We need to move beyond fear-mongering about the costs and start capturing the benefits. ❏

Article 7.4

THE GO-ZONE'S NO-ZONES
After more than five years, a deeply flawed disaster-recovery program has failed to rebuild the Gulf Coast.

BY DARWIN BONDGRAHAM
May/June 2011

In the wake of Hurricane Katrina the federal government created an unprecedented economic recovery program for the Gulf Coast. The precedent it has set, however, is not a positive one. Called the Gulf Opportunity Zone Act of 2005, the centerpiece of this bill, a multi-billion dollar advance of tax-exempt construction bonds, has proven a dismal failure. Federal policymakers claimed the GO-Zone would spur a broad array of private investments, create jobs, and rebuild damaged properties across the hurricane-ravaged Gulf. The GO-Zone has not only failed to stimulate the region's economy, it has been gamed by large corporations and wealthy investors to secure billions for questionable projects that will do little or nothing to benefit disaster stricken communities.

Among the program's many flaws: GO-Zone bonds have been allocated to projects mostly outside the hardest-hit areas; hard-hit areas like New Orleans have had GO-Zone money rescinded; giant petrochemical corporations have consumed most of the bonds, while small companies, especially local firms, have been shut out. Important sectors like agriculture and home construction have secured only small fractions of GO-Zone dollars, while the oil and chemical industries have received the lion's share. In all, the GO-Zone bond program has failed to stimulate investments in a diversified economic infrastructure, especially in the worst flooded areas like Orleans and Jefferson parishes.

Since pro-corporate lobbyists working through the Republican Party wrote the GO-Zone Act, in some sense it worked exactly as planned. The failure therefore wasn't that the policy didn't deliver as intended, but rather that it was not subject to more immediate scrutiny and opposition from grassroots community groups, labor unions, local officials in the most devastated parishes and counties, and their allies in Congress. It's possible that when it was passed in late 2005 the effects the GO-Zone would have were simply unknown. With more than five years of the GO-Zone in action, however, we can now assess its impacts and draw some conclusions about how to create just disaster reconstruction policies.

Opportunities for Capital

The GO-Zone represents perhaps the most perfect expression of extreme neoliberal economic policy. Distilled to its essence, the GO-Zone was intended to spur recovery in southern Louisiana, Alabama, and Mississippi by providing tax incentives for private investment in real estate and capital goods. What the GO-Zone didn't do: it didn't produce economic incentives that small businesses, workers, and communities without access to major pools of capital could use. The very letter and intent of the law shut out the majority of businesses, and literally all workers. As the head of Louisiana's State Bond Commission complained about the GO-Zone: "If you didn't have the money, you couldn't qualify to get the money."

The GO-Zone Act's primary sponsor, Rep. Jim McCrery, was a conservative Republican from Louisiana's 4th District, the northwestern quadrant of the state, which was mostly unaffected by Hurricanes Katrina and Rita. Before politics McCrery worked as a lawyer for the Georgia Pacific Corporation, an Atlanta-based industrial timber and pulp plantation company. This corporate background gave form to everything McCrery accomplished while in Congress, especially the GO-Zone Act.

As a member of the House Ways and Means Committee, McCrery spent the early 2000s crafting tax law for the benefit of corporations and the wealthy. He was a key participant in writing the Bush administration's highly regressive

Tax-Exempt Bonds?

The bond program at the core of the GO-Zone works basically as follows: Congress delegated authority to the states of Louisiana, Mississippi, and Alabama to allocate a total of $14.9 billion in bonds that would be exempt from federal income taxes. Louisiana's share came to $7.9 billion. This bonding authority could only be used in disaster- stricken parishes (Louisiana's version of counties), but the bill dubiously extended this zone across a geographic expanse that included areas with extreme damage such as New Orleans, and other relatively unscathed areas like Baton Rouge.

A developer or company seeking to raise money in order to build real estate or expand their operations could seek a share of this bonding authority from the state, and then sell these bonds to buyers, usually large financial companies. Because Washington would not tax the interest on these bonds, bond buyers are willing to accept lower overall interest rates. This cheaper money theoretically makes financing more available for businesses seeking to invest in the region.

Because they incur a tax expense for the federal government (a decline in expected revenues), tax-exempt bonds are normally reserved for the construction of projects with a broad public purpose like schools. The GO-Zone Act authorized tax-exemption for "private activities," however, so that hotels, movie theaters, and similar for-profit projects could receive tax-free financing.

According to the Government Accountability Office, GO-Zone bonds will result in a $1.6 billion reduction in federal revenue between 2006 and 2015. Another way to understand it is that the GO-Zone has created a $1.6 billion entitlement program for wealthy investors, rationalizing with the logic that these investors will spur economic activity with broad public benefits across the disaster-stricken zone.

Source: "Gulf Opportunity Zone: States are allocating federal tax incentives to finance low-income housing and a wide range of private facilities." Government Accountability Office, July 2008, GAO-08-913 (www.gao.gov/products/GAO-08-913).

tax laws. During his Congressional career McCrery received near perfect scores from corporate political action committees and lobbies, and even founded his own PAC, naming it the Committee for the Preservation of Capitalism. Coming out of McCrery's office, and influenced by his corporate patrons, the GO-Zone Act was less of a disaster-relief bill, and more of the same corporate-friendly tax rollbacks the Congress had been providing since the election of Bush II.

TABLE 1: GO-ZONE BONDS ISSUED BY PARISH
(AS OF DECEMBER 2010)

Rank	Parish	Issued Amount	% total
1	Multiple	$1,165,630,340	17.7%
2	Calcasieu	$1,108,722,000	16.8%
3	St. John	$1,000,000,000	15.2%
4	East Baton Rouge	$969,396,968	14.7%
5	St. James	$911,200,000	13.8%
6	Ascension	$458,000,000	6.9%
7	Orleans*	$227,279,000	3.4%
8	Jefferson*	$188,822,816	2.9%
9	St. Tammany	$165,884,080	2.5%
10	Lafourche*	$158,500,000	2.4%
11	Lafayette	$59,399,520	0.9%
12	Terrebonne*	$58,986,000	0.9%
13	St. Charles	$52,550,000	0.8%
14	St. Bernard*	$29,999,719	0.5%
15	Livingston	$27,733,875	0.4%
16	Iberia*	$7,500,000	0.1%
17	Jefferson Davis	$6,815,000	0.1%
18	St. Mary*	$2,100,000	0.0%
19	Tangipahoa	$1,900,000	0.0%
20	Plaquemines*	$0	0.0%
21	West Baton Rouge	$0	0.0%
22	West Feliciana	$0	0.0%
23	Iberville	$0	0.0%
24	Acadia	$0	0.0%
25	Pointe Coupee	$0	0.0%
26	St. Martin	$0	0.0%
27	Vermilion*	$0	0.0%
	Total	**$6,600,419,318**	**100.0%**

* Coastal parish

Not long after the GO-Zone's implementation, local officials hoping to use the program in hard-hit areas of Louisiana noted severe flaws. For example, members of the State Bond Commission and the Industrial Development Board of New Orleans realized within the first half-year that inland parishes which had experienced a tiny fraction of the damage sustained by coastal parishes had already scooped up GO-Zone bonds by the hundreds of millions, while Orleans and St. Bernard parishes and other centers of devastation were receiving virtually nothing. Developers and companies were, many surmised, choosing not to rebuild in New Orleans and other coastal zones, using the tax-free dollars instead in northern parishes.

After some debate the Louisiana State Bond Commission altered its plan for disbursement; whereas they initially had operated on a first-come first-served basis, they began reserving a portion of GO-Zone bonds for the hardest-hit areas. But it would prove too little, too late.

TABLE 2: TOP TWENTY GO-ZONE PROJECTS (AS OF DECEMBER 2010)

Entity	Parish	Allocation (in millions)	Purpose
Marathon Oil Corp.	St. John	$1,000	Oil Refinery
Leucadia National Corporation	Calcasieu	$1,000	Petroleum Coke Gasification Plant
Nucor Steel	St. James	$600	Iron factory
La. Ethanol Refinery Corp.	Multiple	$600	Oil Refinery
Valero Energy Corp.	St. Charles	$300	Oil Refinery
SeaPoint, LLC	Plaquemines	$300	Port
Exxon	East Baton Rouge	$300	Oil Refinery
Faustina Hydrogen Products	St. James	$250	Petroleum Coke Gasification Plant
Westlake Chemical Corp.	multiple	$250	Chemical Plant
Georgia-Pacific Corp.	East Baton Rouge	$250	Pulp & paper mill
Tiger State Ethanol, LLC	St. James	$200	Ethanol Plant
3CP Associates, LLC	Orleans	$200	Hotel
ExxonMobil	East Baton Rouge	$200	Refinery
International Matex	Ascension	$165	Oil logistics facility
St. Tammany Holdings Corp.	St. Tammany	$150	Real Estate
Southern Intracoastal	Calcasieu	$150	Bio-Diesel Refinery
La. Offshore Terminal Authority	Multiple	$120	Oil logistics facility
St. Francisville Acquisition	West Feliciana	$100	Pulp & paper mill
La. Sugar Refining Project	St. John	$100	Sugar Refinery
Louisiana Sugar Refining, LLC	St. James	$100	Sugar Refinery
Total		**$6,335**	

The Problem with Allocation and Issuance

By the end of 2010 nearly all of Louisiana's $7.8 billion in GO-Zone bonds had been allocated for approximately 298 projects in 23 of the 31 eligible parishes. Eight eligible parishes, all of them rural, with high preexisting rates of poverty, and in desperate need of economic assistance, have been allocated zero GO-Zone bonds: Assumption, Cameron, East Feliciana, Point Coupee, St. Helena, St. Martin, Vermillion, and Washington parishes.

Allocation is only the first step in utilizing tax-free bonds. Even some parishes that have been allocated GO-Zone funds have yet to see economic benefits because the bonds have not been sold to buyers. As of December 2010 about $6.6 billion in GO-Zone bonds have been issued, or sold, by their recipients. The remaining $1.2 billion has not yet been issued. Some of this money, like previous allocations, could be rescinded by the State Bond Commission and given to different projects that are believed to have better prospects for finding a buyer. Reliance on large institutional investors to finance economic recovery through the GO-Zone has stalled and even canceled some major projects. For example, a developer who received $225 million in GO-Zone bonds to re-open the New Orleans Hyatt Hotel was forced to relinquish over $202 million of these funds when buyers could not be found.

So far almost $1 billion in GO-Zone bonds have been rescinded in Louisiana. Fully three-quarters of all rescinded GO-Zone bonds were taken back from commercial real estate projects, including hotels, and tourism and entertainment projects. Because Orleans Parish (the county coterminous with the city of New Orleans) is highly dependent on hotels, tourism, and entertainment, it ranks second among parishes that have lost bonds. Real estate and hotel projects together account for 68% of rescinded GO-Zone bonds, whereas oil and chemical projects have only seen about 6% of their allocations taken back. The pre-Katrina profile of different local economies has therefore negatively affected the pace and level of economic stimulus through GO-Zone incentives. These incentives do not apply equally to different kinds of local economies across the affected region.

Geographic Inequities

Although it was claimed that GO-Zone bonds would stimulate economic activity in the hardest hit areas, most of the funds have gone to parishes that experienced less devastation than those immediately adjacent to the Gulf's waters. Among the top five parishes in terms of GO-Zone bond allocations, only Orleans Parish is coastal and was exposed to the severe flooding which caused the majority of hurricane-related economic damage. Other hard-hit coastal parishes have been allocated few GO-Zone bonds for reconstruction. St. Bernard, for example, ranks 19th among parishes in GO-Zone allocations, even though its damage from the storm was rivaled only by Orleans and Plaquemines parishes.

When the impact of GO-Zone bonds is measured in terms of issuance, that is, how much of the lending authority is actually being put to work, hard-hit coastal parishes fare even worse. Orleans Parish drops from its second rank to seventh, accounting for a mere 3.4% of all GO-Zone bonds, even though it sustained far more damage than any parish. Most other coastal parishes have issued less than 1% of the GO-Zone's total. Table 1 ("GO Zone Bonds Issued by Parish") illustrates the extremely inequitable spread among parishes, resulting in little to no economic stimulus for those parishes that have yet to sell bonds for approved projects.

Calcasieu, St. John, East Baton Rouge, St. James, and Ascension parishes, all of which experienced much less damage than coastal parishes, have virtually monopolized GO-Zone bonds issued in the five years following Katrina. Together with a large category of GO-Zone bonds being spent in multiple parishes, these few areas have issued 85% of all bonds to date.

Oil and Chemical Monopoly

Oil and chemical companies have dominated the GO-Zone bond program. Corporations like ExxonMobil and Marathon Oil were in advantageous positions to utilize these tax-free bonds as a means of dramatically expanding their operations. The majority of GO-Zone bonds issued as of 2010 will be used to expand major oil, gas, and chemical facilities. Table 2 (previous page) lists the top twenty GO-Zone projects.

The oil and chemical industry has gobbled upwards of 65% of the $6.6 billion in GO-Zone bonds issued by the end of 2010. If current allocations proceed without any major changes, then oil and chemical companies may end up consuming at least half of all GO-Zone bonds to build mostly new facilities.

The top ten oil, gas, and chemical projects alone have received $4.3 billion in allocation authority, or 55% of the total GO-Zone bond cap for Louisiana. These projects include a billion-dollar petroleum coke gasification plant in Calcasieu Parish, and a less expensive quarter-billion-dollar gasification plant in St. James Parish, a billion-dollar oil refinery in St. John the Baptist Parish, and other refineries, petroleum storage and processing facilities and chemical plants ranging from $200 million to $600 million in price.

This hugely disproportionate subsidy to petrochemical corporations through the GO-Zone recovery program is especially ironic given last year's second disaster for southern Louisiana, caused by the blowout of BP's Macondo well. Indeed, the oil industry's activities—canal and shipping channel dredging and toxic pollution—are partly responsible for the erosion of coastal Louisiana, which has created vulnerability to disastrous storm surges for New Orleans and other Gulf-bordering parishes.

Trailing far behind oil and chemical firms to round out the top five industries receiving GO-Zone bonds are manufacturing, housing finance, commercial real estate, and tourism and entertainment with 13%, 7%, 3%, and 3% of the total issuances, respectively. Industries with extremely poor levels of GO-Zone bond utilization include health care and education with 2% and 1% of issues so far. The irony here is that tax-exempt bonds are most often used for non-profit educational and health-care facilities.

Lessons to be Learned

After Katrina, the government chose to create huge tax subsidies for big business at exactly the moment when the people of the Gulf Coast most needed direct federal investments in their communities. After a disaster of a different sort—the Great Depression—direct government investment and employment was widely understood as the best recovery policy instead of reliance on the "free market." The Great Depression was viewed as a disaster warranting direct federal economic aid in the form of welfare payments to victims, direct employment of the unemployed to rebuild their communities, and importantly, federally funded construction of public housing, schools, and civic infrastructure. Other responses to natural disasters in the nation's history have set positive examples of what government can do when policymakers at the federal and state levels choose to directly invest in the economy's health.

One of the reasons the GO-Zone may have avoided firm opposition from those who have been harmed by its inequities is that the likely effects were unknown in 2005. This explains why the act passed Congress on bipartisan grounds and elicited little to no concern from local officials, labor unions, and community groups along the Gulf Coast. When the next Katrina-like disaster strikes, workers, small businesses, and local officials must mobilize to demand just reconstruction policies that focus funds on the most affected areas, and for a wide range of purposes. The Gulf Coast also deserves something more. Congress and the president should honestly reassess the GO-Zone's outcome, and make right on the inequities experienced by communities like New Orleans. ❑

Sources: Ariella Cohen, "New Orleans gets table scrap in GO Zone lending feast," The Lens, December 17, 2010 (thelensnola.org/2010/12/17/go-zone-lending-program); "Rep. Jim McCrery." Almanac of the National Journal (www.nationaljournal.com/almanac/2008/people/la/rep_la04.php); Biography of Jim McCrery (www.capitolcounsel.com/bios/JimMcCrery.htm); Jennifer Larino, "Hyatt developers to use private funds, not GO Zone bonds," New Orleans City Business blog, July 12, 2010 (neworleanscitybusiness.com/blog/); "Tax Policy: Tax-Exempt Status of Certain Bonds Merits Reconsideration, and Apparent Noncompliance with Issuance Cost Limitations Should Be Addressed," Government Accountability Office, February 15, 2008, GAO-08-364 (www.gao.gov/products/GAO-08-364).

Article 7.5

THE COSTS OF EXTREME WEATHER

Climate inaction is expensive—and inequitable.

BY HEIDI GARRETT-PELTIER

November/December 2011

Two thousand eleven has already been a record-setting year. The number of weather disasters in the United States whose costs exceed $1 billion—ten—is the highest ever. August witnessed one of the ten most expensive catastrophes in U.S. history, Tropical Storm Irene. An initial estimate put the damages from Irene at between $7 billion and $13 billion. In this one storm alone, eight million businesses and homes lost power, roads collapsed, buildings flooded, and dozens of people lost their lives. Meanwhile, Texas is experiencing its hottest year in recorded history: millions of acres in the state have burned, over 1,550 homes have been lost to wildfires as of early September, and tens of thousands of people have had to evacuate their homes. The devastation caused by the storms and droughts has left individuals and businesses wondering how they'll recover, and has left cash-strapped towns wondering how they'll pay for road and infrastructure repairs.

Extreme weather events like these are expected to become more frequent and more intense over the next century. That's just one of the impacts of climate change, which, according to the consensus of scientists and research organizations from around the world, is occurring with both natural and human causes, but mainly from the burning of fossil fuels. According to NASA, since 1950 the number of record high-temperature days has been rising while the number of record low-temperature days has been falling. The number of intense rainfall events has also increased in the past six decades. At the same time, droughts and heat waves have also become more frequent, as warmer conditions in drier areas have led to faster evaporation. This is why in the same month we had wildfires in Texas (resulting from more rapid evaporation and drought) and flooding in the Northeast (since warmer air holds more moisture and results in more intense precipitation).

In response to these dramatic weather changes, the courses of action available to us are *mitigation*, *adaptation*, and *reparation*. *Mitigation* refers to efforts to prevent or reduce climate change, for example, cutting fossil fuel use by increasing energy efficiency and using more renewable energy. *Adaptation* refers to changing our behaviors, technologies, institutions, and infrastructure to cope with the damages that climate change creates—building levees near flood-prone areas or relocating homes further inland, for example. And as the term implies, *reparation* means repairing or rebuilding the roads, bridges, homes, and communities that are damaged by floods, winds, heat, and other weather-related events.

Of these, mitigation is the one strategy whose costs and benefits can both be shared globally. Moving toward a more sustainable economy less reliant on the burning of fossil fuels for its energy would slow the rise in average global temperatures and make extreme weather events less likely. Mitigation will have the greatest impact with a shared worldwide commitment, but even without binding international agreements, countries can take steps to reduce their use of coal, oil, and natural gas.

According to the Intergovernmental Panel on Climate Change, even the most stringent mitigation efforts cannot prevent further impacts of climate change in the next few decades. We will still need to adapt and repair—all the more in the absence of such efforts. But the costs and burdens of adaptation and reparation are spread unevenly across different populations and in many cases the communities most affected by climate change will be those least able to afford to build retaining walls or relocate to new homes. Farmers who can afford to will change their planting and harvesting techniques and schedules, but others will have unusable land and will be unable to sustain themselves. Roads that are washed away will be more quickly rebuilt in richer towns, while poorer towns will take longer to rebuild if they can at all. The divide between rich and poor will only grow.

Given the high cost of damages we've already faced just this year, mitigation may very well be sound economic planning. But it is also the most humane and equitable approach to solving our climate problem. ❑

Sources: NOAA/NESDIS/NCDC, "Billion Dollar U.S. Weather/Climate Disasters 1980-August 2011"; Michael Cooper, "Hurricane Cost Seen as Ranking Among Top Ten," *New York Times*, August 30, 2011; "Hurricane Irene Damage: Storm Likely Cost $7 Billion to $13 Billion," *International Business Times*, August 29, 2011; Intergovernmental Panel on Climate Change, *Fourth Assessment Report: Climate Change 2007*, Working Group II ch. 19; NASA, "Global Climate Change: Vital Signs of the Planet—Evidence"; U.S. EPA, "Climate Change—Health and Environmental Effects, Extreme Events."

Chapter 8

SOCIAL POLICY: HEALTH CARE, WELFARE, AND SOCIAL SECURITY

Article 8.1

UNIVERSAL HEALTH CARE: CAN WE AFFORD ANYTHING LESS?

Why only a single-payer system can solve America's health-care mess.

BY GERALD FRIEDMAN
July/August 2011

America's broken health-care system suffers from what appear to be two sepa-rate problems. From the right, a chorus warns of the dangers of rising costs; we on the left focus on the growing number of people going without health care because they lack adequate insurance. This division of labor allows the right to dismiss attempts to extend coverage while crying crocodile tears for the 40 million uninsured. But the division between problem of cost and the problem of coverage is misguided. It is founded on the assumption, common among neoclassical economists, that the current market system is efficient. Instead, however, the current system is inherently inefficient; it is the very source of the rising cost pressures. In fact, the only way we can control health-care costs and avoid fiscal and economic catastrophe is to establish a single-payer system with universal coverage.

The rising cost of health care threatens the U.S. economy. For decades, the cost of health insurance has been rising at over twice the general rate of inflation; the share of American income going to pay for health care has more than doubled since 1970 from 7% to 17%. By driving up costs for employees, retirees, the needy, the young, and the old, rising health-care costs have become a major problem for governments at every level. Health costs are squeezing public spending needed for education and infrastructure. Rising costs threaten all Americans by squeezing the income available for other activities. Indeed, if current trends continued, the entire economy would be absorbed by health care by the 2050s.

Conservatives argue that providing universal coverage would bring this fiscal Armageddon on even sooner by increasing the number of people receiving care. Following this logic, their policy has been to restrict access to health care by raising insurance deductibles, copayments, and cost sharing and by reducing access to insurance. Even before the Great Recession, growing numbers of American adults were uninsured or underinsured. Between 2003 and 2007, the share of non-elderly adults without adequate health insurance rose from 35% to 42%, reaching 75 million. This number has grown substantially since then, with the recession reducing employment and with the continued decline in employer-provided health insurance. Content to believe that our current health-care system is efficient, conservatives assume that costs would have risen more had these millions not lost access, and likewise believe that extending health-insurance coverage to tens of millions using a plan like the Affordable Care Act would drive up costs even further. Attacks on employee health insurance and on Medicare and Medicaid come from this same logic—the idea that the only way to control health-care costs is to reduce the number of people with access to health care. If we do not find a way to control costs by increasing access, there will be more proposals like that of Rep. Paul Ryan (R-Wisc.) and the Republicans in the House of Representatives to slash Medicaid and abolish Medicare.

The Problem of Cost in a Private, For-Profit Health Insurance System

If health insurance were like other commodities, like shoes or bow ties, then reducing access might lower costs by reducing demands on suppliers for time and materials. But health care is different because so much of the cost of providing it is in the administration of the payment system rather than in the actual work of doctors, nurses, and other providers, and because coordination and cooperation among different providers is essential for effective and efficient health care. It is not cost pressures on providers that are driving up health-care costs; instead, costs are rising because of what economists call transaction costs, the rising cost of administering and coordinating a system that is designed to reduce access.

The health-insurance and health-care markets are different from most other markets because private companies selling insurance do not want to sell to everyone, but only to those unlikely to need care (and, therefore, most likely to drop coverage if prices rise). As much as 70% of the "losses" suffered by health-insurance providers—that is, the money they pay out in claims—goes to as few as 10% of their subscribers. This creates a powerful incentive for companies to screen subscribers, to identify those likely to submit claims, and to harass them so that they will drop their coverage and go elsewhere. The collection of insurance-related information has become a major source of waste in the American economy because it is not organized to improve patient care but to harass and to drive away needy subscribers and their health-care providers. Because driving away the sick is so profitable for health insurers, they are doing it more and more, creating the enormous bureaucratic waste that characterizes the process of billing and insurance handling. Rising by over 10% a year for the past 25 years, health insurers' administrative costs are among the fastest-growing in the U.S. health-care sector. Doctors in private practice now spend as much as 25% of their revenue on administration, nearly $70,000 per physician for billing and insurance costs.

For-profit health insurance also creates waste by discouraging people from receiving preventive care and by driving the sick into more expensive care settings. Almost a third of Americans with "adequate" health insurance go without care every year due to costs, and the proportion going without care rises to over half of those with "inadequate" insurance and over two-thirds for those without insurance. Nearly half of the uninsured have no regular source of care, and a third did not fill a prescription in the past year because of cost. All of this unutilized care might appear to save the system money. But it doesn't. Reducing access does not reduce health-care expenditures when it makes people sicker and pushes them into hospitals and emergency rooms, which are the most expensive settings for health care and are often the least efficient because care provided in these settings rarely has continuity or follow-up.

The great waste in our current private insurance system is an opportunity for policy because it makes it possible to economize on spending by replacing our current system with one providing universal access. I have estimated that in Massachusetts, a state with a relatively efficient health-insurance system, it would be possible to lower the cost of providing health care by nearly 16% even after providing coverage to everyone in the state currently without insurance (see Table 1). This could be done largely by reducing the cost of administering the private insurance system, with most of the savings coming within providers' offices by reducing the costs of billing and processing insurance claims. This is a conservative estimate made for a state with a relatively efficient health-insurance system. In a report prepared for the state of Vermont, William Hsiao of the Harvard School of Public Health and MIT economist Jonathan Gruber estimate that shifting to a single-payer system could lead to savings of around 25% through reduced administrative cost and improved delivery

TABLE 1: SOURCES OF SAVINGS AND ADDED COSTS FOR A HYPTHETICAL MASSACHUSETTS SINGLE-PAYER HEALTH SYSTEM

Change in health-care expenditures	Size of change as share of total health-care expenditures
Savings from single-payer system	
Administration costs within health-insurance system	-2.0%
Administrative costs within providers' offices	-10.1%
Reduction in provider prices through reducing market leverage for privileged providers	-5.0%
Savings:	-17.1%
Increased costs from single-payer	
Expansion in coverage to the uninsured	+1.35%
Increased utilization because of elimination of copayments, balanced by improvements in preventive care	+/- 0.0%
Total increased costs:	+1.35%
Net change in health-care expenditures:	-15.75%

Source: Calculations by the author from data in OECD Health Data 2010 (oecd.org).

of care. (They have also noted that administrative savings would be even larger if the entire country shifted to a single-payer system because this would save the cost of billing people with private, out-of-state insurance plans.) In Massachusetts, my conservative estimates suggests that as much as $10 billion a year could be saved by shifting to a single-payer system.

Single-Payer Systems Control Costs by Providing Better Care

Adoption of a single-payer health-insurance program with universal coverage could also save money and improve care by allowing better coordination of care among different providers and by providing a continuity of care that is not possible with competing insurance plans. A comparison of health care in the United States with health care in other countries shows how large these cost savings might be. When Canada first adopted its current health-care financing system in 1968, the health-care share of the national gross domestic product in the United States (7.1%) was nearly the same as in Canada (6.9%), and only a little higher than in other advanced economies. Since then, however, health care has become dramatically more expensive in the United States. In the United States, per capita health-care spending since 1971 has risen by over $6,900 compared with an increase of less than $3,600 in Canada and barely $3,200 elsewhere (see Table 2). Physician Steffie Woolhandler and others have shown how much of this discrepancy between the experience of the United States and Canada can be associated with the lower administrative costs of Canada's single-payer system; she has found that administrative costs are nearly twice as high in the United States as in Canada—31% of costs versus 17%.

TABLE 2: GREATER INCREASE IN COST FOR U.S. HEALTH-CARE SYSTEM, 1971-2007

	U.S. vs. Canada		U.S. vs. 5-country average	
	Dollars	Share of GDP	Dollars	Share of GDP
Extra increase 1971-2007	$3,356	5.40%	$3,690	4.72%
Extra adjusted for smaller life expectancy gain	$4,006	5.98%	$4,480	5.73%
	As share of national health expenditures			
Extra increase 1971-2007	45%		49%	
Extra adjusted for smaller life expectancy gain	53%		59%	

Note: The first line shows how much faster health-care spending rose per person and as a share of gross domestic product in the United States compared with Canada and with the average of five countries (Canada, France, Germany, Sweden, and the United Kingdom). The second row adjusts this increase for the slower rate of growth in life expectancy in the United States than in these other countries. The third and fourth rows estimate the degree of waste in our health-care system as the proportion of total expenditures accounted for by the extra increases in health-care expenditures in the United States.

Source: Calculations by the author from data in OECD Health Data 2010 (oecd.org).

The United States is unique among advanced economies both for its reliance on private health insurance and for rapid inflation in health-care costs. Health-care costs have risen faster in the United States than in any other advanced economy: twice as fast as in Canada, France, Germany, Sweden, or the United Kingdom. We might accept higher and rapidly rising costs had Americans experienced better health outcomes. But using life expectancy at birth as a measure of general health, we have gone from a relatively healthy country to a relatively unhealthy one. Our gain in life expectancy since 1971 (5.4 years for women) is impressive except when put beside other advanced economies (where the average increase is 7.3 years).

The relatively slow increase in life expectancy in the United States highlights the gross inefficiency of our private health-care system. Had the United States increased life expectancy at the same dollar cost as in other countries, we would have saved nearly $4,500 per person. Or, put another way, had we increased life

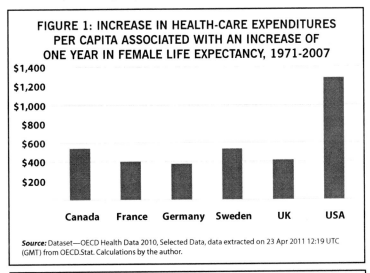

FIGURE 1: INCREASE IN HEALTH-CARE EXPENDITURES PER CAPITA ASSOCIATED WITH AN INCREASE OF ONE YEAR IN FEMALE LIFE EXPECTANCY, 1971-2007

Source: Dataset—OECD Health Data 2010, Selected Data, data extracted on 23 Apr 2011 12:19 UTC (GMT) from OECD.Stat. Calculations by the author.

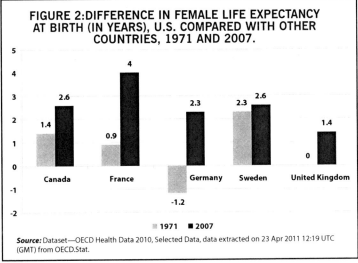

FIGURE 2: DIFFERENCE IN FEMALE LIFE EXPECTANCY AT BIRTH (IN YEARS), U.S. COMPARED WITH OTHER COUNTRIES, 1971 AND 2007.

Source: Dataset—OECD Health Data 2010, Selected Data, data extracted on 23 Apr 2011 12:19 UTC (GMT) from OECD.Stat.

expectancy at the same rate as other countries, our spending increase since 1971 would have bought an extra 15 years of life expectancy, 10 years more than we have. The failure of American life expectancy to rise as fast as life expectancy elsewhere can be directly tied to the inequitable provision of health care through our private, for-profit health-insurance system. Increases in life expectancy since 1990 have been largely restricted to relatively affluent Americans with better health insurance. Since 1990, men in the top 50% of the income distribution have had a six-year increase in life expectancy at age 65 compared with an increase of only one year for men earning below the median.

Rising health-care costs reflect in part the greater costs of caring for an aging population with more chronic conditions. As such, the United States looks especially bad because our population is aging less quickly than that of other countries because of high rates of immigration, relatively higher fertility, and the slower increase in life expectancy in the United States. Countries also buy higher life expectancy by spending on health care; rising health expenditures have funded improvements in treatment that have contributed to rising life expectancy throughout the world. Female life expectancy at birth has increased by nearly nine years in Germany since 1971, by over eight years in France, by seven years in Canada and the United Kingdom, and by six years in Sweden. By contrast, the United States, where female life expectancy increased by a little over five years, has done relatively poorly despite increasing health-care expenditures that dwarf those of other countries. In other countries, increasing expenditures by about $500 per person is associated with an extra year of life expectancy. With our privatized health-insurance system, we need spending increases over twice as large to gain an extra year of life (see Figure 1, previous page).

The international comparison also provides another perspective on any supposed trade-off between containing costs and expanding coverage. In countries other than the United States, almost all of the increase in health-care spending as a share of national income is due to better quality health care as measured by improvements in life expectancy (see Figure 2, previous page). The problem of rising health-care costs is almost unique to the United States, the only advanced industrialized country without universal coverage and without any effective national health plan.

In short, the question is not whether we can afford a single-payer health-insurance system that would provide adequate health care for all Americans. The real question is: can we afford anything else? ❑

Sources: Cathy Shoen, "How Many Are Underinsured? Trends Among U.S. Adults, 2003 and 2007," Health Affairs, June 10, 2008; "Insured but Poorly Protected: How Many Are Underinsured? U. S. Adults Trends, 2003 to 2007," Commonwealth Fund, June 10, 2008 (commonwealthfund.org); David Cutler and Dan Ly, "The (Paper) Work of Medicine: Understanding International Medical Costs," Journal of Economic Perspectives, Spring 2011; Stephen M. Davidson, Still Broken: Understanding the U.S. Health Care System, Stanford Business Books, 2010; P Franks and C M Clancy, "Health insurance and mortality. Evidence from a national cohort," The Journal of the American Medical Association, August 11, 1993; Allan Garber and Jonathan Skinner, "Is American Health Care Uniquely Inefficient?" Journal of Economic Perspectives, Fall 2008; Jonathan Gruber, "The Role of Consumer Co-payments for Health Care: Lessons from the RAND Health Insurance Experiment and Beyond," Kaiser Family Foundation, October 2006 (kff.org); David Himmelstein and Steffie Woolhandler, "Administrative Waste in the U.S. Health Care System in 2003," International Journal of Health Services, 2004; "The Uninsured: A Primer: Supplemental Data Tables," Kaiser Family Foundation, December 2010; Karen Davis and Cathy Shoen, "Slowing the Growth of U.S. Health Care Expenditures: What are the Options?" Commonwealth Fund, January 2007 (commonwealthfund. org); "Accounting for the Cost of Health Care in the United States," McKinsey Global Institute, January 2007 (mckinsey.com); "Investigation of Health Care Cost Trends and Cost Drivers," Office of Massachusetts Attorney General Martha Coakley, January 29, 2010 (mass.gov); Trends in Mortality Differentials and Life Expectancy for Male Social Security-Covered Workers, by Average Relative Earnings by Hilary Waldron, Social Security Administration, October 2007; Richard G. Wilkinson, The Spirit Level, Bloomsbury Press, 2010; William Hsiao and Steven Kappel, "Act 128: Health System Reform Design. Achieving Affordable Universal Health Care in Vermont," January 21, 2011 (leg.state.vt.us); Steffie Woolhandler and Terry Campbell, "Cost of Health Care Administration in the United States and Canada," New England Journal of Medicine, 2003.

Article 8.2

DIFFERENT ANTI-POVERTY REGIME, SAME SINGLE-MOTHER POVERTY

BY RANDY ALBELDA

January/February 2012

Four years into a period of deep recession and persistent economic crisis, only now has the p-word—poverty—finally surfaced. The Census Bureau's September 13 announcement that the U.S. poverty rate had increased to 15.1% in 2010, up from 14.3% in 2009, put the issue of poverty onto page one, albeit briefly. In fact, poverty and how to address it have not been prominent items on the national agenda since the "welfare reform" debates of the 1980s and early 1990s.

"Welfare queens" may have disappeared from politicians' rhetoric, but poor people, disproportionately single mothers and their children, are still around. Single-mother families have been and continue to be particularly vulnerable to being poor. The September report showed the poverty rate for single mothers and their children rose as well: from 32.5% in 2009 to 34.2% in 2010.

It is remarkably hard to be the primary caregiver *and* garner enough income to support a family. This reality was built into the design of the first generation of federal anti-poverty programs in the United States. Developed beginning in the New Deal era, these programs were aimed at families with no able-bodied male breadwinner and hence no jobs or wages—single mothers, people with disabilities, and elders. Putting single mothers to work was thought to be undesirable. Or, white single mothers—there was much less reluctance in the case of black single mothers, who were largely excluded from the various anti-poverty programs until the 1960s.

The most important of the anti-poverty programs for single mothers was the cash assistance program, Aid to Dependent Children (later renamed Aid to Families with Dependent Children, or AFDC), established in 1935—also commonly referred to as "welfare." Other programs developed in the succeeding decades included Food Stamps, Medicaid, and housing assistance.

Then, in 1996, with the support of President Clinton, Congress abolished AFDC, replacing it with a block grant called TANF (Temporary Assistance to Needy Families), and passed a spate of other changes to related programs. The new anti-poverty regime implied a new social compact with the non-disabled, non-elder poor, supported by both conservatives and liberals: to require employment in exchange for—and ultimately be weaned off of—government support. In other words, the new mandate for poor adults, especially single mothers, was to get a job—any job.

And, in fact, in the ensuing years the number of poor families with wages from work increased. Moreover, welfare rolls dropped. And, in the first four years following welfare "reform," the official poverty rate for single-mother families fell too. (It has been increasing since 2000, although not quite back to its 1996 level.) But despite their higher wage income, many single-mother families are no better able to provide for their basic needs today than before the mid-1990s. Even the lower poverty rate may not reflect the real material well-being of many single moms and their children, given that their mix of resources has shifted to include more of the kinds of income counted by poverty measures and less of the uncounted kinds.

While TANF and the other legislative changes promote employment in theory, they did not reshape anti-poverty programs to genuinely support employment. Key programs are insufficiently funded, leaving many without access to child care and other vital work supports; income eligibility requirements and benefit levels designed for those with no earnings work poorly for low-wage earners; and the sheer amount of time it takes to apply for and keep benefits is at odds with holding down a job.

Ironically, there has been little or no talk of revisiting these policies despite the massive job losses of the Great Recession. With job creation at a standstill, in 2010 the unemployment rate for single mothers was 14.6% (more than one out of every seven). For this and other reasons it is time to "modernize" anti-poverty programs by assuring they do what policy makers and others want them to do—encourage employment while reducing poverty. And they must also serve as an important safety net when work is not available or possible. But changes to government policies are not enough. If employment is to be the route out of poverty, then wages and employer benefits must support workers at basic minimum levels.

Ending "Welfare" And Promoting Employment

Among the changes to U.S. anti-poverty programs in the 1990s, the most sweeping and highly politicized involved AFDC, the cash assistance program for poor parents. The 1996 legislative overhaul gave states tremendous leeway over eligibility rules in the new TANF program. For the first time there was a time limit: states are not allowed to allocate federal TANF money to any adult who has received TANF for 60 months—regardless of how long it took to accrue 60 months of aid. And the new law required recipients whose youngest child is over one year old to do some form of paid or unpaid work—most forms of education and job training don't count—after 24 months of receiving benefits.

To accommodate the push for employment, Congress expanded the Earned Income Tax Credit, which provides refundable tax credits for low-income wage earners; expanded the Child Care Development Block Grant, which gives states money to help provide child care to working parents with low incomes, including parents leaving TANF; and established the State Children's Health Insurance Program (S-CHIP), in part out of a recognition that single mothers entering the workforce were losing Medicaid coverage yet often working for employers who provided unaffordable health insurance coverage or none at all. Even housing assistance programs started promoting employment: the Department of Housing and Urban Development encouraged local housing authorities to redesign housing assistance so as to induce residents to increase their earnings.

The strategy of promoting employment was remarkably successful at getting single mothers into the labor force. In 1995, 63.5% of all single mothers were employed; by 2009, 67.8% were. This rate exceeds that of married mothers, at 66.3%. So with all that employment, why are poverty rates still so high for single-mother families? The answer lies in the nature of low-wage work and the mismatch between poverty reduction policies and employment.

Single Mothers and Low-Wage Jobs Don't Mix

There are two fundamental mismatches single mothers face in this new welfare regime. The first has to do with the awkward pairing of poor mothers and low-wage jobs. In 2009 over one-third of single mothers were in jobs that are low paying (defined as below two-thirds of the median hourly wage, which was $9.06). In addition to the low pay, these jobs typically lack benefits such as paid sick or vacation days and health insurance. Many low-wage jobs that mothers find in retail and hospitality have very irregular work hours, providing the employers with lots of flexibility but workers with almost none. These features of low-wage work wreak havoc for single moms. An irregular work schedule makes child care nearly impossible to arrange. A late school bus, a sick child, or a sick child-care provider can throw a wrench in the best-laid plans for getting to and staying at work. Without paid time off, a missed day of work is a missed day of pay. And too many missed days can easily cost you your job.

Medicaid, the government health insurance program for the poor, does not make up for the lack of employer-sponsored health insurance common in low-wage jobs. Medicaid income eligibility thresholds vary state by state, but are typically so low that many low-wage workers don't qualify. Only 63% of low-wage single mothers have any health insurance coverage at all, compared to 82% of all workers. The new Patient Protection and Affordable Care Act (a/k/a Obamacare) may help, depending on the cost of purchasing insurance, but for now many low-wage mothers go without health care coverage.

Finally, there is the ultimate reality that there are only 24 hours in a day. Low wages mean working many hours to earn enough to cover basic needs. Yet working more hours means less time with kids. This can be costly in several ways. Hiring babysitters can be expensive. Relying heavily on good-natured relatives who provide care but may not engage and motivate young children also has costs, as does leaving younger children in the care of older brothers and sisters, who in turn can miss out on important after-school learning. Long work hours coupled with a tight budget might mean little time to help do homework, meet with teachers, or participate in in- and out-of-school activities that enrich children's lives.

A New Mismatch

The first generation of anti-poverty programs were designed on the assumption that recipients would not be working outside the home. Unfortunately, their successor programs such as TANF and SNAP, despite their explicit aim of encouraging employment, still do not work well for working people.

What does it mean that these programs are not designed for those with employment? There are two important features. First, income thresholds for eligibility tend to be very low—that is, only those with extremely low earnings qualify. For example, only two states have income thresholds above the poverty line for TANF eligibility. To get any SNAP benefits, a single mother needs to have income below 130% of the poverty line. Working full-time at $10 an hour (that's about $1,600 a month in take-home pay) would make a single mother with one child ineligible for

Poverty Remeasured

According to the Census Bureau, 46.2 million Americans were poor in 2010. But what exactly does "poor" mean? The academic and policy debates over how to measure poverty fill volumes. Some questions relate to the establishment of the poverty threshold. On what basis should the poverty line be drawn? Is poverty relative or absolute—in other words, if the average standard of living in a society rises, should its poverty threshold rise as well? Other questions concern measuring income. What kinds of income should be counted? Before or after taxes and government benefits? Who is included in the poverty assessment? (For example, those in institutional settings such as prisons are excluded from the official U.S. poverty measure—not a minor point when you consider that nearly 2.3 million adults were incarcerated in the United States as of the end of 2009.)

Established in 1963 by multiplying an emergency food budget by three, and adjusted solely for inflation in the years since, the official U.S. poverty thresholds are notoriously low. A family of four bringing in over $22,314—*including* any TANF cash assistance, unemployment or workers' comp, Social Security or veterans' benefits, and child support—is not officially poor. In many parts of the United States, $22K would not be enough to keep one person, let alone four people, off the street and minimally clothed and fed.

An interagency federal effort to develop a more realistic poverty level has just released its new measure, known as the Supplemental Poverty Measure. The SPM makes many adjustments to the traditional calculation:

It counts the Earned Income Tax Credit and non-cash benefits such as food stamps and housing assistance as income.

It subtracts from income out-of-pocket medical costs, certain work-related expenses (e.g., child care), and taxes paid.

Its thresholds are adjusted for cost-of-living differences by region and are relative rather than absolute—basic expenses that are the building blocks of the threshold are pegged at the 33rd percentile of U.S. households.

The SPM poverty rate for 2009 was 15.7%, somewhat higher than the 14.5% official rate. More dramatic differences between the two poverty rates appeared in some subgroups, especially the elderly: 9.9% by the traditional measure versus 16.1% by the SPM, largely due to their high out-of-pocket medical expenses.

—*Amy Gluckman*

Sources: "Measure by Measure," *The Economist*, January 20, 2011; Ellen Frank, "Measures of Poverty," *Dollars & Sense*, January 2006; Center for Women's Welfare, Univ. of Wash. School of Social Work, "How Does the Self-Sufficiency Standard Compare to the New Supplemental Poverty Measure?"; U.S. Census Bureau, "How the Census Bureau Measures Poverty" and "Poverty Thresholds by Size of Family and Number of Children: 2010."

both programs in all states. Moreover, even if you are eligible, these benefits phase out sharply. With TANF (in most states), SNAP, and housing assistance, for every additional dollar you earn, you lose about 33 cents in each form of support. This means work just does not pay.

Second, applying for and maintaining benefits under these programs often takes a great deal of time. Each program has particular eligibility requirements; each requires different sets of documents to verify eligibility. While some states have tried to move to a "one-stop" system, most require separate applications for each program and, often, one or more office visits. Recertification (i.e., maintaining eligibility) can require assembling further documentation and meeting again with caseworkers. If you have ever applied for one of these programs, maybe you have experienced how time-consuming—and frustrating—the process can be.

In short, the programs were designed for applicants and recipients with plenty of time on their hands. But with employment requirements, this is not the right assumption. Missing time at work to provide more paperwork for the welfare office is just not worth it; there is considerable evidence that many eligible people do not use TANF or SNAP for that reason. Even the benefit levels assume an unlimited amount of time. Until recently, the maximum dollar amount of monthly SNAP benefits was based on a very low-cost food budget that assumed hours of home cooking.

Unlike cash assistance or food assistance, child care subsidies are obviously aimed at "working" mothers. But this program, too, often has onerous reporting requirements. Moreover, in most states the subsidy phases out very quickly especially after recipients' earnings reach the federal poverty line. This means that a worker who gets a small raise at work can suddenly face a steep increase in her child-care bill. (Of course, this is only a problem for the lucky parents who actually receive a child-care subsidy; as mentioned earlier, the lack of funding means that most eligible parents do not.)

The Earned Income Tax Credit is a notable exception. The refundable tax credit was established explicitly to help working parents with low incomes. It is relatively easy to claim (fill out a two page tax form along with the standard income tax forms), and of all the anti-poverty programs it reaches the highest up the income ladder. It even phases out differently: the credit increases as earnings rise, flattens out, and then decreases at higher levels of earnings. Most recipients get the credit in an annual lump sum and so use it very differently from other anti-poverty supports. Families often use the "windfall" to pay off a large bill or to pay for things long put off, like a visit to the dentist or a major car repair. While helpful and relatively easy to get, then, the Earned Income Tax Credit does not typically help with day-to-day expenses as the other anti-poverty programs do.

Has Employment-Promotion "Worked"?

The most striking change in the anti-poverty picture since welfare reform was enacted is that the welfare rolls have plummeted. In 1996, the last full year under the old system, there were 4.43 million families on AFDC nationwide; in 2010, amid the worst labor market in decades, the TANF caseload was only 1.86 million. In fact, when unemployment soared in 2008, only 15 states saw their TANF caseloads increase. The rest continued to experience reductions. Plus, when the TANF rolls fell sharply in the late 1990s, so did Medicaid and Food Stamps enrollments. These programs have since seen increases in usage, especially since the recession, but it's clear that when families lose cash assistance they frequently lose access to other supports as well.

Welfare reform has worked very well, then, if receiving welfare is a bad thing. Indeed, advocates of the new regime tout the rapid and steep decline in welfare use as their main indicator of its success. In and of itself, however, fewer families using anti-poverty programs does not mean less poverty, more personal responsibility, or greater self-sufficiency. During the economic expansion of the late 1990s, the official poverty rate for single mothers and their children fell from 35.8% in 1996 to 28.5% in 2000. It has risen nearly every year since, reaching 34.2% in 2010. But if a successful anti-poverty effort is measured at all by the economic well-being of the targeted families, then that slight drop in the poverty rate is swamped by the 60% decrease in the number of families using welfare over the same period. Far fewer poor families are being served. In 1996, 45.7% of all poor children received some form of income-based cash assistance; in 2009, only 18.7% did. The Great Recession pushed 800,000 additional U.S. families into poverty between 2007 and 2009, yet the TANF rolls rose by only 110,000 over this period.

Data from two federal government reports on TANF, depicted in the chart below, nicely illustrate the dilemmas of the new welfare regime. The chart shows the total average amounts of earnings and the value of major government supports ("means-tested income") for the bottom 40% of single-mother families (by total income) between 1996 and 2005. It is clear that since welfare reform, these families are relying much more on earnings. But despite the additional work effort, they find

EARNINGS AND MEANS-TESTED INCOME FOR THE BOTTOM TWO QUINTILES OF SINGLE-MOTHER FAMILIES, 1996-2005 (IN 2005 DOLLARS)

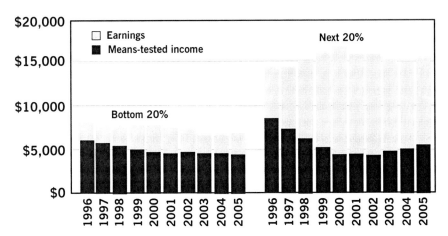

Notes: Those with negative income not included. Means-tested income is the total of Supplemental Security Income, Public Assistance, certain Veteran's Benefits, Food Stamps, School Lunch, and housing benefits.

Source: U.S. Department of Health and Human Services, the Office of Assistant Secretary for Planning and Evaluation, Table 4:3 of TANF 6th Annual Report to Congress (November 2004) and Table 4:2 of TANF 8th Annual Report to Congress (June 2009), using tabulations from the U.S. Census Bureau, 1996-2005.

themselves essentially no better off. The bottom 20% saw their package of earnings and government benefits *fall*: their average earnings have not increased much while government supports have dropped off, leaving them with fewer resources on average in 2006 than in 1996. For the second quintile, earnings have increased substantially but benefits have fallen nearly as much, leaving this group only slightly better off over the period. And that is without taking into account the expenses associated with employment (e.g. child care, transportation, work clothes) and with the loss of public supports (such as increased co-payments for child care or health insurance). These women are working a lot more—in the second quintile about double—but are barely better off at all! So much for "making work pay."

More hours of work also means fewer hours with children. If the time a mother spends with her children is worth anything, then substituting earnings for benefits represents a loss of resources to her family.

What Might Be Done?

Employment, even with government supports, is unlikely to provide a substantial share of single-mother families with adequate incomes. Three factors—women's lower pay, the time and money it takes to raise children, and the primary reliance on only one adult to both earn and care for children—combine to make it nearly impossible for a sizeable number of single mothers to move to stable and sufficient levels of resources.

Addressing the time- and money-squeeze that single mothers faced in the old anti-poverty regime and still face in the new one will take thoroughgoing changes in the relations among work, family, and income.

- *Make work pay by shoring up wages and employer benefits.* To ensure that the private sector does its part, raise the minimum wage. A full-time, year-round minimum wage job pays just over the poverty income threshold for a family of two. Conservatives and the small business lobby will trot out the bogeyman of job destruction, but studies on minimum-wage increases show a zero or even positive effect on employment. In addition, mandate paid sick days for all workers and require benefit parity for part-time, temporary, and subcontracted workers. This would close a loophole that a growing number of employers use to dodge fringe benefits.

- *Reform anti-poverty programs to really support employment.* To truly support low-wage employment, anti-poverty programs should increase income eligibility limits so that a worker can receive the supports even while earning and then phase out the programs more gradually so low-wage workers keep getting them until they earn enough not to need them. Also, streamline application processes and make them more user-friendly. Many states have done this for unemployment insurance, car registration, and driver's license renewal. Why not do the same for SNAP, TANF and Medicaid?

- *Support paid and unpaid care work.* A society that expects all able-bodied adults to work—regardless of the age of their children—should also be a society that shares the costs of going to work, by offering programs to care for children and others who need care. This means universal child care and afterschool programs. It also means paid parental leave and paid time off to care for an ill relative. The federal Family and Medical Leave Act gives most workers the right to take unpaid leaves, but many can't afford to. California and New Jersey have extended their temporary disability insurance benefits to cover those facing a wide range of family needs—perhaps a helpful model.

New anti-poverty regime, but same poverty problems. Most single mothers *cannot* work their way out of poverty—definitely not without the right kinds of supplemental support. There are many possible policy steps that could be taken to help them and other low-wage workers get the most out of an inhospitable labor market. But ultimately, better designed assistance to poor and low-income families, old fashioned cash assistance, and minimal employment standards must be part of the formula. ❑

Sources: Randy Albelda and Chris Tilly, *Glass Ceilings and Bottomless Pits: Women's Work, Women's Poverty*, South End Press, 1997; U.S. Census Bureau, *Historical Tables on Poverty*; Kaiser Family Foundation, "Income Eligibility Limits for Working Adults at Application as a Percent of the Federal Poverty Level by Scope of Benefit Package," statehealthfacts.org, January 2011; U.S. Dept. of Health and Human Services, *TANF 6th and 8th Annual Report to Congress,* November 2004 and July 2009; U.S. Dept. of Health and Human Services, *Estimates of Child Care Eligibility and Receipt for Fiscal Year 2006*, April 2010; Thomas Gabe, *Trends in Welfare, Work, and the Economic Well-being of Female Headed Families with Children: 1987-2005*, Congressional Research Service Report RL30797, 2007; Randy Albelda and Heather Boushey, *Bridging the Gaps: A Picture of How Work Supports Work in Ten States,* Center for Social Policy, Univ. of Mass. Boston and Center for Economic and Policy Research, 2007; Author's calculations from the U.S. Census Bureau's Current Population Survey, various years.

Article 8.3

THE "OBAMACARE" TAX HIKE AND REDISTRIBUTION

BY JOHN MILLER
May/June 2010

OBAMACARE'S WORST TAX

Opponents [of ObamaCare] should go down swinging, and that means exposing such policy debacles as President Obama's 11th-hour decision to apply the 2.9% Medicare payroll tax to "unearned income."

That's what savings and investment income are called in Washington, and this destructive tax wasn't in either the House or Senate bills, though it may now become law with almost no scrutiny.

For the first time, the combined employer-worker Medicare rate would be extended beyond wages to interest, dividends, capital gains, annuities, royalties and rents for individuals with adjusted gross income above $200,000 and joint filers over $250,000.

Earning even a single dollar more than $200,000 in adjusted gross income will slap the tax on every dollar of a taxpayer's investment income, creating a huge marginal-rate spike that will most hurt middle-class earners, as opposed to the superrich.

—Wall Street Journal editorial, March 17, 2010

There are plenty of legitimate complaints about "ObamaCare," but its tax hike on unearned income is surely not one of them.

The new tax does take a bite out of the income of the rich. It adds 0.9 percentage points to the current hospital-insurance tax on most wage-income above $200,000. It also levies a 3.8% tax on investment income (e.g., dividends and capital gains). Only the richest 5% of taxpayers, with 2009 incomes above $231,179, will pay the new tax. And the richest 1%, with incomes in excess of $624,396 in 2009, will pay 85% of the tax hike.

That is a good thing, doing a bit to reduce the great income inequalities that have developed in recent decades. But the new tax hardly constitutes soaking the rich. Even after the tax, the rich will hand over a smaller portion of their income in federal income taxes than they did before three decades of pro-rich tax cutting. According to the Tax Policy Center, the new tax would push up the tax burden of the richest one percent by 1.3 percentage points, to 33.6% of their income, still well below their 37.0% effective tax rate in 1979. In any case, the rich can surely afford it. The incomes of the top 1% roughly doubled from 1979 to 2009 (after correcting for inflation).

Beyond that, the new tax was a compromise. It replaced the 5.4% tax on any income above $1 million in the House healthcare bill. That tax would have been paid exclusively by the richest 1%. So the *WSJ* editors should be happy that its friends got off as well as they did. Also the new tax postponed the start date for the excise tax on high-cost healthcare plans in the Senate bill, but didn't eliminate it. When it goes into effect in 2018, the tax on "Cadillac" healthcare plans will fall mostly on better-off households, but nonetheless will collect one-third of its taxes from individuals who currently have incomes between $50,000 and $100,000.

What really has the *WSJ* editors in a lather is levying hospital-insurance taxes on non-wage, or "unearned," income. They claim that middle-income taxpayers, not the super-rich, will ultimately bear the burden of the tax. Why? Because by taxing savings and investment income, the new tax will put a stopper in "trickle-down economic growth" (not that we have seen much trickling down over recent decades).

But economic evidence suggests that they are just plain wrong. First, unearned income is not the same thing as savings and investment. Take stock-trading, the source of most capital gains. From 1998 to 2007, $27 in stocks was traded on the U.S. exchanges for very dollar corporations invested in plant and equipment, according to a recent study by economists Robert Pollin and Dean Baker. The bulk of the gains of financial investors, therefore, comes from trading existing assets, not financing investment in new assets. Second, there is no solid evidence that lower taxes on unearned income do much to spur economic growth. Economist Joel Selmrod, director of the Office of Tax Policy Research at the University of Michigan, reports: " I know of no evidence that establishes a connection between prosperity and the rate we tax capital gains." Finally, the *WSJ* editors fail to take into account that the new tax hike will go to expand health insurance coverage for families with incomes below four times the poverty level.

Health-care reform surely could have done more to redistribute income and economic power, by squeezing out private insurers' massive overhead costs and profits, and relying on the House tax on income over $1 million. But even as is, ObamaCare should do more than any legislation in many years to help generate the bottom-up economic growth that could replace the "trickle-down" economic growth that has rewarded so few with so much. ❑

Sources: David Leonhardt, "In Health Bill, Obama Attacks Wealth Inequality," *New York Times*, March 23, 2010; Robert Pollin and Dean Baker, "Public Investment, Industrial Policy, and U.S. Economic Renewal," Political Economy Research Institute, December 2009; Tax Policy Center, "The Medicare Tax as Proposed in H.R. 3590 (Senate Health Bill) and H.R 48723 (Reconciliation Act of 2010)," March 19, 2010.

Article 8.4

GO AHEAD AND LIFT THE CAP
Assessing a Campaign Flyer on Social Security

BY JOHN MILLER
March/April 2008

> **Barack Obama.** A plan with a trillion dollar tax increase on America's hard-working families. Lifting the cap on Social Security taxes to send more of Nevada families' hard-earned dollars to Washington. Senator Obama said, "I think that lifting the cap [on Social Security taxes] is probably going to be the best option."
>
> **Hillary Clinton.** A blueprint to rebuild the road to middle-class prosperity. Provide tax relief for the middle class and address Social Security without putting burdens on hard-working families or seniors. Strengthen Social Security and the economy by returning to balanced budgets.
>
> —*Official campaign flyer distributed*
> *by Nevadans for Hillary, January 2008*

Back in January [2008], even before things got really nasty in the Democratic primary, Barack Obama and Hillary Clinton were already going after each other about taxes and Social Security.

The Clinton campaign sent a flyer to Nevada voters before that state's January 19 Democratic caucuses, accusing Obama of planning to impose "a trillion dollar tax increase on America's hard-working families" by lifting the cap on income subject to Social Security taxes. Clinton, the flyer claimed, does "not want to fix the problems of Social Security on the backs of middle-class families and seniors."

The truth was something different. First, Obama did not exactly propose removing the cap, which was $97,500 in 2007. (In other words, employers and employees each pay a flat percentage of the first $97,500 of each employee's salary, but no tax on the income above that.) He did discuss adjusting it as "the best way to approach this [reforming Social Security]," preferable to either cutting benefits or increasing the retirement age, later adding that he would consider keeping the exemption from $97,500 to around $200,000, lifting it only for any income above $200,000.

More important, lifting the cap would in no way increase the tax burden on middle-income families. Just under 6% of U.S. wage earners make more than $97,500 in wages, so even removing the cap altogether would raise taxes only for that small group.

Now, there is a legitimate progressive objection to Obama's discussion of fixing Social Security by adjusting the cap: any talk of reforming Social Security inevitably plays into the hands of those out to privatize it by trumping up a phony crisis. But that hardly seems to be the point of the Clinton campaign flyer.

Too bad it wasn't. Clinton gets it: in the past she herself has warned that acting as if Social Security is in crisis is "a Republican trap." Yet last October, an Associated Press reporter overhead her telling an Iowa voter that she would consider lifting the cap on payroll taxes as long as wages between $97,500 and $200,000 remained exempt—precisely the proposal she derides in the Nevada flyer.

Inside Social Security

Let's remind ourselves that Social Security, which cut poverty rates among the elderly from 35% in 1960 to 9.4% in 2006, is no Robin Hood plan that robs the rich to pay for the retirement of the working class. Rather, it is a mildly redistributive public retirement program financed by contributions from the wages of working people. In fact, Social Security taxes fall far more heavily on the poor and working class than on the well-to-do. Payroll taxes are a fixed 12.4% (actually 6.2% on employees and 6.2% on employers); they are levied only on wage income, not on property income; and the cap on wages subject to the tax (the subject of the debate between Clinton and Obama) means that while most workers pay the tax on every dollar of their income, the highest earners pay it only on a part.

Even FDR acknowledged that relying on payroll contributions to finance Social Security was regressive, although he famously argued that with those contributions in place, "no damn politician can ever scrap my Social Security program."

George W. Bush's 2005 push to privatize Social Security only underscored FDR's point. Bush made more than 40 trips around the United States to stump for his plan, but fewer people supported Social Security privatization afterwards than before he started. Ironically enough, the only aspect of Social Security reform that has generated widespread support is lifting the cap: in a February 2005 Washington Post poll, 81% of respondents agreed that Americans should pay Social Security taxes on wages over the cap.

This is no radical or hare-brained idea. It has the endorsement of the AARP, the largest seniors' lobby. And there is a clear precedent. A similar cap used to apply to the payroll tax that funds Medicare, but a 1993 law removed that cap and now every dollar of wage income is taxed to pay for Medicare. It certainly does not warrant the derision heaped on it by the Clinton campaign or the unwillingness of the Obama campaign to embrace it. In fact, lifting the cap would rewrite this one rule to favor working people more—just what the Obama campaign claims to support.

Lifting the cap on Social Security taxes would raise a significant amount of revenue: $1.3 trillion dollars over ten years according to the libertarian Cato Institute, and $124 billon a year according to the left-of-center Citizens for Tax Justice. Long term, lifting the payroll tax cap would just about cover the shortfall Social Security will face if economic growth slows to a snail's pace in the decades ahead, as forecast by the Social Security Administration (SSA). (See "The Social Security Administration's Cracked Crystal Ball" and "Social Security Isn't Broken," in this volume, for critiques of the SSA's forecasts.) According to Stephen Goss, the SSA's chief actuary, lifting the cap while giving commensurate benefit hikes to high-income taxpayers once they retire would cover 93% of the SSA's projected shortfall in Social Security revenues over the next 75 years. Removing the cap without raising

EFFECT OF REMOVING THE EARNINGS CAP ON SOCIAL SECURITY TAXES BY INCOME CATEGORY

RESULTING SOCIAL SECURITY TAX INCREASE AND TOTAL SOCIAL SECURITY TAX AS SHARES OF TOTAL INCOME IN 2007

Income Group	Increase in Social Social Security Tax	Revised Total Security Tax Paid
$0 – 10K	—	6.8%
$10K – 20K	—	6.2%
$20K – 30K	—	7.8%
$30K – 40K	—	8.7%
$40K – 50K	—	9.0%
$50K – 75K	—	9.4%
$75K – 100K	+0.0%	9.7%
$100K – 150K	+0.5%	9.6%
$150K – 200K	+1.5%	9.1%
$200K – 300K	+2.7%	8.3%
$300K – 400K	+4.1%	7.7%
$400K – 500K	+4.5%	7.4%
$500K – 750K	+4.7%	6.9%
$750K – 1M	+4.7%	6.4%
$1M – 2M	+4.4%	5.5%
$2M – 5M	+4.0%	4.5%
$5M – 10M	+3.8%	4.0%
$10M – 20M	+3.2%	3.3%
over $20M	+2.7%	2.7%

Source: "An Analysis of Eliminating the Cap on Earnings Subject to the Social Security Tax & Related Issues," (Citizens for Tax Justice, November 30, 2006).

those benefits would actually produce a surplus in the system over the same period—even if the economy creeps along as the SSA predicts it will.

Finally, the combination of the cap and the unprecedented inequality of the last two decades has shrunk the Social Security tax base. Some 90% of wages fell below the cap in 1983. Today, with the increased concentration of income among the highest-paid, that figure is down to 84%—even as the number of workers with earnings above the cap has dropped. The cap would have to rise to $140,000 just to once again cover 90% of all wages; the additional revenues resulting from just this change would close about one-third of the long-term Social Security deficit projected by the SSA.

Hardly Soaking the Rich

Making high earners pay the Social Security tax on all of their wage income, as low- and middle-income earners already have to, might not strike you as class warfare—but the high flyers sure think it is. Just listen to the financial establishment squeal. Investment Management chairman Robert Pozen, architect of the benefit-cutting proposal endorsed by the Bush administration (and deceptively labeled "progressive indexing"), warns that lifting the cap would represent "one of the greatest tax increases of all time" and "is so crazy it's beyond belief." The editors of the *Wall Street Journal* agreed. And the conservative Heritage Foundation ginned up numbers purporting to show that lifting the cap would impose a "massive 12.4 percentage point tax hike" that would return federal tax rates to levels not seen since the 1970s.

Just how wet would the rich get if the cap on Social Security taxes was lifted? The data suggest they would get damp, but hardly soaked.

For starters, lifting the cap affects just 5.9% of wage-earners. This group benefited massively from three rounds of Bush tax cuts, as evidenced by the fact that the effective federal tax rate (i.e., the share of income actually paid in federal taxes, once all deductions and exemptions have been taken) on the richest 5% of taxpayers fell from 31.1% in 2000 to 28.9% in 2005, according to the Congressional Budget Office.

So, lifting the wage cap on Social Secu-rity taxes would not do much more than reverse those tax giveaways to the wealthy. And the wealthiest taxpayers, those with incomes over $1 million, would still be paying a smaller portion of their income in payroll taxes than all other taxpayers. (See table.) For the top 5% of taxpayers, lifting the cap would push their effective federal tax rate up to 31.5%, a bit above where it was when Bush took office but still below the 31.8% level they paid back in 1979, before nearly three decades of pro-rich tax cutting. The top 1% would pay an effective federal tax rate of 33.8% —again, higher than it was in 2000 but still well below its 1979 level of 37.0%.

That is hardly soaking the rich. In any case they can afford it. The best-off 5% of households had an average income of $520,200 in 2005, some 81% higher than in 1979 after correcting for inflation. The richest 1%, with an average income of $1,558,500 in 2005, saw their after-tax income rise a whopping 176% over the same period.

Lifting the cap on payroll taxes would not only resolve any alleged crisis in Social Security, but also help to right the economic wrongs of the last few decades. And it is popular to boot. Isn't that an idea any progressive politician should seriously consider? ❏

Sources: M. Sullivan, "Budget Magic and the Social Security Tax Cap," *Tax Notes*, March 14, 2005; "Social Security: Raising or Eliminating the Taxable Earnings Base," Congressional Rsch Svc, May 2, 2005; R. Dederman et al., "Keep the Social Security Wage Cap; Nearly a Million Jobs Hang in the Balance," Center for Data Analysis Report #05-04 (Heritage Foundation, April 22, 2005); Robert C. Pozen, "A 'Progressive' Solution to Social Security," *Wall Street Journal*, March 15, 2005; "Social Security Progressives," *Wall Street Journal*, March 15, 2005; Greg Ip, "Wage Gap Figures in Social Security's Ills," *Wall Street Journal*, April 11, 2005; "Social Security Memorandum to Stephen C. Goss," February 7, 2005; "An Analysis of Eliminating the Cap on Earnings Subject to the Social Security Tax & Related Issues," (Citizens for Tax Justice, November 30, 2006); "Obama: Clinton Also Considering $1 Trillion Social Security Tax Hike on Wealth," (Associated Press, January 16, 2008); "Barack Obama on Social Security," *On the Issues*; "Effective Federal Tax Rates, 1979 to 2005," Congressional Budget Office, December 2007.

Article 8.5

HARD WORK AT AN ADVANCED AGE

BY AMY GLUCKMAN
September/October 2010

A mong the many proposals that the Social-Security-is-in-crisis crowd is touting is an increase in the retirement age. The Social Security "full retirement age" was 65 from the program's inception until 1983, when Congress legislated a gradual increase, based on year of birth, to 67. The 1983 amendments did not change the age of earliest eligibility for Social Security retirement benefits, which remains 62. However, those who opt to start receiving benefits before they reach the full retirement age for their cohort face a lifetime cut in their monthly payment.

At first glance, it seems reasonable to push the retirement age upward in line with average life expectancy, which rose rapidly in the United States during the 20th century. But that rise in life expectancy owes a great deal to sharp drops in infant and child mortality. For those who survive to adulthood and especially to old age,

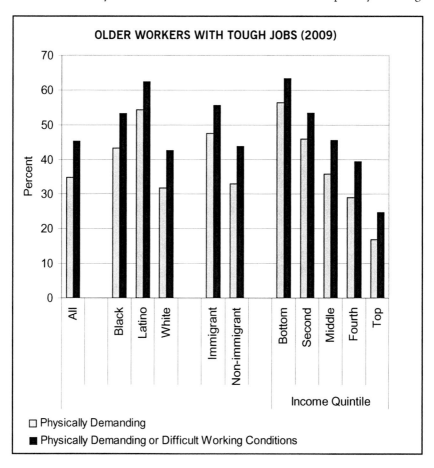

OLDER WORKERS WITH TOUGH JOBS (2009)

the change is far less dramatic. People who turned 65 in 1940, the first year monthly Social Security retirement benefits were paid out, could expect to live to nearly 79; those who turned 65 in 1990 had a life expectancy only about four years longer.

What would it mean to ratchet up the full retirement age further? The answer is: It depends. Some 60- and 70-somethings can readily continue working and postpone receiving Social Security benefits; a few have sufficient personal savings and/or private pensions that they will never need to rely on Social Security at all. But for the millions of older custodians, cooks, cashiers, construction workers, and others who do physically demanding work, having to put in even a few more years on the job before they can receive their full Social Security benefits is a different story.

A surprising number of older workers have these kinds of jobs, as a study by Hye Jin Rho of the Center for Economic and Policy Research shows. Following the classifications used in the U.S. Labor Department's Occupational Information Network database, the study defines "physically demanding" jobs as those that require significant time standing or walking, repetitive motions, or handling and moving objects. "Difficult working conditions" include outdoor work, use of hazardous equipment, and exposure to contaminants. Of the 18.8 million U.S. workers who are 58 or older, over 45% have physically demanding jobs and/or difficult working conditions. The rate is even higher for the 5.2 million workers 66 and up (48.2%).

Certain groups of older workers perform these tough jobs at disproportionate rates (see figure). Not surprisingly, the workers who can least afford to take an early-retirement penalty in their monthly Social Security check are often those who are most likely to reach their mid-60s saying, "Time to quit!" ❑

Sources: Hye Jin Rho, "Hard Work? Patterns in Physically Demanding Labor Among Older Workers," Center for Economic and Policy Research, August 2010; U.S. Social Security Administration, "Life Expectancy for Social Security"; Laura Shrestha, "Life Expectancy in the United States," Congressional Research Service, August 2006.

Chapter 9

INEQUALITY, TAXES, AND CORPORATIONS

Article 9.1

NEARLY $2 TRILLION PURLOINED FROM U.S. WORKERS IN 2009

BY JAMES M. CYPHER
July/August 2011

In 2009, stock owners, bankers, brokers, hedge-fund wizards, highly paid corporate executives, corporations, and mid-ranking managers pocketed—as either income, benefits, or perks such as corporate jets—an estimated $1.91 *trillion* that 40 years ago would have collectively gone to non-supervisory and production workers in the form of higher wages and benefits. These are the 88 million workers in the private sector who are closely tied to production processes and/or are not responsible for the supervision, planning, or direction of other workers.

From the end of World War II until the early 1970s, the benefits of economic growth were broadly shared by those in all income categories: workers received increases in compensation (wages plus benefits) that essentially matched the rise in their productivity. Neoclassical economist John Bates Clark (1847-1938) first formulated what he termed the "natural law" of income distribution which "assigns to everyone what he has specifically created." That is, if markets are not "obstructed," pay levels should be "equal [to] that part of the product of industry which is traceable to labor itself." As productivity increased, Clark argued, wages would rise *at an equal rate.*

The idea that compensation increases should equal increases in *average* labor productivity per worker as a matter of national wage policy, or a wage norm, is traceable to the President's Council of Economic Advisors under the Eisenhower and Kennedy administrations. This *macroeconomic* approach was anchored in the fact that if compensation rises in step with productivity growth, then both unit labor costs and capital's versus labor's share of national income will remain constant. This "Keynesian Consensus" never questioned the fairness of the initial capital/labor split, but it at least offered workers a share of the fruits of future economic growth.

As the figure below shows, both Clark's idea of a "natural law" of distribution and Keynesian national wage policy have ceased to function since the onset of the neoliberal/supply-side era beginning in the early 1970s. From 1972 through 2009, "usable" productivity—*that part of productivity growth that is available for raising wages and living standards*—increased by 55.5%. Meanwhile, real average hourly pay *fell* by almost 10% (excluding benefits). As a group, workers responded by increasing their labor-force participation rate. To make the calculation consistent over time, employment is adjusted to a *constant participation rate* set at the 1972 level. Had compensation matched "*usable*" productivity growth, the (adjusted) 84 million non-

INDEX OF WAGES, COMPENSATION, PRODUCTIVITY, AND "USABLE" PRODUCTIVITY OF U.S. NON-SUPERVISORY WORKERS, PER HOUR, 1972-2009 (1972=100)

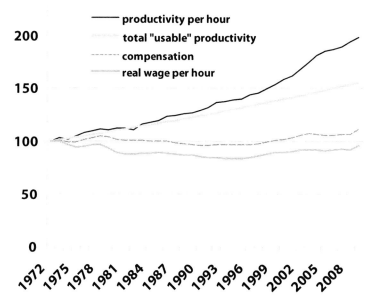

Sources and Calculations: This calculation is based on the 1972 average real hourly wage expressed in 2009 dollars, $17.88, plus $2.95 per hour in benefits, with total compensation [wages + benefits] equal to $20.83 per hour for non-supervisory workers (U.S. Department of Labor, 2010a, 2010b: 85-90; Economic Policy Institute, 2011). The growth of private productivity from 1972 to 2009 was 92.7%. Adjusting the productivity figure (downward) to account for lower economy-wide productivity, consistent deflation in both producer prices and consumer prices, and a rising rate of depreciation, the net growth of "usable" productivity was 55.5% (Baker 2007). If workers had been paid the value of their annual productivity increases (as they essentially were prior to the early 1970s) they would have received an average of $35.98 per hour in compensation in 2009 instead of the $23.14 they actually received. The differential was $12.84. Workers worked an average of 39.8 hours per week in 2009, so $511 of compensation that they would have received under conditions prior to the early 1970s instead was diverted. On an annual basis of 1,768 hours worked per year, according to the OECD, each worker lost to capital an average of $22,701. Adjusting the 88,239,000 production and non-supervisory workers employed in 2009 to the lower 1972 labor force participation rate equivalent of 84,180,000 workers, the total of purloined workers' compensation for 2009 comes to $1.91 trillion (Council of Economic Advisors, 2010: Tables B-47, B-49; U.S. Department of Labor, Bureau of Labor Statistics, 2011 Table B-6).

supervisory and production workers in 2009 would have received roughly $1.91 *trillion* more in wages and benefits. That is, 13.5% of the nation's Gross Domestic Product in 2009 was transferred from non-supervisory workers to capitalists (and managers) via the gap of 44.4% that had opened up between compensation and "usable" productivity since 1972.

As expected, neoclassical (or mainstream) economists offer tortured justifications for the new *status quo*. The erstwhile dauphin of neoclassical economics, Harvard economist Gregory Mankiw agrees with Clark's formulation. But he says that even though "productivity has accelerated, workers have *become accustomed to the slow rate of wage growth since the 1970s*." Why "accustomed"? Well, believe it or not, neoclassical economists claim that today's workers suffer from "low wage aspirations." Mankiw equates the wage that workers aspire to with the wage they consider fair. So, according to this very strange formulation, workers consider that they are getting a fair shake today, even though their compensation increases lag behind their productivity increases. Yet a few decades earlier, they considered it fair (as did Clark and Mankiw) for compensation growth to keep up with productivity increases.

Some economists simply deny that any change has occurred. Noted neoclassical conjurer Martin Feldstein believes that the "productivity-compensation gap" is merely a matter of bad measurement: by dropping the Consumer Price Index as the appropriate yardstick, Feldstein alchemically transforms the way wages are adjusted for inflation. His soothing Panglossian recalibration *raises* workers' "real" income; *et voilà!*—the productivity-compensation gap all but disappears.

Leaving aside such statistical prestidigitation, a vast upward transfer of income is evident. That transfer is directly related to the rupture of the so-called "Treaty of Detroit"—an understanding between capital and labor, pounded out during the Truman administration, wherein employers accepted the idea that compensation could grow at the rate that productivity increased. In 1953 union strength was at its high point; 32.5% of the U.S. labor force was unionized. With the profit squeeze of the early 1970s and the onset of Reaganism, unionization rates began to fall—to 27% in 1979, then to 19% in 1984. By 2010 the rate was down to 11.9% (and only 6.9% in the private sector). Off-shoring, outsourcing, vigorous (and often illegal) corporate tactics to stop unionization drives, and an overall political climate of hostility to free and fair union elections have deprived workers of the countervailing power they once held. The result is that without unions struggling to divide the economic pie, non-supervisory and production workers (78% of the private-sector workforce) have been deprived of a minimal level of economic distributive justice.

The upward redistribution has remained as hidden as possible. The forms it has taken—as bonuses, bloated salaries, elephantine stock options, padded consulting fees, outsized compensation to boards of directors, sumptuous conferences, palatial offices complete with original artwork, retinues of superfluous "support" staff, hunting lodges, private corporate dining rooms, regal retirement agreements, and so on—defy exact categorization. Some would appear as profit, some as interest, some as dividends, realized capital gains, gigantic pension programs, retained earnings, or owners' income, with the remainder deeply buried as "costs of doing business."

In the final analysis, the $1.91 trillion figure is only an approximation, designed to make more concrete a concept that has lacked an important quantitative dimension. Of course, had compensation increases matched "usable" productivity increases, workers would have paid taxes on the wage portion of their compensation, leaving them with much less than the $1.91 trillion in their pockets. Meanwhile, as these funds are shifted over to capital (and management salaries), federal, state, and local taxes are paid on the portion which appears as declared income. This results in a considerable drop in the *net after-tax* transfer amount actually pocketed by capital through their appropriation of the productivity increases of non-supervisory workers. Even so, their haul remains a staggering—even astonishing—sum. ❏

Sources: Dean Baker, "The Productivity to Paycheck Gap," Center for Economic and Policy Research, 2007 (cepr.net); Lawrence Ball and Gregory Mankiw, "The NAIRU in Theory and Practice," *Journal of Economic Perspectives*, V. 16, No. 14: 115-136 (2002); Council of Economic Advisors, *Economic Report of the President, 2010*, Washington, D.C.: USGPO; Economic Policy Institute, "Wages and Compensation Stagnating," chart from *The State of Working America*, 2011 (stateofworkingamerica.org); Martin Feldstein, "Did Wages Reflect Growth in Productivity?" paper presented at the 2008 American Economics Association meetings (aeaweb.org); Steven Greenhouse, "Union Membership Fell to a 70-Year Low," *New York Times*, January 22, 2011; E.K. Hunt, *History of Economic Thought*, Belmont, Calif.: Wadsworth (1979); David Cay Johnston, "Plane Perks," *Perfectly Legal*, New York: Penguin (2005); T.C. Leonard, "A Certain Rude Honesty: John Bates Clark as a Pioneering Neoclassical Economist," *History of Political Economy* vol. 35, no. 3: 521-558 (2003); U.S. Department of Labor, Bureau of Labor Statistics, *Economic News Release: Table B-6, Employment of Production and Non-Supervisory Employees*, January 7, 2011 (bls.gov); Bureau of Labor Statistics, Table A: Employer Cost for Employee Compensation, USDL-10-1687, December 8, 2010 (bls.gov); Bureau of Labor Statistics, "Current Labor Statistics," *Monthly Labor Review*, Vol. 133, No. 7, July 2010 (bls.gov).

Article 9.2

A DIRTY JOB NO ONE SHOULD DO

A lawyer's self-serving defense of Wall Street pay doesn't add up.

BY JOHN MILLER
May/June 2011

WALL STREET LAWYER: DON'T BLAME PAY

Steve Eckhaus just wanted to get some deals done. He has negotiated hundreds of high-profile pay packages, some of which were met with scorn and scrutiny in Washington and beyond.

"I hate to say it, but I have friends who blame me for the financial crisis," says Mr. Eckhaus, who estimates he has negotiated well over $5 billion in banker pay over the years, including several $100 million pay deals.

"It was understandable why there was anger," says Mr. Eckhaus, but "the crisis was not caused by Wall Street fat cats." In general, he said his clients are "pure as the driven snow" and doing work that supports the economy and justifies their pay.

"There's nothing helpful or healing in the midst of a financial crisis to talk about Wall Street 'fat cats,' " added Mr. Eckhaus. "To blame Wall Street for the financial meltdown is absurd."

—Steve Eder, "Wall Street Lawyer: Don't Blame Pay," *Wall Street Journal*, February 5, 2011

Pure as the driven snow? How about as dirty as what remains of the Northeast's snow piles, covered with filth a month after record storms? Eckhaus and his fat-cat clients richly deserve the scorn that even his friends have heaped upon them. The pay packages Eckhaus negotiated are obscene. They cushioned financial fat cats from the often-disastrous consequences of their actions. And Eckhaus's protestations notwithstanding, the finance industry's compensation structures lie at the heart of the financial crisis. Banking execs and other key decision-makers all along the mortgage securitization process were induced to take excessive risks because of the way they were compensated.

Let's start with the first link in the process—the people who made the mortgage loans to homebuyers. It's standard practice to pay mortgage brokers based on the volume of loans they originate, not the performance or quality of those loans. And since the banks and mortgage companies who employ the brokers bundled up the loans and sold them off as mortgage-backed securities, they too had little interest in the quality of the loans.

The fees garnered by the financial-services industry from home mortgage lending and mortgage securitization were enormous, as much as $2 trillion in the six years from 2003 to 2008, according to estimates by economist James Crotty. That figure includes the fees paid to mortgage brokers as well as the fees collected by investment bankers who packaged the loans into securities, the fees paid to the ratings agencies who gave the securities their seal of approval, and the fees paid to yet others who serviced the securities. Those massive sums were paid out for short-term success even when the decisions those sums rewarded resulted in long-term losses or failures, a point Securities and Exchange Commission chair Mary Schapiro confirmed for the Financial Crisis Inquiry Commission, the ten-member panel appointed by Congress to examine the causes of the financial crisis.

That the compensation system has "no rhyme or reason" is the conclusion Andrew Cuomo, then attorney general of New York, reached in his 2009 report on compensation practices in the U.S. banking system. The record of Bank of America, for Cuomo, shows just how little compensation had to do with bank performance. In 2006, as the bank raked in profits during the housing bubble, it paid out $18 billion in compensation. In 2008, after the bubble had burst, Bank of America continued to make compensation payments at the $18 billion level—even as its net income plummeted from $14 billion to $4 billion. That fall Bank of America took over Merrill Lynch, which had just brought a new investment banking chief on board—Mr. Eckhaus's client Tom Montag—by guaranteeing him a $39.4 million bonus.

Those giant bonuses paid out to Wall Street high rollers provoked the ire of many, especially when they came from financial firms that received TARP (Troubled Asset Relief Program) bailout funds from the federal government, as was the case with Mr. Montag's millions. The Cuomo report pays special attention to the bonuses paid out by the original TARP recipients. For two of the nine, Citigroup and Merrill Lynch, the disconnect between the banks' earnings and executive bonuses was especially alarming. Together, these two corporations in 2008 lost $54 billion, paid out nearly $9 billion in bonuses, and then received TARP bailouts totaling $55 billion. At Merrill Lynch, 700 employees received bonuses in excess of $1 million in 2008. The top four recipients alone received a total of $121 million. Merrill's reported losses for 2007 and 2008, as Crotty points out, were enough to wipe out 11 years of earnings previously reported by the company.

The Cuomo report rails against this "heads I win, tails you lose" bonus culture. As Cuomo put it, when banks did well, executives and traders were showered with bonuses. When the banks lost money, taxpayers bailed them out, and bonuses and overall compensation remained sky-high.

The consequences of such a perverse compensation system are disastrous, as Crotty explains:

> It becomes rational for top financial firm operatives to take excessive risk in the bubble even if they understand that their decisions are likely to cause a crash in the intermediate future. Since they do not have to return their bubble-year bonuses when the inevitable crisis occurs and since they continue to receive substantial bonuses even in the crisis, they have a powerful incentive to pursue high-risk, high-leverage strategies.

So go ahead and blame Wall Street for the crisis. Not to would indeed be absurd. The bonuses Eckhaus's clients and others took home were the most deformed element of a compensation system that enabled the risk-taking that pushed the financial industry into crisis. Those bonus babies deserve your scorn. Throwing them out with their dirty bathwater, the whole compensation system, is the first step toward curbing the destructive behavior they helped to perpetuate. ❏

Sources: Steve Eder, "Wall Street Lawyer: Don't Blame Pay," Wall Street Journal, February 5, 2011; James Crotty, "The Bonus-Driven 'Rainmaker' Financial Firm," Political Economy Research Institute Working Paper 209, revised August 2010 (www.peri.umass.edu/236/hash/468a9ba021/publication/386/); Andrew Cuomo, No Rhyme Or Reason: The Heads I Win, Tails You Lose Bank Bonus Culture, State of New York, 2009 (www.scribd.com/doc/17849813/Andrew-Cuomos-Bonus-Report); The Financial Crisis Inquiry Report: Final Report of the National Commission on the Causes of the Financial and Economic Crisis in the United States, January 2011 (www.fcic.gov/report).

Article 9.3

NO FOOLING—CORPORATIONS EVADE TAXES
Forbes Finally Notices what has Been Obvious For Years

BY JOHN MILLER
May/June 2011

> WHAT THE TOP U.S. COMPANIES PAY IN TAXES
>
> Some of the world's biggest, most profitable corporations enjoy a far lower tax rate than you do—that is, if they pay taxes at all.
>
> The most egregious example is General Electric. Last year the conglomerate generated $10.3 billion in pretax income, but ended up owing nothing to Uncle Sam. In fact, it recorded a tax benefit of $1.1 billion.
>
> Over the last two years, GE Capital [one of the two divisions of General Electric] has displayed an uncanny ability to lose lots of money in the U.S. (posting a $6.5 billion loss in 2009), and make lots of money overseas (a $4.3 billion gain).
>
> It only makes sense that multinationals "put costs in high-tax countries and profits in low-tax countries," says Scott Hodge, president of the Tax Foundation. Those low-tax countries are almost anywhere but the U.S. "When you add in state taxes, the U.S. has the highest tax burden among industrialized countries," says Hodge. In contrast, China's rate is just 25%; Ireland's is 12.5%.
>
> —Christopher Helman, "What the Top U.S. Companies Pay in Taxes," *Forbes*, April 1, 2011

When *Forbes* magazine, the keeper of the list of the 400 richest Americans, warns that corporations not paying taxes on their profits will raise your hackles, you might wonder about the article's April 1 dateline. If it turns out *not* to be an April Fool's joke, things must be *really* bad.

And indeed they are. As *Forbes* reports, General Electric, the third largest U.S. corporation, turned a profit of $10.3 billion in 2010, paid no corporate income taxes, and got a "tax benefit" of $1.1 billion on taxes owed on past profits. And from 2005 to 2009, according to its own filings, GE paid a consolidated tax rate of just 11.6% on its corporate rates, including state, local, and foreign taxes. That's a far cry from the 35% rate nominally levied on corporate profits above $10 million.

Nor was GE alone among the top ten U.S. corporations with no tax obligations. Bank of America (BofA), the seventh largest U.S. corporation, racked up $4.4 billion in profits in 2010 and also paid no corporate income taxes (or in 2009 for that matter). Like GE, BofA has hauled in a whopping "tax benefit"—$1.9 billion.

For BofA, much like for GE, losses incurred during the financial crisis erased it tax liabilities. BofA, of course, contributed mightily to the crisis. It was one of four banks that controlled 95% of commercial bank derivatives activity, mortgage-based securities that inflated the housing bubble and brought on the crisis.

And when the crisis hit, U.S. taxpayers bailed them out, not once but several times. All told BofA received $45 billion of government money from the Troubled Asset Relief Program (TARP) as well as other government guarantees. And while BofA paid no taxes on their over $4 billion of profits, they nonetheless managed to pay out $3.3 billion in bonuses to corporate executives. All of that has made BofA a prime target for US Uncut protests (see p. 6) against corporate tax dodging that has cost the federal government revenues well beyond the $39 billion saved by the punishing spending cuts in the recent 2011 budget deal.

These two corporate behemoths and other many other major corporations paid no corporate income taxes last year, even though 2010 U.S. corporate profits had returned their level in 2005 in the midst the profits-heavy Bush expansion before the crisis hit.

An Old Story

But why is *Forbes* suddenly noticing corporate tax evasion? After all, corporations not paying taxes on their profits is an old story. Let's take a look at the track record of major corporations paying corporate income before the crisis hit and the losses that supposedly explain their not paying taxes.

The Government Accounting Office conducted a detailed study of the burden of the corporate income tax from 1998 to 2005. The results were stunning. Over half (55%) of large U.S. corporations reported no tax liability for at least one of those eight years. And in 2005 alone 25% of those corporations paid no corporate income taxes, even though corporate profits had more than doubled from 2001 to 2005.

In another careful study, the Treasury Department found that from 2000 to 2005, the share of corporate operating surplus that that U.S. corporations pay in taxes—a proxy for the average tax rate—was 16.7% thanks to various corporate loopholes, especially three key mechanisms:

- Accelerated Depreciation: allows corporations to write off machinery and equipment or other assets more quickly than they actually deteriorate.

- Stock Options: by giving their executives the option to buy the company's stock at a favorable price, corporations can take a tax deduction for the difference between what the employees pay for the stock and what it's worth.

- Debt Financing: offers a lower effective tax rate for corporate investment than equity (or stock) financing because the interest payments on debt (usually incurred by issuing bonds) get added to corporate costs and reduce reported profits.

Corporate income taxes are levied against reported corporate profits, and each of these mechanisms allows corporations to inflate their reported costs and thereby reduce their taxable profits.

And then there are overseas profits. U.S.-based corporations don't pay U.S. corporate taxes on their foreign income until it is "repatriated," or sent back to the parent corporation from abroad. That allows multinational corporations to defer payment of U.S. corporate income taxes on their overseas profits indefinitely or repatriate their profits from foreign subsidiaries when their losses from domestic operations can offset those profits and wipe out any tax liability, as GE did in 2010.

Hardly Overtaxed

Nonetheless, Scott Hodge, the president of the right-wing Tax Foundation, steadfastly maintains that U.S. corporations are overtaxed, and that that is what driving U.S. corporations to park their profits abroad (and lower their U.S. taxes). Looking at nominal corporate tax rates, Hodge would seem to have a case. Among the 19 OECD countries, only the statutory corporate tax rates in Japan surpass the (average combined federal and state) 39.3% rate on U.S. corporate profits. And the U.S. rate is well above the OECD average of 27.6%.

But these sorts of comparisons misrepresent where U.S. corporate taxes stand with respect to tax rates actually paid by corporations in other advanced countries. Why? The tax analyst's answer is that the U.S. corporate income tax has a "narrow base," or in plain English, is riddled with loopholes. As a result U.S. effective corporate tax rates—the proportion of corporate profits actually paid out in taxes—are not only far lower than the nominal rate but below the effective rates in several other countries. The Congressional Budget Office, for instance, found that U.S. effective corporate tax rates were near the OECD average for equity-financed investments, and below the OECD average for debt-financed investments. And for the years from 2000 to 2005, the Treasury Department found the average corporate tax rate among OECD countries was 21.6%, well above the U.S. 16.7% rate.

Current U.S. corporate tax rates are also extremely low by historical standards. In 1953, government revenue from the U.S. corporate income taxes were the equal of 5.6% of GDP; the figure was 4.0% of GDP in 1969, 2.2% of GDP from 2000 to 2005, and is currently running at about 2.0% of GDP.

By all these measures U.S. corporations are hardly over-taxed. And some major corporations are barely taxed, if taxed at all.

Closing corporate loopholes so that corporate income tax revenues in the United States match the 3.4% of GDP collected on average by OECD corporate income taxes would add close to $200 billion to federal government revenues—more than five times the $39 billion of devastating spending cuts just made in the federal budget in 2011. Returning the corporate income tax revenues to the 4.0% of GDP level of four decades ago would add close to $300 billion a year to government revenues.

The cost of not shutting down those corporate loopholes would be to let major corporations go untaxed, to rob the federal government of revenues that could, with enough political will, reverse devastating budget cuts, and to leave the rest of us to pay more and more of the taxes necessary to support a government that does less and less for us. ❑

Sources: "Corporate Tax Reform: Issues for Congress," by Jane G. Gravelle and Thomas L. Hungerford, CRS Report for Congress, October 31, 2007; "Treasury Conference On Business Taxation and Global Competitiveness," U.S. Department of the Treasury, Background Paper, July

23, 2007; "Six Tests for Corporate Tax Reform," by Chuck Marr and Brian Highsmith, Center on Budget and Policy Priorities, February 28, 2011; "Tax Holiday For Overseas Corporate Profits Would Increase Deficits, Fail To Boost The Economy, And Ultimately Shift More Investment And Jobs Overseas," by Chuck Marr and Brian Highsmith, Center on Budget and Policy Priorities, April 8, 2011; and, "Comparison of the Reported Tax Liabilities of Foreign and U.S.-Controlled Corporations, 1998-2005," Government Accounting Office, July 2008.

Article 9.4

TAXES AND ECONOMIC GROWTH

BY ARTHUR MacEWAN
July/August 2011

> Dear Dr. Dollar:
>
> It seems to be an article of faith amongst the "serious people" that low taxes on dividends and capital gains will stimulate the economy. While most economists (I understand) pretty much agree that any reduction in taxes will have some positive effect on the economy by stimulating demand, is there any empirical evidence that these particular tax cuts help the economy by encouraging productive investment (as opposed to increasing demand)?
> —*Stuart E. Baker, Tallahassee, Fla.*

In 1993, when Clinton and the Democrats in Congress increased taxes, Republicans screamed that this action would stifle economic growth. The remaining seven years of the Clinton administration saw the economy grow at the relatively high rate of 4% per year.

After the 2001 recession, the Bush tax cuts were enacted as "The Economic Growth and Tax Relief Reconciliation Act of 2001." Then, between 2001 and 2007, the economy expanded at only 2.7% per year, the slowest post-recession recovery on record. So the general experience of the last two decades is hardly a brief for the positive impact of tax cuts on economic growth.

The Clinton tax increase mainly affected society's highest income groups. The Bush tax cuts were focused on the wealthy and included specific reductions in tax rates on capital gains and dividends. So these two cases provide some empirical evidence—albeit crude empirical evidence—that tax cuts on these categories of income do not generate more productive investment and more rapid economic growth, and that tax increases on these categories of income do not curtail investment and growth. (Moreover, no one should expect much impact on demand, one way or the other, from changes in taxes on high-income groups because their expenditures are not very sensitive to changes in their incomes.)

There is also more finely focused evidence that lowering taxes on capital gains and dividends does not have much, if any, positive impact on economic growth. For example, in a 2005 "Tax Facts" piece from the Tax Policy Center, economists Troy Kravitz and Leonard Burman point out that "Capital gains [tax] rates display no contemporaneous correlation with real GDP growth during the last 50 years."

One reason that preferential tax treatment for capital gains does not have much, if any, positive impact on productive investment is that this treatment creates strong incentives for the wealthy to invest in non-productive tax shelters. Burman, who is the author of *The Labyrinth of Capital Gains Tax Policy*, comments: "…the creative energy devoted to cooking up tax shelters could otherwise be channeled into something productive."

Also, when tax reductions for the rich result in an increase in the federal deficit, as is generally the case, and thus more government borrowing, the result could be higher interest rates. And the higher interest rates would tend to negate any positive impact of the tax reduction on investment.

A useful summary of the issues, including references to relevant studies, is the November 2005 report by Joel Friedman of the Center on Budget and Policy Priorities, "Dividend and Capital Gains Tax Cuts Unlikely to Yield Touted Economic Gains."

Those who support the reduction of taxes on the wealthy, capital gains taxes, and taxes on dividends do tout studies that tend to support their position. And there is no denying the fact that people's behavior is affected by tax policy, including the investment behavior of those with high levels of income. Yet the evidence we have does not support the argument that tax adjustments on capital gains and dividends are major factors affecting the course of the economy.

Many of these issues were examined by Joel Slemrod, professor of business economics and public policy, director of the Office of Tax Policy Research at the University of Michigan, and a leading expert on tax issues, in a 2003 interview in *Challenge* magazine. Slemrod summed his view thus: "there is no evidence that links aggregate economic performance to capital gains tax rates." ❏

Sources: Troy Kravitz and Leonard Burman, "Capital Gains Tax Rates, Stock Markets, and Growth," *Tax Notes*, November 7, 2005 (taxpolicycenter.org); Leonard Burman, "Under the Sheltering Lie," Tax Policy Center, December 20, 2005 (taxpolicycenter.org); Joel Friedman, "Dividend and Capital Gains Tax Cuts Unlikely to Yield Touted Economic Gains," Center on Budget and Policy Priorities, November 2005 (cbpp.org); "The Truth about Taxes and Economic Growth: Interview with Joel Semrod," *Challenge*, vol. 46, no. 1, January/February 2003, pp. 5–14 (challengemagazine.com).

Article 9.5

MONOPOLY CAPITAL AND GLOBAL COMPETITION

BY ARTHUR MacEWAN
September/October 2011

> Dear Dr. Dollar:
> Is the concept of monopoly capital relevant today, considering such things as global competition?
>
> *—Paul Tracy, Oceanside, Calif.*

In 1960, the largest 100 firms on *Fortune* magazine's "annual ranking of America's largest corporations" accounted for 15% of corporate profits and had revenues that were 24% as large as GDP. By the early 2000s, each of these figures had roughly doubled: the top 100 firms accounted for about 30% of corporate profits and their revenues were over 40% as large as GDP.*

The banking industry is a prime example of what has been going on: In 2007 the top ten banks were holding over 50% of industry assets, compared with about 25% in 1985.

If by "monopoly capital" we mean that a relatively small number of huge firms play a disproportionately large role in our economic lives, then monopoly capital is a relevant concept today, even more so than a few decades ago.

Global competition has certainly played a role in reshaping aspects of the economy, but it has not altered the importance of very large firms. Even while, for example, Toyota and Honda have gained a substantial share of the U.S. and world auto markets, this does not change the fact that a small number of firms dominate the U.S. and world markets. Moreover, much of the rise in imports, which looks like competition, is not competition for the large U.S. firms themselves. General Motors, for example, has established parts suppliers in Mexico, allowing the company to pay lower wages and hire fewer workers in the states. And Wal-Mart, Target, and other large retailers obtain low-cost goods from subcontractors in China and elsewhere.

Economics textbooks tell us that in markets dominated by a few large firms, prices will be higher than would otherwise be the case. This has generally been true of the auto industry. Also, this appears to be the case in pharmaceuticals, telecommunications, and several other industries.

Wal-Mart and other "big box" stores, however, often do compete by offering very low prices. They are monopsonistic (few buyers) as well as monopolistic (few sellers). They use their power to force down both their payments to suppliers and the wages of their workers. In either case—high prices or low prices—large firms are exercising their market power to shift income to themselves from the rest of us.

Beyond their operation within markets, the very large firms shift income to themselves by shaping markets. Advertising is important in this regard, including, for example, the way pharmaceutical firms effectively create "needs" in pushing their products. Then there is the power of large firms in the political sphere. General

Electric, for example, maintains huge legal and lobbying departments that are able to affect and use tax laws to reduce the firm's tax liability to virtually nothing. Or consider the success of the large banks in shaping (or eliminating) financial regulation, or the accomplishments of the huge oil companies and the military contractors that establish government policies, sometimes as direct subsidies, and thus raise their profits. And the list goes on.

None of this is to say that everything was fine in earlier decades when large firms were less dominant. Yet, as monopoly capital has become more entrenched, it has generated increasingly negative outcomes for the rest of us. Most obvious are the stagnant wages and rising income inequality of recent years. The power of the large firms (e.g., Wal-Mart) to hold down wages is an important part of the story. Then there is the current crisis of the U.S. economy—directly a result of the way the very large financial firms were able to shape their industry (deregulation). Large firms in general have been prime movers over recent decades in generating deregulation and the free-market ideology that supports deregulation.

So, yes, monopoly capital is still quite relevant. Globalization does make differences in our lives, but globalization has in large part been constructed under the influence and in the interest of the very large firms. In many ways globalization makes the concept of monopoly capital even more relevant. ❑

* The profits of the top 100 firms (ranked by revenue) were quite low in 2010, back near the same 15% of total profits as in 1960, because of huge losses connected to the financial crisis incurred by some of the largest firms. Fannie Mae, Freddie Mac, and AIG accounted for combined losses of over $100 billion. Also, the revenues of all firms are not the same as GDP; much of the former is sales of intermediate products, but only sales of final products are included in GDP. Thus, the largest firms' revenues, while 40% as large as GDP, do not constitute 40% of GDP.

CONTRIBUTORS

Randy Albelda is a professor of economics at the University of Massachusetts-Boston and a *Dollars & Sense* Associate.

Sylvia A. Allegretto is an economist and deputy chair of the Center on Wage and Employment Dynamics at the Institute for Research on Labor and Employment, University of California, Berkeley.

William K. Black is executive director of the Institute for Fraud Prevention and teaches economics and law at the University of Missouri at Kansas City.

Darwin BondGraham is a sociologist, historian, and staff member of the Los Alamos Study Group.

Roger Bybee, the former editor of the union weekly *Racine Labor*, is now a consultant and freelance writer whose work has appeared in *Z Magazine*, *The Progressive*, *Extra!*, and *In These Times*.

James M. Cypher, co-editor of this volume, is a *Dollars & Sense* Associate. He is a professor at California State University-Fresno and at Universidad Autónoma de Zacatecas, Mexico.

Elissa Dennis is a consultant to nonprofit affordable housing developers with Community Economics, Inc., in Oakland, Calif.

Josh Eidelson is a freelance writer based in Philadelphia.

Anne Fischel teaches media and community studies at the Evergreen State College in Olympia, Wash.

Mike-Frank Epitropoulos teaches sociology at the University of Pittsburgh.

Gerald Friedman is a professor of economics at the University of Massachusetts at Amherst.

Heidi Garrett-Peltier is an economist and research associate at the Political Economy Research Institute at the University of Massachusetts-Amherst.

Fadhel Kaboub is an assitant professor of economics at Denison University.

Tim Koechlin is a visiting associate professor of economics at Vassar College.

Rob Larson is an assistant professor of economics at Tacoma Community College in Tacoma, Wash. and has written for *Z Magazine* and *The Humanist*.

Arthur MacEwan is professor emeritus of economics at the University of Massachusetts-Boston and is a *Dollars & Sense* Associate.

Steven Maher is a Washington, D.C.-based freelance journalist whose work has appeared in *The Guardian*, *Extra!*, Truthout, and the Electronic Intifada.

John Miller is a member of the *Dollars & Sense* collective and professor economics at Wheaton College.

Lin Nelson teaches environmental and community studies at the Evergreen State College in Olympia, Wash.

Steven Pitts is a labor policy specialist at the University of California Berkeley Center for Labor Research and Education, where he focuses on strategies for worker organizing and labor-community alliances.

Robert Pollin teaches economics and is co-director of the Political Economy Research Institute at the University of Massachusetts-Amherst. He is also a *Dollars & Sense* Associate.

Ethan Pollack is a policy analyst at the Economic Policy Institute.

Smriti Rao, co-editor of this volume, teaches economics at Assumption College in Worcester, Mass., and is a member of the *Dollars & Sense* collective.

Dan Read is a freelance jounralist based in London.

Alejandro Reuss, an economist and historian, is a former editor of *Dollars & Sense* and a *D&S* Associate.

Katherine Sciacchitano is a former labor lawyer and organizer. She is also a professor at the National Labor College and a freelance labor educator.

Chris Sturr, co-editor of this volume, is co-editor of *Dollars & Sense.*

Jeffrey Thompson is an assistant research professor at the Political Economy Research Institute at the University of Massachusetts-Amherst.

Jeannette Wicks-Lim is an economist and research fellow at the Political Economy Research Institute at the University of Massachusetts-Amherst.

Richard D. Wolff is professor emeritus of economics at the University of Massachusetts-Amherst and author of *Capitalism Hits the Fan: The Global Economic Meltdown and What to Do About It.*

Marty Wolfson teaches economics at the University of Notre Dame and is a former economist with the Federal Reserve Board in Washington, D.C.